Christianity for a New Age

# FAITH AND FRAGMENTATION

**J. PHILIP WOGAMAN**

**FORTRESS PRESS**                    **PHILADELPHIA**

**Library of Congress Cataloging in Publication Data**

Wogaman, J. Philip.
    Faith and fragmentation.

    Bibliography: p.
    Includes index.
    1. Christianity—20th century. 2. Apologetics—
20th century. I. Title.
BR479.W64   1986    209'.04    85–47712
ISBN 0–8006–1864–5

1714C85   Printed in the United States of America   1–1864

To
Walter G. Muelder
and
L. Harold DeWolf

# CONTENTS

# PREFACE

This book is addressed to people who wonder whether Christian faith makes sense in light of the sweeping changes of our age. Some of these people are inside the church but occasionally wonder why. Others are outside, either having abandoned formal religion or never having been attracted to it. Such people, whether presently church members or not, live in a world that is different from all other times. It is a pluralistic world, with many different religions and ideologies clamoring stridently for human allegiance. It is a sophisticated world, offering exciting new discoveries in physics and biology, astronomy and psychology. It is a dangerous world, torn by murderous conflict and perilously close to self-destruction. It is a deeply troubled world, unsure of its basic values and lacking a clear sense of direction. It is a world in which many people suffer while others prosper. What are thoughtful people to make of such an age?

A principal thesis of this book is that the real test of any religious faith is not so much whether it makes people feel good as whether it brings all aspects of life into focus. Does it unify our experience, making it possible for us to live deeply and with integrity? Or do we have to be dishonest with ourselves in order to be religious? Does it ask us to forget what we have learned about molecular biology and astronomy and to ignore the implications of moral evil and natural catastrophe? Or does it truly illuminate such things, providing us with purpose and direction? Does it help us face religious pluralism creatively, or does it commit us to fanaticism?

I write this book as a Christian, yet knowing that I also live in this age as a human being. As human beings, we must have courage to abandon ideas and institutions that no longer reflect our deeper values and our actual experience—and it is particularly important for writers to be honest and not intentionally mislead. In this work I have sought to be very honest about Christianity, both to myself and to the reader. But this also means taking Christian faith seriously and exploring its possibilities with openness. Intellectual and spiritual maturity require us to consider issues of faith without either arrogance or embarrassment.

Most of my previous writing has been in Christian ethics. Viewed from that perspective, this book is an examination of the foundations ultimately making Christian ethics possible. But I have not written the present book with a specialized academic audience in mind. There have been all too few writings on the great general questions gnawing at the minds and spirits of people in our time. One does not have to be an academic specialist to think seriously about issues of faith and to try to relate faith to all aspects of human experience. The general character of this book heightens my consciousness of how dependent I am upon the contributions of people in many different fields of knowledge. How important it is for all of us to try to draw together the threads of knowledge and human existence into a fabric of wholeness! The real function of a book like this is not to state finally the whole truth but to stimulate every reader to think with wholeness and integrity about things that truly matter.

My own thought process has been aided by several opportunities to explore the major themes of this book before responsive audiences. This included the Palmer Lectures at the University of Puget Sound, the Balmer Showers Lecture at Lebanon Valley College, and a study group at Metropolitan Memorial, the National United Methodist Church in Washington, D.C., as well as my own students and colleagues at Wesley Theological Seminary. These audiences were generous in their hospitality, patient with a tentative addressing of issues, and helpful in their criticism and suggestions. Two of my colleagues at Wesley Theological Seminary, Professors John D. Godsey and Larry L. Rasmussen read the entire manuscript and contributed valuable insights. I am grateful to Emily, Stephen, Jean, and Diane Wogaman for suggestions on parts of the manuscript and to my wife Carolyn for reading it and being my best critic and source of encouragement. While improving the work, none of these good people is to be blamed for errors or infelicities in the book. I wish also to record my thanks for secretarial assistance to Jane Phillips and Virginia Hamner and to Wesley Theological Seminary for a sabbatical leave during which most of the writing was completed. Harold W. Rast, Davis Perkins, and Therese D. Boyd of Fortress Press have provided indispensable encouragement and editorial suggestions.

I have dedicated the book to two of my great teachers, Walter G. Muelder

and L. Harold DeWolf, in gratitude for their wisdom, support, and friendship through many years.

J. PHILIP WOGAMAN

Wesley Theological Seminary
Washington, D.C.

# 1

## END OF AN ERA?

The world is rapidly approaching the end of the second millennium of what some have been pleased to call the Christian era. The year 2000 *anno Domini* will mean different things to different people. For some, who do not identify themselves with Christianity in any of its forms, it may come as an unpleasant reminder that dating systems pay lasting tribute to the cultural victories of some groups over others. For those who are indifferent to religious history or current religious conflict, the date may have only the impressiveness we find in large round numbers and the marking off of great segments of time. To Christians, among whom the years are celebrated as years of the Lord, this will no doubt be a time for considerable reflection.

It will clearly be a time for gratitude, among Christians, that so much good has come to the world and to them out of this two-thousand-year history. There will also be sober reminders of the evils that have sometimes been visited upon humanity by those bearing the Christian name. Some celebrations will be trivial and nostalgic; others will challenge Christians to new vision and recommitment. Some may give themselves over to renewed eschatological expectations, a response that was popular around the year 1000. Already writers have attracted millions of readers with such speculations,[1] although we may doubt that very many people really believe a divinely initiated end of the world to be just around the corner—whatever the likelihood may be for human initiation of such an event. Most people do not think of events and consummations deferred for two thousand years to be probable in their own lifetimes. The tendency in twentieth-century biblical scholarship to take the eschatological orientation of the earliest Christians seriously—that, for instance, St. Paul really *did* expect the end of the age to occur during or shortly after his own lifetime and that in this he may have been following the expectations of

Jesus himself—now leads more to reinterpretation than to literal belief among sophisticated Christians.

But this also suggests a broader problem. Is the Christian faith, taken as a whole, one that can bear the weight of indefinitely extended time? Is this faith sustainable in a pluralistic world of constantly accumulating knowledge and experience, a world in which contrasting faiths are accessible to the eye and mind of all as never before? Will the first two thousand years of Christian history be viewed increasingly as the solid foundation for a great new creative thrust by Christianity in the third millennium? Or will it be seen as an era drawing to a close amidst the gathering of new post-Christian energies? Will the parable of Jesus concerning the difficulty of containing new wine in old wineskins soon find ironic confirmation in the inability of the Christian wineskin to contain new wine in a new age?

Certainly the cultural and linguistic forms associated with Christian tradition do not always seem to fit too well. For instance, in a celebrated passage in Colossians, Christ is referred to in the following way:

> He is the image of the invisible God, the first-born of all creation; for in him all things were created, . . . whether thrones or dominions or principalities or authorities—all things were created through him and for him. He is before all things, and in him all things hold together. (Col. 1:15–17)

This is extraordinary language! Is there any sense in which it is also true? Can people who live in an age of nuclear physics and space travel be faulted for not seeming to believe that kind of thing any more? How indeed would one set about showing that it is a true statement? Indeed, does such a statement even *mean* anything? I suppose not very many people have studied the linguistic analysts, such as Alfred Ayer, who concluded that religious and moral language is essentially meaningless. But whether or not people possess that level of sophistication, they may join Ayer and others in treating religious language like the Colossians passage as the language of feeling—not as meaningful statements about anything that is objectively real. For such language seems far removed from the realities of New York and Calcutta and Moscow. It does not bring readily into focus the anguish of malnutrition in the Third World, the threat of nuclear war, the realities of unemployment and inflation, the depletion of energy resources, the horrors of genocide, the insecurities of revolution and counterrevolution, the experimental life styles of a new generation, the ennui of an older one. It does not seem to have evidential rootage in the realms of science, and it seems irrelevant to the developments of recent technology; it does not appear to bring such worlds into meaningful focus. Nor does it readily touch the spiritual malaise with which many people of our time have been seized. Nor does it seem particularly relevant to the daily occupations of contemporary people, to their patterns of work and home life, their education and recreation. What really does Christian faith have to offer to these times that helps bring life into focus?

## THE BROKEN CUP

Insofar as this has been a Christian society in the past we may now be very close to the situation described by the anthropologist Ruth Benedict in her classic study, *Patterns of Culture*. She reports there on a conversation she had half a century ago with a chief of the Digger Indians of California. The chief sought to explain what it meant to have the old cultural frame of reference collapse with the intrusion of Western culture. These were his words:

> In the beginning God gave to every people a cup, a cup of clay, and from this cup they drank their life. They all dipped in the water, but their cups were different. Our cup is broken now. It has passed away.[2]

Through this compelling figure of speech, the chief referred to those central beliefs and practices that are formative of culture: those basic values, those perceptions of reality that give meaning to personal and social activity. Ultimately, the "cup" referred to the organizing religious perspective on the basis of which human experience is interpreted and evaluated. The chief may have understood a very important point: Religion cannot be an isolated, specialized aspect of human life. It must be the basis for holding everything else in a context of meaning. It is what gives point to the entire fabric of human thought, feeling, and action; without it life is futile. The tragedy of his people was the shattering of a whole cultural viewpoint, the loss of its sense of meaning and value, as a result of the contact between his people and an alien civilization. His "cup" was broken, and nothing was able to replace it. That drama has, of course, been reenacted throughout the world in the twentieth century as traditional societies have felt the impact of Western cultural intrusion.

But it has also become a serious question whether this may not also be true now of the Christian faith. Is the Christian "cup" broken in the modern world? While lingering for a time here and there—and even prospering for a time here and there—is Christianity fatally disintegrated and doomed to pass away like the culture of which the chief of the Diggers spoke? There are people who think so. One of the characters in a Tom Robbins novel puts it this way:

Christianity is dying of its own accord. Its most vital energies are already dead. We are living in a period of vast philosophical and psychological upheaval, a rare era of evolutionary outburst precipitated by a combination of technological breakthroughs. . . . And when we come out of this period of change—provided that the tension and trauma of it doesn't lead us to destroy ourselves—we will find that many of the old mores and attitudes and doctrines will have been unrecognizably altered or eliminated altogether. One of the casualties of our present upheaval will unquestionably be Christianity. It is simply too ineffectual (on a spiritual level) and too contradictory (on an intellectual level) to survive.[3]

The same character, evidently reflecting the author's own point of view, remarked earlier that "the discernible activity in the modern church, the modern ecumenism, social activism, militancy and debates about the state of God's health are merely the nervous twitchings of a cadaver. The handsome new church buildings, the plush pulpits and wall-to-wall carpets are no more than funeral trappings. It's all over. The Christian faith is dead."

Active, church-going Christians will not agree with that assessment. But those who are closest to the institutional life of the church may be the ones who are most tempted to mistake the trappings for the real thing. The crucial question is not whether there is evidence of institutional health, but whether Christian faith as a whole can any longer provide a very profound basis for integrating the experience of contemporary humanity: our personal hopes and dreams, our social/political life together, our new intellectual horizons. Can it even survive a neutrally rigorous examination of Christianity itself, through research into biblical and historical sources and the disciplines of sociology and psychology of religion? If not, then it may simply be a matter of time before it will have to be announced by honest Christians that our cup is broken now—it has passed away.

The prospect would be welcomed by some who, caught up in immature rebellion against the constraints of what they perceive to be an outworn creed and institution, think no further than the liberation of humanity from such restricting anachronism. But humanity's problem needs to be seen in deeper perspective. The broken cup is personal and social tragedy. It is the loss of a personal center of meaning and, at the social level, it is the loss of a basis for shared purpose and just relationships. The late twentieth-century world has been characterized by murderous conflict of nations and races, of classes and tribes. The problems underlying the conflicts are difficult enough, but they are made all the more intractable by the lack of shared meanings and values on the basis of which a new era of peace with justice could be built. The world has become a much more dangerous place, for without common values the only arbiter left is naked force—and there is altogether too much of that available for the use of warring parties.

A new, more satisfactory cup is always a possibility, but new religious and cultural perspectives cannot be created out of whole cloth. Most of all they must be rooted profoundly in a new conception of ultimate reality, and there is little evidence of any such thing in the offing. None of the major contemporary alternatives to Christian faith—such as other great world religions or Marxism—can claim greater credibility when tested in the crucible of the whole range of human moral and intellectual experience. But that fact, too, should give the Christian no satisfaction. For humanity needs above all else an integrating center of life.

## RECENT RELIGIOUS REVIVAL

There is, of course, some evidence of religious revival during these closing decades of the twentieth century.

A Gallup survey of religion in America in the 1970s notes more than a doubling of the percentage of Americans believing in an increased influence of religion in American life. The same survey shows that nine out of ten Americans state a specific religious preference. Moreover, church attendance has remained remarkably high, with 41 percent of American adults attending some kind of religious service each week.[4] The evidences of renewed interest in Christianity appear to be even more dramatic in some other parts of the world. For example, the Centre for the Study of World Evangelization reported in 1979 that there were six million new converts to Christianity in Africa during 1978–79 and that some 34.8 million Asians were evangelized during the same period. The director of that Centre predicted that more people would be won to Christian faith during the decade of the 1980s than in all previous history.[5] While these figures and that prediction may well be on the high side, they show that a surprisingly positive trend may in fact be operating now in terms of the institutional success of Christianity.

Of course, people are also abandoning the faith. It is estimated that almost a million North Americans abandoned Christianity in 1978–79, and that almost two million Europeans did so during the same period.[6] This more sobering reality, projected into the years ahead, suggests that more practicing Christians might defect during these coming years than in any comparable previous era—although, again, church attendance is up and Gallup surveys in America indicate little change in the basic beliefs of

Americans. The number of professing Christians in the United States in fact greatly exceeds the number who participate actively in the life of the nation's churches. Gallup found that eight out of ten Americans believe in Christ as a manifestation of God and nine out of ten pray to God at least occasionally—figures nearly double the already remarkable 41 percent who attend church services at least once a week.[7] Do such data presage great new cultural vitalities as more and more people interpret and organize life on the basis of Christian faith?

We should pause before leaping to that conclusion. Gallup himself concluded that the two overriding reasons for the religious revival revealed in his 1977 survey were "the general turning inward to seek refuge from everyday pressures" and "a search for non-material values in light of the fading American Dream."[8] If that is so, these reasons sound more like a reaction to a "broken cup" phenomenon than like a recovery of wholeness of vision. A retreat into the "spiritual" may be a recovery of something profound that had been lost; but it may also reflect a failure to cope with everyday life and to come to terms with the material aspects of experience on the basis of deeper values. That is to say, the "religious revival" might itself be a manifestation of the brokenness of contemporary life—and the brokenness of Christianity itself. We cannot be sure of that, either; but we should pause before taking statistical manifestations of revival at face value.

Earlier in the decade of the 1970s, Dean M. Kelley's book *Why Conservative Churches Are Growing*[9] advanced the thesis that mainline Protestant denominations—the kinds represented in the National Council of the Churches of Christ—were losing members while evangelical, less ecumenically-inclined churches and sects were gaining. The reason seemed to be because the latter groups presented a message of ultimate answers and placed serious demands upon their members, requiring a total commitment. The mainline denominations, on the other hand, were suffering declines because they presented a more relativistic faith and a more laissez faire attitude toward the meaning of church membership. Interpreted on one level, that thesis would seem to suggest that the more conservative and sectarian religious groups have tapped into the longing of large numbers of people for a spiritual home and for a cause capable of enlisting the whole self—while, at the same time, the mainline churches fail to touch more than a segment of the life experience of their members, and that only superficially. But one notes that the churches that are growing present the widest variations of world view, including Southern Baptists, Jehovah's Witnesses, Moon's Unification Church, the Latter-day

Saints, and various Eastern religious groups. Can all such groups commend themselves equally well as religious *perspectives*? If so, how are we to decide which, if any, is the "true" perspective and even which, in the long run, really represents the wave of the future? If the exclusiveness and totality of the claims made upon the believer really account for the numerical success of these groups, then the adequacy of their various perspectives may be, for the moment at least, a secondary question. But the moment will pass; and the staying power of religious groups based upon what may come to be seen as very inadequate world views and social vision may prove limited.

One might also argue that because the mainline churches regard the inclusive faith perspective as the primary question, they have found it impossible to make exclusive claims and demand total commitment in an age when this is difficult to achieve. The mainline churches, by and large, recognize that they are not the sole repositories of truth and guardians of society's moral standards—hence their interest in ecumenical activities and interfaith dialogues. It is difficult to make new converts if one recognizes a certain legitimacy, a certain truth in the position already held by those whom one wishes to convert. And it may be difficult to retain the allegiance of some if all one has to offer is a *relatively* true picture of God and world in an age when people are yearning for spiritual wholeness and commitment to loyalties beyond themselves.

Thus, the situation of the mainline denominations may not be enviable, but it would be decidedly premature to conclude that the more single-minded denominations and sects that are currently growing most rapidly also best represent the shape of the future. One could argue equally well that it is precisely those latter groups that reflect most the religious despair of our age, the fragmentation of the Christian cup. One could also argue that it is the mainline denominations that, for all their current weakness, have the greatest opportunity to put together a holistic vision for our time. For while they currently experience much frustration, they are at least seeking to face the real issues. In the main, they have not allowed themselves to become avenues of escapism, although (as the next chapter will suggest) they do provide certain escapist temptations unique to their form of organization. They have sought to be honest about science and the views of other religions, and they have struggled with the realities of human oppression and hunger and the threat of nuclear war; and they have not been unaware of the hazards and temptations of nationalism and culture religion in its various forms. One could not honestly record that the mainline churches have yet put together a theological vision of wholeness sufficient to command the intellectual respect and commitment of the late twentieth-century world. My point is that they are struggling with elements that must be encompassed in any such vision, while the more rapidly growing denominations and sects are, by and large, ignoring those elements. Whether *any* Christian group can develop a perspective capable of organizing the experience of humanity in our time may not yet be clear. The cup may be broken beyond repair. But there is little promise in loyalties that demand that one turn one's back upon truth, goodness, and beauty in any of its forms, nor upon the needs and hurts and aspirations of people who are not of one's own group.

In any event, we do not want to place too much stock in statistical trends. The problem we are addressing cuts much deeper. Anybody who wished to predict the future religious life of the Roman Empire at the time of Christ would have been badly misled by even the most dependable survey of religious preferences. Christianity would scarcely have been mentioned. Various sects, cults, and philosophical creeds would have looked like the wave of the future. But most of these were virtually dead within five hundred years! Christian faith swept over the face of the Mediterranean world and thence into northern Europe like a brushfire. Why? Largely because it was able to bring life into focus for vast numbers of people who found no such belongingness and completeness in the mythical and philosophical alternatives of that time. A new wineskin was needed for the new wine. A new cup was needed to contain the life experience of a new age. Again our question: Does that cup still suffice now as we complete the second millennium? Or has the Christian cup been fatally fragmented by the actual experience of our era?

## FOUR TRAPS AVOIDED BY
## EARLY CHRISTIANITY

It may be instructive in assessing the problems facing contemporary Christianity to remember that early Christians had to confront four fundamental problems, each representing a potential pitfall which might have ruined the future possibilities of Christianity as integrating center of Western culture.

The first was the temptation to identify the church exclusively with the Hebrew covenant and law. While there are important respects in which Christian faith and church were incomprehensible apart from the Hebrew background, the apostle Paul saw very clearly that to treat the church simply as a part of the Jewish religious community—as many of the original Christians sought to do—would effectively shut out most of the non-Jewish (Gentile) world. Primarily through his leadership, the church was able to make direct appeal to Gentiles, bypassing Jewish initiation rites and other nonessential legal and ritualistic requirements and observances. There is thus a certain cultural sense in which Christianity can be interpreted as the formula that opened up the broader reaches of Mediterranean civilization to inclusion in the deeper meaning of the Hebrew covenant, although the meaning of that covenant would itself be at issue in such an interpretation. Many Christians and Jews alike might be quite offended by such an interpretation, thereby perhaps overlooking some of the profound similarities and differences between Christian and Jewish faiths. Paul perceived that some aspects of his own Jewish faith could only be regarded as arbitrary religious requirements by potential Gentile converts. But the basic covenantal model of reality had broad appeal in a world of crude anthropomorphic cults and abstract philosophical creeds. That appeal might not have resulted in Christianity's becoming the integrating faith of the Mediterranean world had the covenantal view been tied to the nonessential requirements.

The second potential trap the early church avoided was anti-intellectualism. A good deal of the religious life of the period was purely emotional, and there is evidence in the New Testament that some of the first Christians responded primarily on the level of feeling—prompting Paul to remark that he would rather speak five words with his mind in order to instruct others than ten thousand words in tongues, and then to challenge his readers that they should "in thinking be mature." That advice was followed with spectacular results by the early church fathers, particularly those of the Alexandrian school. These early theologians of the church were able to make use of the most sophisticated philosophical systems of the day, particularly Stoicism, in developing a rational presentation of Christian faith. Whether anything of theological importance was sacrificed in the process is still debated among Christian thinkers. But the willingness of those early theologians to face the issues posed by the higher philosophies of the time made it possible for Christianity to be a world view in the most inclusive sense. Purely irrational creeds and cults, on the one hand, and purely rational philosophies, on the other, were not able to bring together the ultimate focus of faith and understanding needed to form a religious "cup."

The third trap avoided in the early church, though only after much internal struggle, was that of antimaterial spiritualism. While uniting faith and reason, some early Christians did so by interpreting the faith in

gnostic or docetic terms. Christ was presented as an other-worldly, imma-
terial spirit, and the material world itself was taken to be the work of some
force other than the God of Jesus Christ. Gnosticism had very great appeal
in the Mediterranean world, and during the second century A.D. fully half
of those calling themselves Christians may have been followers of the
gnostic Christian leader Marcion. But had this kind of spiritualistic interpretation of the faith ultimately prevailed it likely would have doomed
Christianity to irrelevance in a world that is, after all, material.

The fourth trap the church ultimately avoided was sectarian aloofness
from the responsibilities and dilemmas of secular power. It is quite arguable that early Christianity struck too easy an accommodation to Roman
political interests during the Constantinian period and thereafter, and the
triumphalism of "Christendom" is legitimately criticized by many theologians today. Nevertheless, to treat political power as simply evil or unre-
lated to issues of faith is to locate large areas of human existence outside
the purview of the Christian perspective, contributing further to the
fragmentation of human life. Political power is a universal aspect of
human society. The only question is whether it can be made responsive to
values derived from a profound faith.

It would be an interesting exercise to explore other pitfalls that were
avoided or not avoided in the subsequent centuries of Christian development and to see how success or failure in avoiding them affected the
Christian "cup" as a basis for encompassing the breadth and depth of life
in those cultures most affected by Christianity. But our concern now is in
the present tense. Is the Christian cup really broken now, beyond repair?

# 2

---

## FRAGMENTS OF BROKEN FAITH

If, for a moment, we may continue to use the "broken cup" figure of speech to refer to a religious perspective that has been shattered, it is well to remind ourselves that many people continue to cling to fragments of the cup long after it has "passed away." The religious appearance of the fragment and the devotion with which the fragment is grasped easily convey the impression of profound faith. But, in the old chief's manner of speaking, the vessel no longer holds the water of life; it is no longer able to contain life experience as a whole. It no longer serves as the organizing vision and center of value that we all need to give perspective and purpose to everything else. The fragments serve as a comforting distraction from the actual experience of meaninglessness. So one clings to some *aspects* of the old religion as a more or less specialized thing, no longer as a basis of integration. Now people center themselves around this fragmentary thing, to the extent they are able; but they find large areas of their lives no longer capable of being related to the fragment. They themselves are fragmented.

Many people in our time cling to particular aspects of faith or church without really finding it possible to organize their lives as a whole on such a basis. Regardless of the intensity with which the fragments are held, the partial loyalty stands in contradiction to whole areas of temporarily suppressed experience. Indeed, the very intensity of devotion sometimes helps reveal the specialized, not integrative, character of a fragmented faith. So it was in ancient Rome, when devotion to the mystery cults could scarcely conceal the conflict between the substance of those cults and the realities of an emerging, sophisticated world civilization. In that setting, as we have noted, the least useful way of predicting the future shape of Western culture would have been a numerical census of the various religious groups. While the critics of Christianity in that setting bitterly condemned the new faith for undermining Rome by eroding traditional religious loyalties, apologists like St. Augustine made clear that Rome's vulnerability had deeper roots.[1]

In our own time it is similarly beside the point to measure the numerical successes and failures of the rich spectrum of cults and gurus and ideologies, the fads and fantasies and fanaticisms of an age in disarray—except as any of these give promise of the actual integration of human life experience at its deeper levels. And which of them do? Even within mainstream Christianity there are unmistakable evidences of disintegration—of people clinging to fragments of Christian faith and culture in compensation for the loss of the Christian cup as a whole.

There is, to be sure, a certain sense in which Christians have always best understood themselves and their culture most truly in the acceptance of their brokenness, recognizing that one should have no aspiration to possess the whole vision and where, indeed, the pretension of actually having the "whole view" is only an enlarged, but this time concealed, fragment of broken life. I take this to be Hans Küng's point when he writes that "like all human knowledge, the knowledge of faith is also fragmentary. Only when faith remains aware of this does it remain free from arrogance, intolerance and false zeal."[2] But lest we make a virtue of fragmentation too quickly, let it be said that the only claim of such humility is that it leads us home to that center of being that offers promise of reconciliation and enlarged life purpose. The presupposition of such humility is secure faith in a transcendent source of goodness and meaning, not the disintegration of such a faith. The fragments of which we speak in this chapter are the *wreckage*. They are a pale substitute for holistic faith. All the same, we do well to avoid moralism in examining them, as though fragmentary faith were only to be judged and blamed from some superior vantage point. Clearly such fragments must be criticized insofar as they stand between contemporary humanity and wholeness. But we must not forget that when people cling to fragments of the broken cup it is in compensation for a very great loss.

## FRAGMENT 1: THE NOSTALGIC VISION

We may compensate for the loss of a holistic faith by clinging to a nostalgic vision of piety and church life as we knew it before or as we fancy others knew it before. It is faith turned inward and backward, seeking to capture anew the lived experience of Christians of another time or place. In purely personal terms, it may recollect that "no spot is so dear to my childhood as the little brown church in the dale," the cherishing of familiar sentimental hymns, the clinging to childhood images of faith and childhood expressions of prayer. In every other respect, one may have outgrown one's childhood, but not in religion! Consequently, religion is utterly unable to relate to, much less to integrate, those other aspects of life in which one has grown to adult status. A little segment of one's childhood is replayed periodically, but most of the time it is out of sight and mind. The further question of whether Christian faith is generally nostalgic insofar as it projects a divine image derived, ultimately, from warm relationships of childhood memory must be explored more fully in the next chapter. But, regardless of the outcome of the question, there clearly is a good deal of popular religion based upon personal nostalgia alone.

Nostalgia can be reflected in the authority one accords to historical models and leading figures. Among Roman Catholics it may reflect a vision of what the church was in the high medieval period or as reflected in the unchallenged sacramental routines of the church of one's childhood. In a pluralistic world, rent with conflict and divided loyalty, the vision of an imagined Christendom—or even of a real one—in the past may have particular attractiveness. *Then,* at least, was a time when the faith truly dominated and integrated the world; perhaps that same faith could dominate and integrate the world again, just as it did before. In some respects, T.S. Eliot's *Christianity and Culture* expresses this nostalgia, as does Christopher Dawson's *The Historical Reality of Christian Culture*.[3] In the latter book, for instance, Dawson speaks glowingly of the Christian civilization that "actually existed for a thousand years, more or less." This civilization "was a living and growing organism—a great *tree of culture* which bore rich fruit in its season." Whether or not that is a true characterization we may leave to the balanced judgments of the medievalists; but the point is that it is scarcely a model that could be applied to our time without the most serious modification. Many lay Catholics, for whom the overall vision of a Christian civilization would have little meaning, have reacted on a more personal level to the loss of personal religious pattern and vision in the reforms of the post–Vatican II period. Ironically, the reforms in worship and practice, such as saying the Mass in the vernacular, which were intended to bring the church closer to the actual experience of ordinary people had the immediate effect of disorienting many of those same people. But that fact is itself revealing of how far the religious expression had gone toward being a specialized part of life. For the attempt to make the Mass more relevant to the actual experience of people represented an invasion of spheres of their existence that had become thoroughly secularized. Similar comments could be recorded concerning the negative reactions of some Episcopalians and Anglicans to the revision of their prayer book.

Among Lutherans nostaliga may center on the veneration of Martin Luther, and it may allow Luther to settle twentieth-century theological questions in the preserved modes of sixteenth-century expression—so that a scholastic quotation lifted from some writing of Luther's is taken to be decisive. Presbyterians and others of the Reformed tradition may similarly esteem John Calvin. Among Methodists there is a notable turning again to the figure of John Wesley as the source of United Methodist theological and spiritual identity. On one level this is presented as a veneration of particular artifacts and edifices associated with Wesley; on another, more serious plane it is an organizing of Methodist theological work more exclusively around the Standard Sermons and Journals of the founder. There is much to be said, of course, for bringing one's actual roots into awareness and celebration and for sharing one's particular heritage in the wider religious forum. The question is whether any of these particularisms of religious heritage can actually bring contemporary existence into a holistic focus or whether (and to what extent) they function nostalgically to provide comfort in a segment of one's life.

In the Soviet Union many churches have been turned into antireligious museums. That may be equally but more ironically true in the West! In England, for instance, the principal sign of vitality in some village churches is a poster detailing the conditions and regulations under which visitors (mostly North American) can do brass rubbings on the medieval plaques commemorating various saints and sinners. That does not seem far different, in principle, from some of the religious shrines to be found in many other countries—certainly including the United States—where religious life may also be treated as object of nostalgia. And this is not to mention the pins and rings and tie clasps and items of clothing emblazoned with the emblems of this or that denomination which help to establish a sense of identity among the members.

These words are not intended to belittle the jewels of historical memory, for we all need some sense of historical rootage; without that we truly cannot be integrated persons in an integrated society. True integration of self and society includes integration of personal and social history and tradition. But we do need to ask whether such jewels actually provide anybody in the twentieth century with an encompassing frame of reference, with a cup that is capable of holding the water of life in our time.

## FRAGMENT 2: RELIGIOUS FEELING

Shallow pietism can also burst forth in spirit and song. Feeling, too, can be a fragment of the cup. In the moment of high emotion feelings can be all-encompassing, all-consuming. How can there be anything inauthentic that *feels so good*? In the moment of intense feeling one wonders how there can be any reality except that expressed in the moment. It is no wonder that the persistent tendency of charismatic Christians has been to deny the authenticity of the faith of anybody who does not share their feelings—as expressed through the "spirit" and the "gift of tongues." Charismatic Christians deny resolutely that the spiritual gifts are only an emotional expression; but is it not the intensity of the emotion that finally authenticates this reality for them? And does not the dominant wish of other, non-Charismatic Christians, to "be inspired" by religious worship often place emotional feeling in the center of life, even though this may be feeling of a more restrained kind, as evoked by soft organ music and the aesthetic appearances of stained glass and stately arch? Among Protestants, especially, pulpit oratory is sometimes tested above all else by its capacity to evoke good feelings—only secondarily, it would seem, by its capacity to convey truth and moral vision.

But even the noblest or most intense feelings represent but a part of life. The problem is that feelings come and go, attaching themselves to objects and occasions of all kinds. As Küng sarcastically remarks, "If we rely on feelings, the name can be changed as desired: instead of Che Guevara with the Jesus look we can have Jesus with the Guevara look, and again vice versa."[4] We can have the intense feelings of a victory in football, the solemn feelings of a fraternity ritual, the happy feelings of the wedding feast, the dedicated feelings of the political party worker (of any party), the pious feelings evoked by the songs of one's religious childhood. But do any of these feelings persist long enough to afford overall integrity to our lives and unity to our experience? And what is it about the feelings themselves that marks them specifically as Christian?

In the 1950s a leading Methodist church in Atlanta, Georgia had a huge billboard by its front door, visible for a long distance, which advertised *Happy Sunday Nights*. No doubt many people did experience happiness in that setting. But that very church turned black people away from attendance or membership, clearly demonstrating that the feelings of many of its members were incapable of encompassing the realities of a new day in the American South, much less of expressing Christian theological integrity.[5] It is regrettably difficult even to distinguish between moral goodness and the demonic in feelings. One recalls old newsreels showing the happy throngs of people greeting Adolf Hitler, the fatherly kindness with which he embraced the children who had brought him flowers, and the vast throngs of Nazis congregated at Nuremberg joyfully singing their devotion to the new Reich with words set to one of Haydn's noblest melodies!

It is no wonder that prophetic twentieth-century theologians like Karl Barth raised serious questions about the tendency in some nineteenth- and twentieth-century theology to define religion largely in terms of feelings.

Any "cup" must be able to contain the whole range of human feeling, and a part of the fragmentation of much contemporary life consists precisely in the inadequacy of people to integrate their feelings with the rest of their experience and with their basic values. Feelings remain very important. But feeling alone is not enough to integrate human life.

### FRAGMENT 3: LITURGICAL FORMALISM

By "liturgical formalism" I mean treating particular forms of liturgy as the essence of the faith. Worship itself is not a sign of brokenness, at least not necessarily. Worship is the center of all religious faith, for it is bringing to the center of one's own being the source of meaning and value by which one lives. It entails the celebration of good and the acknowledgment of struggle to overcome evil. So long as the reality celebrated in worship is profound enough to encompass and interpret all other realities without illusion, worship is itself the essence of the whole cup.

But forms of worship, taken as ends in themselves, are characteristic fragments among many who have lost a sense of the wholeness of faith. Again, sound reasons exist why particular forms of worship may be chosen rather than others. For such reasons to be "sound" they must reflect a desire to preserve the wholeness of faith. For example, the elimination of the unilateral pledge by the bride to "obey" her husband has frequently been replaced in the contemporary church by language symbolizing the equality of partners in the marriage covenant. At the same time, the retention of the words "till death us do part" symbolizes the unity and dependability of that covenant. In both cases, liturgical form brings important realities into profounder focus.

But people can continue to cling to particular observances long after the point of those observances has been lost. A particular order of service, a given form of vestment, certain designated liturgical colors or designated sacramental observances, when turned into absolutes may reflect a fragmented faith. Paul skillfully avoided this "trap" in the early church by treating the rites and rituals of Jewish tradition as dispensable among the Gentiles who were attracted to the new Christian faith. But it remains a potential trap today. Some of the banners and balloons of contemporary worship in many churches of recent years are difficult to classify. Much of this came about as a reaction against older, less lively forms of worship and as a liberation of life to new levels of celebration and joy. And yet all this celebration, too, can be fragmentary. It can be avant garde for avant garde's sake or aestheticism for aestheticism's sake, and not a reflection of wholeness of faith and life. It can be irrelevant to the deepest currents of human experience, including tragedies of sin and death and misery; it can express an escape from unpleasant everyday experience, and it can convey a subtle anti-intellectualism.

A key test, helping to identify whether particular forms of liturgy do in fact function as fragmentary faith, is to ask whether any particular forms could be set aside for the sake of a fuller realization of the faith in a given circumstance or whether it is "inconceivable" that a particular form could be abandoned by real Christians. Could one substitute something else for wine in the Eucharist if no wine were available or if use of wine were physiologically undesirable for particular people? Would one regard a Quaker meeting as a liturgically acceptable form of Christian worship in that community of faith? Does one believe that particular liturgical practices have been set forth by God and that deviation is sinful disobedience? For Christians, that question may be particularly relevant when applied to the sacraments, which are often taken to be divinely appointed. It is doubtful that contemporary humanity, by and large, is prepared to take such a claim at face value, however meaningful sacramental observances may be in the life of the church.

Of course, the trap of liturgical formalism is often a disguised form of the nostalgia of which we have already spoken. It can represent sentimentally meaningful habit patterns or nostalgic re-creations of an image one has of the church as it has always been. Or, it can all come down to a simple matter of taste, with one's own particular taste being absolutized. A somewhat vivid illustration of the latter was provided by a New England church of my acquaintance, where a prominent (and very wealthy) old member threatened to resign from the church because a new minister, in leading the Lord's Prayer, had pronounced "trespasses" as tres-páss-es and not as trés-passes. That was, he said, the last straw. And so it was!

## FRAGMENT 4: INSTITUTIONAL ACTIVISM

Again, the church as an organization, as an institution, can claim our fragmented loyalty. The institution and its buildings, programs, and structure of leadership roles can be a tangible, sometimes comforting fragment. There is certainly nothing wrong with institutions, buildings, programs, and leadership as such. No society could long do without them. But it is another matter when these things become definitive of one's understanding of Christian faith. People can devote large quantities of energy to these institutional and programmatic interests, assuming the religious significance of such action, while remaining relatively unaffected by this in the remainder of their life experience. It is interesting that Gordon Allport and other social psychologists have documented the tendency of many active church participants to be more inclined toward racial prejudice and other forms of intolerance than those having no connection with religious groups at all.[6] This research is a telling reminder that people can flee into organizational activity as a way of avoiding the difficult tasks of coping with unfamiliar realities and unappreciated people. Institutional activism can buttress a rigid personality which, in turn, reflects deep underlying anxiety.

Even Christians whose institutional activities are in no sense pathological may find such activity fulfilling socially but not the focal point for their ultimate values and the overall integration of their lives. For some active church people, church activity may be the functional equivalent of any other good hobby or organizational activity, except that this hobby may be mildly tinctured with a sense of doing good. Church activity, in other words, can be to participants much the same thing as PTA activity, or scouting, or politics, or service club activity. And people can aspire to leadership and status within the church for precisely the same reasons they seek such things in other institutional contexts. All such activity may be very good in itself, contributing something to human good in general, while still it remains only a fragmentary representation of Christian faith.

The fact that this can be so should lead us to caution in assessing the religious differences between the United States and Europe. Active church participation in Europe is very much lower than in America. This has led some to suppose that Europe has already entered a secular post-Christian era and that America, in time, may follow. But the point is that in some respects America may already be there. The much higher levels of church participation are not wholly convincing evidence to the contrary until it can be established that such participation expresses the profound integration of people's personal and social existence. The differences between America and Europe may have to do with more superficial factors, including the great religious pluralism in America and the contrast between forms of support for European state churches and America's voluntary institutions. America's churches may prosper more because they typically provide more opportunity for active social involvement. But that involvement does not always cut very deeply.

All religious institutions fulfill social and psychological functions. To note that much religious activity is on that plane does not by itself mean that the "cup" of religious activists is broken. My point is simply that since religious institutions do fulfill such functions they may retain a basis for continued existence long after a deeply religious purpose has become fragmented. The decisive test is to ask what is the relationship between church participation and the overall fabric of one's existence, including one's basic beliefs and attitudes. From a Christian standpoint, a good deal of contemporary church activity doubtless fails that kind of test.

## FRAGMENT 5: FUNDAMENTALISM

Particular religious doctrines can also be grasped tenaciously as fragments of the Christian cup, whether or not those doctrines bear any resemblance to observable experience and whether or not they are even relevant to the deeper questions of the human spirit.

The resurgence of fundamentalism within Christianity and some other religions is often mistakenly understood as a great new wave of religious revival when in fact it may be nothing more than a fragmented response of religious despair. It may be the abandonment of the possibility of a unified world view encompassing the factual, rational, emotional, and moral experience of contemporary humanity. Its appeal is necessarily arbitrary and dependent upon sources of external authority. People do not believe the doctrines because they are persuaded of their truth so much as because of the need for some external support to shore up a very insecure faith. The points about which the fundamentalist is most contentious (the "fundamentals") characteristically represent the points in an inherited faith view that are least defensible and must thus be defended most in order to preserve a largely obsolete perspective. In our way of speaking, the structure is already broken, for it can no longer integrate important areas of living experience and emerging realms of human knowledge.

In the North American context, Christian fundamentalism is largely defined by belief in the literal truth of the entire contents of the Bible. Such attitudes can also be found in other religions, notably within Islam, a religion similarly oriented toward a single sacred scripture, the Qur'an. Thus, Islamic fundamentalism has a view of the Qur'an that is substantially interchangeable with a Christian fundamentalist view of the Bible, except for the actual differences of content of the two books. The Christian fundamentalist would find it utterly impossible to appeal to literal biblical authority in conversation with a Moslem fundamentalist, and vice versa, for neither is prepared to subject the written authority to a more universal test of truth. It does no good to quote particular verses of sacred scripture—of any sacred scripture—to close an argument with people who do not accept the authority of the scripture.

The tendency of Christian fundamentalists to accept the literal, factual truth of everything contained in the Bible leads to strained attempts to preserve belief in even the most problematic statements of fact or moral teaching. If the whole Bible is literally "God's word," then it is blasphemous to question any part of the written message, with small concessions to unimportant errors in translation. If we cannot accept all the Bible, how can we believe any of it?—a test one would scarcely apply to any other writing, but quite revealing of the mistrust of the human mind to make discriminating judgments on the basis of experience and thought. Such literalism leads to strained attempts to deal with contradictions within the Bible and to difficulties in interpreting conflicts between the Bible and observable factual data. When strained interpretations fail, the fundamentalist appeals to authority alone: the Bible is true because it says it is true (at least that implication can be drawn by a narrow reading of 2 Tim. 3:16: "All scripture is inspired by God" if one is willing to overlook the fact that the New Testament as such did not even exist at the time that was written). Such an authoritarian use of scriptural materials was alien to the mind of the early church,[7] but acceptance of the literal truth of all parts of the Bible is the decisive test of Christian faith for the fundamentalist. Battle lines therefore tend to form around those aspects of Scripture that seem most difficult to accept. Then, whether a given story is literally true becomes the most important thing about it.

Illustrating the point, the newly elected president of a large American denomination sought to rally the faithful in support of biblical literalism by proclaiming his belief that "Jonah was a literal person, swallowed by a literal fish, spit out of a literal stomach, and in a literal mess." Thus he totally misconstrued the import of a profound but doubtless fictional writing in the Old Testament. An editorial in the publication of the conservative caucus of another leading American denomination insisted that belief in the virgin birth of Jesus is an important test of the seriousness of Christian faith: "Evangelicals believe that the Bible is a reliable record of things that really did happen and will happen. We believe that nothing false is found from Genesis to Revelation."[8] Since God is infinite in power, the editorial noted, who are we mortals to question God's ability to create a child without a human father? How can we believe in the deity of Jesus without the virgin birth? "If Jesus' mother and father were both human beings, then He would be no different from you and me . . . a great man, but certainly not God."

A North American band of fundamentalists recently embarked on a major campaign to require the teaching of stories of creation in the Book of Genesis alongside evolutionary theories in public school biology classes, treating both as equally valid scientific theories. One of the leaders of this movement, Henry Morris, is quoted as saying, "It is only in the Bible that we can possibly obtain any information about the methods of creation, the order of creation, the duration of creation, or any of the other details of creation." He also says that "the Bible teaches that the earth existed before the stars, that it was initially covered by water, that plant life preceded the sun, that the first animals created were the whales, that birds were made before insects, that man was made before woman. . . . If the Bible is really the word of God . . . then evolution and its geological age-system must be completely false."[9]

The intellectual failings of fundamentalism seem so obvious that one is hard pressed to account for its considerable cultural successes in recent years. But the social power of the movement should not be too surprising and the wrong conclusions should not be drawn from it. On the surface, one is tempted to be impressed by the success (though still limited) of the scientific creationism campaign and similar movements. And the impressive union of fundamentalist religion with conservative political movements (as in the American Moral Majority) might lead one to suppose that fundamentalism is more creative and integrative in the contemporary world than it really is.

Great movements and great political power can be generated out of anxiety over the fragmentation of human culture. Such movements can be particularly mean-spirited in the way in which they exercise power and deal with their opponents. At that deeper level of cultural integration or disintegration to which the metaphor "cup" applies, such movements can be both weak and profoundly destructive at the same time. They are weak in that they lack the power of true cultural creativity and integration; they are destructive in that they impose particular meanings and values upon unpersuaded people through power politics. Thus fundamentalism may do more than illustrate the brokenness of faith; it can contribute to further disintegration. Ironically, the greatest long-term damage done by fundamentalist movements may be to Christianity itself.

## FRAGMENT 6: RELIGIOUS NATIONALISM

We have already noted the occasional union of fundamentalism with conservative political movements. That should not be surprising, if at bottom the endeavor of fundamentalism is to shore up what is perceived to be a collapsing way of life. Change itself is threatening; and there is a heightened sense of group identification among those experiencing a disintegration of their whole way of life. Logically, biblical fundamentalism would appear to be antithetical to nationalism, since the Bible's frame of reference is beyond the nation. But the connection is psychologically understandable all the same. The connection is highly visible in Middle Eastern politics, where nationalism in countries like Iran is deeply intertwined with the Islamic fundamentalism of the Shiite sect, and where some forms of Jewish fundamentalism are indistinguishable from Israeli nationalism.

In the United States, movements like the Moral Majority are deeply nationalistic. Appeals to return society to trusted and now threatened moral values are inextricably linked with appeals to nationalism—as in one fund-raising letter in which the Rev. Jerry Falwell, head of Moral Majority, asserted that "our grand old flag is going down the drain" because of a series of moral corruptions (mostly related to sex) and such political sins as that "we gave away the Panama Canal, to prevent 'offending' a leftist government!" In another such letter Falwell spoke vigorously against disarmament efforts and said that "we Americans who are in favor of a strong national defense must speak out now—before it's too late," noting that the Moral Majority's Washington, D. C. staff was standing by for "the task of monitoring, lobbying, and researching what Congress is and is not doing to support President Reagan's defense program."[10]

Such statements have many historical antecedents in this and other lands; the identification of God with national chauvinism is scarcely a recent invention. Nor is it always to be characterized as a fragmentary faith, as we have been using that term. Robert Bellah has noted that there is need for a civil religion of sorts marking a common realm of shared values and traditions among the people of a nation uniting them despite other conflicts of creed and practice.[11] Some of the great figures of American history—one thinks instinctively of Abraham Lincoln and Martin Luther King, Jr.—appealed effectively to such a common realm of shared values. But whether such a "civil religion" is being a part of a holistic cup may be dependent upon whether the civil religion is confirmed by or in conflict with one's ultimately inclusive faith allegiance. Lincoln and King in fact appear to present such a wholeness. Their public statements reflect a deep integrity between their conception of the nation's best traditions and ideals and the (some would say, profoundly) Christian faith they shared. But statements like those of Falwell paint a different picture. There is a narrowness of appeal: One no longer has Lincoln's and King's sensitivity to God's righteous judgment of all, one's own nation included, nor the sense of tragedy about war and the recognition that even the nation's adversaries are a part of God's concern. Wrapping the flag around oneself is another way of shoring up a broken faith; patriotism of the narrow kind continues to be the last resort not only of scoundrels—as the saying has it—but also of many who can find no more inclusive reality to live for.

## FRAGMENT 7: RELIGIOUS RATIONALISM

The obverse side of the fundamentalist problem for Christianity may well be a certain style of rationalism that defines reality narrowly in terms of certain rational methods and their intellectual results. For example, the biblical scholarship of the past few generations has developed immensely fruitful methods of sorting out the background of particular writings—the historical setting, the scribal accretions, the motives for writing, and, in some instances, the actual authorship. But religious writings, like poetry, may have deeper levels of meaning, with possibilities for bringing contemporary problems into focus that purely factual scholarship cannot wholly grasp. Writings sometimes point to levels of meaning that are more profound even than what was consciously in the mind of the writer at the time of writing. Preoccupation with detail can lead to loss of deeper truth. I referred to this as the obverse side of the fundamentalist problem because such rationalism may appear to be completely at odds with the irrational appearance of fundamentalism. But actually religious rationalism may have much in common with fundamentalism. Both are preoccupied with surface problems, not with deeper levels of meaning. A fundamentalist may be concerned only with the literal truth of the whole Bible while a certain kind of rationalist may only be concerned to negate such superstitious views. But both can be preoccupied with problems of detail to the neglect of more profound truth.

Secularism may be more inclusive than the kind of rationalism I am characterizing here, but it sometimes appears more as rational negation of certain rejected religious ideas than as a new and holistic vision of meaning. One such humanistic writing, purporting to speak for humanists in general, asserts that

> instead of basing our attitude toward life upon a dogma, a spiritual assumption, or an imaginary law of God, we based it upon life itself. Instead of answering problems with a text from the Bible, we solve them in the light of verified knowledge of the physical, intellectual, and moral constitution of man.[12]

"In the past," this writer continues, "the fears and hopes alike of religion taught man to deny life, to despise it, to evade it. . . . But our religion is one which says 'yea' to life here and now." Such statements might appear not to be fragments off the Christian cup since they explicitly disavow Christian views. And yet, the fact that they are so largely defined by negative reference to Christian faith is telling. The sweeping dismissal of past religion is a clue that this new humanist faith does not wholly integrate aspects of life that found expression, no matter how imperfectly, in previous religious traditions. And while "life" is appealed to as the foundation of the new faith, the appeal to "verified knowledge" may be more revealing of an essentially rationalist approach to reality.

## FRAGMENT 8: SOCIAL ACTIVISM

One reaction to the loss of confidence in an inclusive religious perspective is to pour oneself into activity designed to improve the human lot, to rectify injustices, to support causes of great importance for the well-being of oppressed and suffering peoples. Such purposeful activity has clear meaning. But it, too, can be a fragment of the cup if it only reflects a general spiritual rootlessness. Such fragmentary social action can be revealed in the haste with which particular causes are adopted and the corresponding speed with which the activist either burns out or moves on to some other preoccupation. It can also be revealed in a tendency to subordinate one's social conscience to that of activist groups and movements—that is, in the lack of confidence in a transcendent source of values. The question is whether the particular social cause is an expression of the deeper integrity of Christian faith or only a fragment of concern seized upon to provide some transient meaning to life's little day. The objectives of fragmented Christian activism are less an outgrowth of the wholeness of faith and more a matter of arbitrary fixation on some attractive goal or cause— sometimes with a measure of self-righteousness added to the mix.

Social activists are often accused of substituting a "social gospel" for the real gospel, by which such critics generally mean that concern for improvements in particular social, economic, and political structures has replaced concern for real people in the depth of one's being—that impersonal, objective systems and laws have replaced human beings in their spiritual nature, and that social activists believe improvement in social structures will automatically take care of important spiritual needs. In religious terms this is a serious charge, for it suggests that a rootless activism has replaced wholeness of religious perspective. I suspect the charge is not always leveled in good faith. Those who make it may have concealed ideological reasons to oppose more equitable distribution of economic benefits and broader sharing in social power. Also, they may have embraced the deviant form of Christianity known as docetism, the denial of the material aspects of life to which we have already referred. But without conceding that all social activism expresses this kind of fragmentation, we may readily acknowledge that *some* does. The fact that people do "burn out" is plainly observable, as is the detachment of others from responsible theological thought and holistic worship.

Such fragmentation can be reinforced at the intellectual level, too, when theological thought is treated purely as a function of social location. Sociology of knowledge (the study of how social factors influence and limit our intellectual life) has much to contribute to critical philosophy and theology. The unique perspective of a black person or a woman or a person from a Third World country may be important correctives to theology as conducted by white male theologians from North America and Europe. But if all truth is entirely relative to one's unique social background, then all that remains is the social struggle. If, for instance, a white woman cannot understand the theological position of a black man, if a poor person cannot understand a rich one, if a North American cannot understand a Brazilian—and vice versa—then a shared holistic perspective is no longer possible and we must be content with fragments of social conflict and action.[13]

To ignore social concerns is to hold a fragmented faith, and many of the social concerns of the social activist must be encompassed in any theological perspective promising a restoration of the Christian cup. But those concerns, taken by themselves, cannot constitute that cup.

## FRAGMENT 9: THEOLOGY AND PHILOSOPHY
## LIMITED TO HISTORY

We may note, finally, the existence of theological and philosophical tendencies that avoid altogether the question of what is ultimately and objectively real. The "death of God" theologies of the 1960s which utilized the metaphor of death to characterize the idea of God as no longer being applicable to real life issues may be viewed in this way. In one form, this borrowed from Ludwig Feuerbach's idea that "God" is only a personification of love in human relationship and, indeed, that "God" leads one to alienation from our true humanity by mislocating and misdefining love.[14] In another, the loss of God celebrated human freedom and creative independence.[15] But generally missing from these theologies was any grappling with the character of ultimate reality.

Similar characterization could be offered of some forms of phenomenology and existentialism portraying humanity as self-actualizing. Religious symbols are taken to be a reflection of historical process in some way, not as reference to the objectively real character of the source of being. Such theological tendencies, which I characterize only broadly, are clearly an important reminder of the significance of action and responsibility in history, without which theological perspective can be curiously abstract and detached from real life. Yet, insofar as such tendencies avoid issues of ultimate truth, including truth beyond history, they lack the mooring points for an understanding of history itself. The point may be illustrated in the work of Jean-Paul Sartre, who portrays the drama of life as each person's struggle to be authentic through assuming full responsibility for the choices that make us what we are.[16] To make responsible decisions and to live by their consequences is to form one's personhood. Life is not something that happens to us—we happen to it. We do not live as created but as self-creating; not as aspects of being but as instances of doing. Authenticity appears in this scheme of things as a fundamental value, as surely it is; but it is rather assumed that humanity is definitely on its own in an otherwise impersonal universe. This characterization of things makes it difficult to gather all aspects of experience in the holistic perspective except insofar as it is frankly a perspective of one's own subjective choosing. This also tends to be very individualistic, even though some existentialists, such as Sartre, sought to combine it with a social perspective.

Consider, too, the linguistic philosophies to which passing reference was made in the first chapter. According to some, such as Ayer, religious language per se is not only untrue, it is meaningless. Those who opt for that judgment not only do not linger over fragments of the cup, they deny that the cup ever had any meaningful reality at any time. Other linguistic analysts eschew metaphysics or theology while seeking to say meaningful things about ethics. And indeed, a discernible tendency in most philosophical ethics of the past thirty years has been to detach ethical judgments from metaphysical or ontological views, so that the ethics itself cannot be an expression of a holistic conception of reality.[17]

Clearly more would have to be said about such theological and philosophical tendencies before entering into serious criticism. But our purpose here is the more limited one of noting that these tendencies offer fragments to which people can cling when an overall vision of the meaning of reality no longer seems possible.

## THE PATHOS OF FRAGMENTATION

Almost every aspect of the contemporary religious scene can be held as a fragment of faith, expressing, ironically, a denial of the wholeness of faith. I have not wished to lampoon or ridicule fragmentary attitudes and activities, even though some may have profoundly destructive effects. They spring from a kind of pathos in the felt disintegration of a Christian cultural setting. An analysis such as this must spring more from compassion than from moralistic judgment, the same kind of compassion summoned forth even by the anti-Christian Karl Marx when he characterized religion as the "opium of the people." For Marx perceived clearly that humankind alienated from itself and from reality *needs* a narcotic to help bear the unbearable pain of its existence. So it is with fragments of the cup! Are they not better, humanly speaking, than no cup at all? Do they not at least provide us with something to hold onto during a period of great uncertainty? Do they not, each of them, still convey some part of the truth, some germ of goodness, some hint of meaning that needs to be and can be affirmed? Yes, of course. But insofar as they mask the condition of brokenness they may obstruct our true condition.

Like Marx, though perhaps not with his world view, we should conclude that hard reality is preferable to pleasant illusion. In the insistence upon honesty, the existentialists are right. It is better to be honest in our quest for truth in all its wholeness, hoping that we shall find the undergirding basis of life or that it will somehow find us. It is not a good thing to lie to ourselves and to others, even when we think it for the greater glory of God! We should not fudge on the deeper questions as a way of bringing more credit to Christ! We cannot substitute "cheap grace" (Bonhoeffer) and mellow feelings, nor even heroic actions, for the profound searching and deeper assurances of what Christians have called the Holy Spirit. The faith of Christians must be capable of encompassing the whole of their experience or it will not finally help them much with any of it.

But are we moving into a post-Christian era? Has the Christian cup been decisively broken, now at the conclusion of its second millennium? Are the currents and energies of humankind pouring out beyond those confines into something altogether different, altogether new? Is the voice of the church to this age only the voice of nostalgia, or of rudderless activism, or of mindless fanaticism, or sweet but meaningless feelings, or fragmented philosophies and theologies?

A final word on that subject may not be possible for any of us yet. But a final point must be registered before concluding this chapter. While many people in our time really have abandoned the idea that Christian faith can nurture and sustain the wholeness of life, there remains a vast reservoir of hope that somehow it can. Humankind does not cheerfully settle for fragmented life. It yearns for wholeness and purpose grounded in truth. Knowing themselves to be broken, women and men yet seek to understand the prayer of St. Augustine: "Thou hast made us for thyself and our hearts are restless until they find their rest in thee." Large numbers of people suspect that that is so. But this age has not yet found that rest.

# 3

## PARTIAL TRUTHS AND THE
## WHOLE TRUTH

During the summer of 1969, less than a year after the Soviet invasion destroyed the democratic reform movement now known as the Prague Spring, I found myself in Czechoslovakia with a small group of concerned Americans. It was an unforgettable experience. Everywhere we went we encountered the lingering effects of the brief renaissance of Czech freedom and creativity; and everywhere we also found bitter disappointment that this reassertion of the national spirit had been crushed so decisively.

The night before we left Prague, three of us wandered up Wenceslaus Square to the great old national museum. There, seated in the shadows of a doorway, we encountered a young Czech. Despite linguistic problems, we fell into a conversation alternating between English and German. We asked what were the little pockmarks that could be seen dotting the façade of the splendid old building. "Russian tanks," he replied simply. We asked why. He answered, "There was no reason." In further conversation he related that he was a philosophy student at Charles University, that he was a Marxist, that he had been a member of the Communist Party until the Soviet invasion. He had resigned from the party in disillusionment after the defeat of "socialism with a human face," although he continued to regard himself as a Marxist and a socialist. He was well informed about world events in general. We shared with him our own anguish about the then-current war in Vietnam and about other problems in American life. The conversation ranged into deeper philosophical matters. As we finally turned to go, he asked us in halting English, "What really is there to believe?"

I continue to be haunted by those words. They voice the deeper questioning of thoughtful people of many lands in a troubled era of human history. For what really is there to believe?

Easy answers leap to mind. Indeed, answers to that question are all lined up, clamoring for the world's attention! But no answer could have claimed the young Czech's assent that did not take into fullest account the depths of his disillusionment, the strength of his commitment to social justice, the sophistication of his grasp of secular sources of knowledge. His question clearly sought for more than a fragmentary representation of any outworn faith. He would have the whole cup or none. An answer to him would have to be able to encompass and make sense of all his values and perceptions; it would have to claim his whole being. So what answer could possibly be given?

## LIMITS TO HUMAN KNOWLEDGE

We do well to remember one very important point, holding it in mind throughout the rest of this book: There is no way to truth and goodness without risk, and no way to be absolutely certain that we have gotten there. That is simply the human condition. Religion, philosophy, or science cannot set aside the fact that we are limited, mortal human beings. This means that the basis upon which any human cup can be founded— confidence that we understand reality and that we know what is ultimately good—is, at best, subject to limitation.

The limits to human knowledge have been recognized by philosophers virtually since the beginning of human thought about knowing. It was recognized very early that our perceptions of the objective world must travel through our senses before registering with our minds and that faulty sense impressions lead to faulty knowledge. It is necessary to have confidence in our senses in order to believe that our perceptions accurately reflect the objective world. The point was sharpened in the British empirical tradition which radically questioned common-sense notions of the relationship between objects and perceptions and ideas. To George Berkeley, for instance, the essence of things lies in their perception; he did not shrink from the conclusion that objects have no independent existence outside the minds of thinking beings. The only things we can perceive are our own sensations and ideas.[1] To David Hume, all ideas are but the reflection of impressions made up of sensations, passions, and emotions, and ideas represent the images of impressions in thinking and reasoning. The idea of objective substance can only be derived from impressions; and this idea he characterized as "nothing but a collection of simple ideas that are united by the imagination, and have a particular name assigned them."[2] Both Berkeley and Hume found ways of resolving the problem of knowledge without recourse to pure subjectivism, but neither could escape the conclusion that our perceptions are in our minds and the only *direct* contact the mind has with anything is through its own perceptions and ideas.

Immanuel Kant developed his theory of knowledge from the same point, concluding that the mind cannot know the external thing in itself. Our modes of perception are shaped into concepts about reality by the structure of the mind itself. Such conceptual categories as space and time and causation represent the mind's own structure. We cannot *know* objective reality as it is in itself *directly*. All knowledge is mediated knowledge; that is, it is mediated through the mind's own nature. Again, whether Kant's own way of resolving the problem of knowledge is adequate does not need to detain us here as long as we grasp, with him, the point that there is no reason to believe that our sensory perceptions and mental constitution are capable of objectively grasping external reality—that is, grasping it apart from what is mediated to us through our senses and shaped by our minds.

An interesting and possibly illuminating rejoinder to this trend of thinking was provided by Friedrich Engels. Engels, anxious to preserve confidence in the objective validity of science (and with it his and Marx's conception of scientific socialism) replied to Kant that it is indeed possible to know objective reality. If one knows all the qualities of a thing, as they are presented to the senses, then everything important about a thing is known and it only remains to be said that the thing itself is not physically present inside one's head. Our confidence in our perceptions of the qualities of things, Engels insisted, is founded on the fact that we can observe them producing the same effects repeatedly under identical circumstances through scientific method.[3]

The objection may be valid, but it is superficial. Berkeley, Hume, and Kant all accepted the validity of scientific method—insofar as it had advanced during their respective lifetimes. The issue they pose is not whether our perceptions of reality function in accordance with orderly laws and sequences or not, but rather it is the degree to which we can grasp the essence of objects apart from their effects upon our perceptions. How is one to prove that our perceptions are *complete*? To put the question back to Engels, how is one to know that we do know *all* the qualities of a thing? In accordance with the state of nineteenth-century science, Engels could have known certain of the qualities of hydrogen, but he could not have had the slightest inkling of the vast energy-releasing potential of hydrogen through nuclear fusion. By the same token, any electrician can say what electricity "is," but a physicist cannot! There are at least practical reasons for being confident that our perceptions of many of the qualities of many things do indeed accurately reflect objective realities outside our minds (due allowances having been made for common human mistakes). But one simply cannot leap from that to the conclusion that we have got it *all*. Even the simplest object presents itself to us through particular effects upon our senses. There is no way to be sure that we have perceived all of the possible effects of an object and that we truly know it—that is, conclusively know it—as it exists in itself. We can legitimately say that we know the contents of our minds, but we cannot *know* that the contents of our minds accurately exhibit the objective world.

If that is the situation so far as our knowledge of the *parts* of reality is concerned, what about the whole of it? What can we know about reality as a whole? Here we confront not only a problem of processing particular impressions from the external world through our senses and our minds; we also confront the fact that we are severely limited in the extent of our contact with potential data. None of us has ever experienced all of reality; no one has ever experienced more than a tiny portion of *everything*. We are, of course, very clever with our minds. Human beings are good at adding two and two and coming up with E equals MC squared. We experience data—more, doubtless, than Berkeley or Hume supposed—and marshal evidences for propositions, and then relate proposition to proposition logically. We probe the frontiers of astronomy and of microscopic dust. We are very good at analyzing the individual psyche and the behavior of crowds. We invent technological wonders on the foundations of our discoveries, threading astronomical needles with our space vehicles at distances of a billion miles, and hastening the evolution of species through mastery of genetics. We are really very clever! But with all that, the frontiers of the unknown keep expanding before the onrush of knowledge: The more we know, the more it appears that we do not know. And the character of the whole of reality and the interconnectedness of its aspects remain enshrouded in mystery.

Conceding that reality does manifest itself through the things we can observe—as, with qualification, we must—our problem is that reality remains so much greater than the sum of its observable parts. Whenever people claim to know everything worth knowing that is fairly good evidence that they have settled for some little corner of truth while shutting out the rest. Great minds are not offended by their own inherent limitations; they are big enough to pause from time to time to wonder at the vast unknown that far exceeds the contents of any human brain. Note, for instance, the words of Albert Einstein:

> The most beautiful thing we can experience is the mysterious. It is the source of all true art and science. He to whom this emotion is a stranger, who can no longer pause to wonder and stand rapt in awe, is as good as dead; his eyes are closed. This insight into the mystery of life, coupled though it be with fear, has also given rise to religion. To know that what is impenetrable to us really exists, manifesting itself as the highest wisdom and the most radiant beauty which our dull faculties can comprehend only in their most primitive forms— this knowledge, this feeling, is at the center of true religiousness. . . . It is enough for me to contemplate the mystery of conscious life perpetuating itself through all eternity, to reflect upon the marvelous structure of the universe which we can dimly perceive, and try humbly to comprehend even an infinitesimal part of the intelligence manifested in nature.[4]

While Einstein, in the omitted portion of this quotation, criticized certain traditional religious beliefs, he did so in the name of a bigger conception of reality than he associated with traditional beliefs; he called for a world view less bound to superficial certainties and egocentric attitudes as he understood them. We have partial truths enough to give us a sense of the rationality and grandeur and mystery of the whole. But the whole truth is not available to us.

## DOES THE WHOLE TRUTH MATTER?

Is it not a little bit pretentious, then, for us even to worry about the nature of the "whole of reality"? Since we cannot know everything, why should we care about the character of the whole? Why should "ultimate" reality, whatever that may mean, concern us?

A good deal of mid-twentieth-century philosophy has raised exactly that question. It is therefore not an accident that twentieth-century philosophy has often avoided metaphysical speculation altogether. Much of it has concentrated instead upon analysis of human existence and the integrity of decisions whereby we constitute our own being as authentic persons. While existentialism in its various forms is very much interested in ultimate questions, these questions are not characteristically questions about the nature of reality as a whole but rather questions about human integrity and the meanings we create and sustain in our own existence. We live only once; our ultimate choice is whether to live lives that matter or to waste our lives. Life lived on the basis of metaphysical speculations is misplaced. Such a life tends to be alienated from the human relationships that really do matter and the creative accomplishments we really might be able to undertake. Existentialism thus seeks to preserve our humanity from abstraction, which it sees to be the negation of all that is truly ultimate about us.

Other forms of philosophy, including especially those influenced most by Marxism, have been preoccupied with social questions. Personal authenticity is here subordinated to, or at least defined by, the quest for social justice. The meaning of life is social relationship. Whether from a Marxist perspective or some other (such as that of Rawls[5]), it seems possible to address the meaning of life without reference to the ultimate character of reality. Even the atheism of Marx is increasingly perceived by Marxists as irrelevant to the main concern of Marxism, which is praxis leading to social transformation. For the latter, it seems unnecessary to venture final judgments about the nature of ultimate reality. The only things that matter are material, the dialectics of history, and the possibilities of human society once the contradictions of historical oppression have been overcome. Again, it is all very much on a human plane.

Such tendencies in twentieth-century thought can be criticized for not being consistent enough. They imply that life really does matter and that personal authenticity or social justice lay ultimate claims upon us. They present the strongest kind of moral appeal; to them, the contrast between good and evil is stark and clear, and to be wholly human is to choose good and join in the fight against evil. *Meaning* is to be found in such choices and struggles. But in a universe that is, in Bertrand Russell's phrase, "blind to good and evil" it would appear that nothing ultimately matters. All moral endeavor would appear to be the building of castles of sand, defending them against adversaries. But still the relentless tides must come to efface even the grandest structure, and all will again be as before when no human hand had touched the sand. If all of our accomplishments and all of our relationships—not to say all of our thoughts and feelings— are written upon the sand, what meaning can there be in face of the eternal sea?

Or again, is not such a universe rather like a football game? It is filled with meaning, both for players and for spectators. One can measure success or failure by the defense of one's goal and the conquest of the opponent's. Rules give ordered regularity, and moral behavior can be marked by respecting them. One's entire being is totally engrossed in the intensity of the struggle within this self-contained system of meaning. But a year, a generation later, how many people will remember? (I wonder whether there are as many as a thousand people on earth today who could supply the name of even one victor in the ancient Olympic games.[6]) In the moment, one plays or watches in such a way as to imply that the very stars in their courses have stood still to await the outcome; but then, in time, it is all gone. And so it seems to be with so many of the games and hobbies and occupations with which people mark off the meaning of their days.[7] And yet I wonder whether there may not also be an unconscious assumption among the more humanistic thinkers of our time that there really is something that registers in the center of being when issues of personal authenticity and social justice are on the line. Do they assume that there is something at the very center of reality that will be affected in a lasting way by the outcome? Or is it all a game to be joined as participant or spectator, to be played before the vast, unconscious tides of history make it as though such a game had never been? The distinct possibility that humanity might be obliterated altogether in a nuclear holocaust poses the problem vividly. If such an unspeakable tragedy were to occur, wiping out every trace of human civilization, would it literally be as though it all had never been? Would the entire historical record then be reduced to the few tiny space probes blindly coursing through eternity?

To raise the question in these terms is to see why the nature of the whole of being really does matter. For that question is also finally the question of meaning. If the universe really is "blind to good and evil," impervious to every human accomplishment as to grains of sand, then our lot is truly a tragic one. Persons of nobility and compassion and creativity will still seize the moment of their existence and make it a good moment. But the meaning of that moment will necessarily be different, for soon it will be lost in the wasteland of cosmic space and time. Things that do not matter in the long run matter less in the short run.

The logical positivists may at least be more consistent about all of this. I am thinking of those who, like Alfred Ayer,[8] question whether value questions are ever meaningful in any form. As we have already noted, the only statements that are meaningful to Ayer are those that can be verified factually (e.g., water will boil at one hundred degrees centigrade at sea level) or those that express abstract mathematical or logical relationships (e.g., two plus two equals four). Statements such as "this is good" or "that is God's will" cannot be verified and may be taken to exist only as emotional utterances. Ethical and religious statements may be useful as psychological or sociological data, but they do not signify anything in themselves.

Views like this have supplied a generation or two of Christian apologists with a nice rhetorical target, but not all critics have been able to provide serious answers. In order to do so they either must demonstrate the validity of some other kind of meaning system or they must show that the substance of religious language is ultimately factual. It is beyond our purpose to enter systematically into this debate at this point, but it may be noted that Ayer himself provides an interesting opening for considering religious language to be factual and verifiable. That opening lies in his distinction between practical verifiability and verifiability in principle. We say that something is practically verifiable if we actually have the means available to verify our factual statements. But a statement may also be verifiable "in principle," according to Ayer, even if we do not have means of verification at hand, if it is something that theoretically *could* be verified. For instance, Ayer himself spoke of the nature of the far side of the moon as something that was not (at his time of writing) practically verifiable: there was no way to get there and no telescope could provide a view from earth since the far side of the moon was always tilted away from the earth. But since we could be reasonably sure that the far side of the moon does exist, Ayer noted that its character is verifiable *in principle*. If a means could be devised for traveling there it would be possible to check the accuracy of theories about it. Therefore, statements about the far side of the moon, whether true or false, could be said to be meaningful. When the astronauts went to the moon they found the far side of the moon to be there.

The distinction between verifiability in principle and in practice may create an opening for religious language insofar as the latter purports to make true statements about the whole of reality. There is no doubt that the whole of reality exists and that it has a character of some kind. Clearly it is beyond practical verification, if we mean factual observation of reality in all of its aspects, for that is beyond human capacity. But still, the whole of reality remains verifiable in principle. If we could but experience all of it as it actually is then we would know how our lives and our activities find their place in it—and meaning, if only derived from frustration and tragedy, would be clear. Therefore, statements about the whole of reality are meaningful, whether they are false or true. So we can at least consider the What is there to believe? question to be a meaningful one.

The related question of what is ultimately *good* is more complex and subtle. To say that something is "good" implies both a subjective judgment and an objective frame of reference. All of us experience some things to be good and other things to be evil, even though we may disagree about which is which. But when we say that this or that *is* good we are saying something more than that we like it or that it feels good to us. We are saying that it has grounding of some kind in reality as a whole.[9] This, too, poses a meaningful question, although it is one that finally lies beyond practical verification.

Our problem as human beings is that we cannot simply leave such questions with an acknowledgment of our ignorance. We remain haunted by the meaning of reality and our place within it. While we cannot experience and know reality as a whole, the meaning of our lives and the values by which we live depend upon what is ultimately true and what is ultimately good. At stake is our personal identity and destiny, the meaning of our life in community, the character of our civilization, the interrelationships of nature with humanity, and the far reaches of cosmic time and space. The deeper questions of meaning and value cannot be pushed aside while we live simple lives at the biological level. Better, said John Stuart Mill, to be Socrates unhappy than a fool satisfied. To be a human being and to live on that plane is to seek to live meaningfully, even if we are finally condemned to frustration and unhappiness in our quest. But in that quest we still cannot overcome the limits of our humanity. So where do we find the answer to the nature of reality providing us with that ultimate context of meaning?

## FROM PARTIAL TRUTH TO THE WHOLE TRUTH

Obviously we have only particles of experience to go by. We have to interpret the whole on the basis of inferences we can draw from some parts of the whole. There is no question that the whole of being exists; it is its character that is but partially known. Our knowledge of the whole depends upon the adequacy of the clues we take to be its best disclosures. We are something like the old story of the three blind men who experienced different parts of the elephant and described the whole animal in terms of those parts. Each was partly right, but the perception of each was also very incomplete. That is the situation everybody is in. There may be great differences of knowledge among the world's people, but there is no privileged sector, no privileged vantage point from which total disclosure is afforded. Nobody has experienced everything.

It would seem, therefore, that we have only two choices. Either we must retreat from the deeper questions of human existence—as some people in every age have done—or we must live on the basis of those pieces of the larger picture that are available to us. The question is, which are the decisive clues? Which provide the basis on which we can best relate ourselves to the unknown and the practically unknowable? If we are not simply to retreat from the problem, we shall have to commit ourselves to an understanding of reality based upon some aspects of experience, believing that some things are more dependable than others in relating us to that vaster realm of things we have not experienced. We may speak of this as a metaphorical approach to ultimate reality, if by "metaphor" we mean some human experience or symbol which we take to be like the unknown.[10]

It may help in understanding this situation to remember that we often have to interpret the unknown on the basis of partial clues. In some respects we are like ancient mariners or explorers, eagerly probing earth and sky and sea for hints revealing location and weather. To the experienced eye, a cloud in the sky or a bird or the feel of the air might be enough to tell all that needed to be known. People who find themselves in unfamiliar social situations also must rely upon little clues to reveal the character and intent of others. Among strangers, one looks especially for signs of friendliness or hostility, and one is likely to interpret the behavior of others on the basis of similar behavior one has experienced before. One may be right or wrong in such interpretations.

For example, during the tense days following the assassination of Dr. Martin Luther King, Jr., a memorial demonstration was scheduled in Memphis, Tennessee, where he had been killed. As thousands of people lined up to begin the march, one young man was seen writing something on the back of the official placard he had been given to carry. Over the youth's shoulder an onlooker could barely make out the letters I HA . . . that he had begun to write. By a kind of free association, the anxious onlooker interpreted this as the beginning of the slogan "I HATE WHITEY," and the fear began to grow that the demonstration would add to racial conflict. When the onlooker could see a few more letters, the sign now read, "I HAVE A. . . ." Aha, he thought, it is going to say "I HAVE A GUN." But in fact, when the youth had completed his work and elevated the sign what it really said was, "I HAVE A DREAM." One's interpretation of clues can be very wrong! The last clue, words from a King speech, turned out to be a dependable one for interpreting the hopeful, peaceful character of the young man and of the demonstration as a whole. Sometimes we must puzzle over a strange situation for a long time, and then suddenly something happens to make sense out of all of it.

Another illustration: The Rev. Billy James Hargis, who gained fleeting notoriety in the United States as one of the leaders of a militant anticommunist movement, accounted for his own considerable following with these words:

> They wanted to join something. They wanted to belong to some united group. They loved Jesus, but they also had a great fear. When I told them that this fear was Communism, it was like a revelation. They knew I was right, but they had never known before what that fear was. They felt better, stronger, more secure

in the knowledge that at last they knew the real enemy that was threatening their homes and their lives. They came to me and I told them.[11]

The metaphor of communism served as interpretive clue to bring a whole bundle of anxieties into focus. Given the climate of the times (the world of the late 1950s and early 1960s) it is more than doubtful whether that was an adequate clue. But followers of leaders like Hargis clearly considered it to be so.

Much depends upon the metaphors we use to interpret reality. They do not construct the world in itself, but they refashion it in our minds. Time and further experience may either confirm the adequacy of the mental construction or require us to change it. Sometimes, having settled upon a particular interpretation of reality, we do not allow ourselves to contemplate change. In this context, the broken cup to which we have referred represents an interpretation that no longer seems viable, though we may still cling to its fragments.

Alfred North Whitehead argued that the most important decision a philosopher can make is in the choice of those metaphors by means of which the basic character of reality is to be interpreted.[12] By a process that he termed "imaginative rationality," Whitehead understood the work of philosophy as beginning with a certain range of facts or experiences and testing the broader applicability of generalizations drawn from those initial facts or experiences. In a famous passage he speaks of "the true method of discovery" as being "like the flight of an aeroplane. It starts from the ground of particular observation; it makes a flight in the thin air of imaginative generalization; and it again lands for renewed observation rendered acute by rational interpretation."[13] "The success of the imaginative experiment," he continues, "is always to be tested by the applicability of its results beyond the restricted locus from which it originated." Thus, for example, "the partially successful philosophic generalization will, if derived from physics, find applications in fields of experience beyond physics."[14] He was able to point out how philosophy over the past few centuries has taken its decisive metaphors from various of the sciences as they developed and achieved success and prestige. Mathematics, astronomy, physics, biology—each has become in due course the basis upon which thinking people interpreted other things. The rest of reality was modeled, so to speak, on these sciences.

The adequacy of such a model of reality depends, of course, upon its interpretive power beyond the original frame of reference, as Whitehead claimed. Thus, during the period when the biological doctrine of evolution was used to explain everything, its usefulness in the form of social Darwinism depended not upon biological evidence but upon its capacity to move beyond biology in interpreting *social* reality. Social Darwinism did not, in fact, turn out very well as a basis for bringing social reality into coherent focus. The "survival of the fittest" exacerbated the already great competitive brutalities of the industrial revolution and proved an inadequate tool for interpreting the social nature of humanity and its need to give and receive love. Contemporary debates over the sociobiology of Edward O. Wilson and the behaviorism of B. F. Skinner raise similar questions about the applicability of biological models to psychological and sociological phenomena.[15] In both instances, though in very different ways, essentially biological metaphors have been taken to understand other forms of reality.

When we believe that a scientific theory or idea has been inappropriately applied beyond its own sphere, we may say that a thinker has been guilty of the fallacy of reductionism, that he or she has "reduced" or diminished the reality to which the scientific metaphor has been applied. Reality has been forced to fit into a procrustean bed for which it is illsuited. There is too much reality to fit into the theory. No doubt, that happens all the time when ideas from one area of experience are thoughtlessly applied to another. But when it comes to interpreting reality as a whole, we really have little choice but to seek out the best available metaphors. We simply cannot know it all directly.

The ancient Greek nature philosophers help illustrate the essential problem for us. In the face of the incompatibility of an obsolete mythological system with emerging social experience, insight, and morality, these philosophers attempted to locate that physical aspect of nature that constitutes its essential quality. That natural phenomenon was then taken by them to be the decisive clue unlocking the mystery of everything else. Thus for Thales, reality is all ultimately water; and given the limitations of ancient scientific method and the complexities of form and function observable in water, that may not have been a completely illogical conclusion. Heraclitus, impressed by the impermanence of all things, regarded perpetual change and fire as the important interpretive clues. Parmenides, by contrast, saw reality as permanence. Empedocles reduced all reality to the four elements of Earth, Water, Air, and Fire; and Democritus saw reality as minute, irreducible atoms (in a striking anticipation of modern nuclear physics). Later Hellenistic philosophies developed subtler and profounder metaphors of characterized reality. For the Epicureans, it was an adaptation of Democritus's materialism and the principle of maximizing pleasure and minimizing pain. For Plato and the Stoics (and other rational traditions) it was the life of reason in itself. For Aristotle it was a teleological conception, in which reality is presented as a hierarchy of beings. Later on, medieval Christendom was significantly influenced by specifically Christian ideas, but it was also inclined to adapt social hierarchy as a metaphor of reality.

Almost everything has been made to serve as an interpretive metaphor in the contemporary world, including impersonal order, chaos, conflict, sex, evolution, personal decision, pluralism, race, dialectical relationship, loyalty, process, personhood, maleness or femaleness, power, creativity, asceticism, money, astrology, mechanical engineering, military life, democracy, commercial exchange, atoms, waves, relativity. Anything can be taken as the decisive clue to the meaning of reality if one is sufficiently impressed by it.

## REVELATION

People come about truth in different ways. Some, perhaps the majority, rest easily upon inherited verities and the sometimes painfully acquired lessons of common sense. Some, no doubt a minority, go about the quest for truth with methodical discipline, carefully adding building blocks to a solid foundation in erecting a trustworthy edifice of knowledge. Others grasp knowledge through flashes of intuition. All, however, ultimately depend upon limited experience to interpret the greater unknown. Does this not exclude claims of religious revelation on the face of it? No doubt it does if we mean by direct revelation any incontestably authentic communications coming to us directly from God. Whatever the ultimate source, knowledge is mediated through our perceptual and cognitive faculties. We may believe that the truth has gotten into our minds because God put it there directly, but we can scarcely say we *know* that that is so.

Consider the revelation claims made by most religions: It is noteworthy that not everybody heard the message in quite the same way. Or that the recipient was the only witness. Or that it has come through the medium of dreams, which anybody may choose to believe or disbelieve. Claims of revelation delivered in miraculous ways, through disruption of the normal processes of nature, are especially questionable. Most people routinely question such claims when they are made on behalf of religions other than their own. Even the ancients, credulous though they might be about such things, were sometimes skeptical about magic shows purporting to express divine communication. In the intriguing account of God's visiting various plagues upon Egypt in order to back up Moses' efforts to liberate the Hebrews, Pharaoh is first impressed by the turning of a rod into a serpent, but then his own magicians did the same thing. Later, official magicians duplicated the feat of turning the water of Egypt into blood and the multiplying of frogs. And so Pharaoh "hardened his heart." The magicians, however, were not able to duplicate later miracles; but even so, Pharaoh was not overly impressed. Phenomena occurring in the world of space and time can always be interpreted in different ways, and no intervention in the phenomenal world can compel the unreceptive mind to draw religious conclusions. Of course, there is also the problem that many religious traditions, some of them mutually exclusive, make claims based upon miracle stories. It is quite difficult to adjudicate among the conflicting miracle claims without taking refuge in nonmiraculous forms of verification and interpretation. But then, it does no good to explain special miracles (such as the Nile turning to what appeared to be blood) in terms of natural phenomena not understood by the ancients (such as a natural process turning the river red)—for then it turns out not to have been a miracle after all!

We cannot rely upon direct, miraculous messages from on high to convey ultimate truth to us. We still have to interpret reality on the basis of limited experience and metaphor.

But that is exactly what revelation can be understood to mean: A limited range of experience that suddenly or gradually comes to impress us as being what ultimate reality is like. It is something that brings everything else into focus. When something strikes us with the "force of revelation" it generally means something that suddenly makes sense out of a previously incoherent mass of facts or something that forces us to change our minds quite radically. The Watergate tapes struck many of President Richard M. Nixon's previous supporters with the force of revelation. While representing only the tip of the iceberg of the thousands of hours of conversation in the White House, they required a radical revision of judgment about the basic character of the President and his administration. When Einstein discovered his theory of relativity it unlocked new ways of understanding and interpreting space and time. Einstein himself remarked that ultimate value questions "come into being not through demonstration but through revelation, through the medium of powerful personalities."[16] It is said that when Gautama, having previously led a quite sheltered life, first encountered real suffering it crystallized a whole new understanding of existence. Indeed, every religious revelation, almost by definition, is of this sort. For religion represents a characterization drawn from some event or experience which, for the believer, brings everything else into perspective.

Among contemporary theologians, Sallie McFague is particularly sensitive to the importance of metaphor in religious language. Defining metaphor simply as "seeing one thing *as* something else" or "spotting a thread of similarity between two dissimilar objects, events, or whatever, one of which is better known than the other, and using the better-known one as a way of speaking about the lesser known," McFague finds the religious use of metaphor very similar to that of poetry:

> Poets use metaphor all the time because they are constantly speaking about the great unknowns—mortality, love, fear, joy, guilt, hope, and so on. Religious language is deeply metaphorical for the same reason and it is therefore no surprise that Jesus' most characteristic form of teaching, the parables, should be extended metaphors.[17]

Indeed, she continues, "the life and death of Jesus of Nazareth can be understood as itself a 'parable' of God."[18]

This general way of understanding religious revelation is not unfamiliar in earlier twentieth-century theology. H. Richard Niebuhr speaks of revelation in history as

> that special occasion which provides us with an image by means of which all the occasions of personal and common life become intelligible. What concerns us at this point is not the fact that the revelatory moment shines by its own light and is intelligible in itself but rather that it illuminates other events and enables us to understand them.[19]

Very few theologians believe either that human minds can know everything or that revelation can be discussed entirely apart from its relationship to other kinds of knowledge. Revelation is the "unveiling" of ultimate truth; but that unveiling must be transmitted through particular experiences. Experience strikes us with the force of revelation, not because it takes us away from everything else but because it brings everything else into focus.

## CAN REVELATION BE TESTED?

Sometimes the language used by theologians suggests that revelation claims must be on a simple "take it or leave it" basis. If revelation must meet some test, then it appears to be subordinate to the rational principles used in the testing. This may be the meaning of Karl Barth's comment:

> According to Holy Scripture God's revelation is a ground which has no sort of higher or deeper ground above or behind it, but is simply a ground in itself, and

therefore as regards man an authority from which no appeal to a higher authority is possible. . . . Revelation is not real and true from the standpoint of anything else, either in itself or for us. It is so in itself, and for us through itself.[20]

A passage like this reminds us of Paul Tillich's remark that Barth throws Christianity at us like a rock through a window. But that may not be quite fair. Remember that we are dealing with the nature of ultimate truth, unknown as such to any of us through rational processes since our minds can never include everything that is. One almost has to say that whatever we take to be ultimate speaks to us from beyond our ability finally to put it to conclusive tests. Revelation, in that sense, always involves some degree of taking it on faith. The writer of Hebrews appears to have understood this point in his words that "faith is the assurance of things hoped for, the conviction of things not seen," and that "by faith we understand . . . that what is seen was made out of things which do not appear."[21] And Paul writes in his famous poem on love, "Now we see in a mirror dimly, but then face to face. Now I know in part; then I shall understand fully, even as I have been fully understood."[22] These New Testament writers understand that, so far as this life is concerned, no test of revelation could be developed that would demonstrate its truth conclusively.

Taken to the extreme, however, would this mire us in hopeless subjectivism? Could there be any way to sort out the contending revelation claims which, in this as in all epochs, do not seem to be in short supply?

We have already, in effect, suggested an important general test: Does revelation in fact bring reality into focus for us? Can we live and think and act and feel on the basis of what it says to us? Does it make "sense" of our world, not in exclusively rational terms but in terms that also include our best thinking? Barth himself appears to apply such a test by acknowledging that while we cannot gain ultimate truth through natural reason, revelation illuminates our understanding of the nature of things a posteriori. Revelation unlocks for us the true meaning of ordinary things. For instance, we understand the natural world as "creation" in light of Christian revelation. It is seen now in a new light, not as existing purely in and of itself but as an expression of divine creative purpose. If a revelation claim could not illuminate the factual world successfully in this a posteriori sense or, worse, if it blatantly contradicted important aspects of our ordinary experience, we would not find it persuasive in the long run. Augustine finally had to abandon a nine-year infatuation with Manichaeanism because he was not able to get convincing answers to important questions through its dualism.[23] Similarly, a number of twentieth-century writers have found that they had to abandon Marxism because it did not illuminate the deeper realities of the human spirit as they experienced them.[24] It would be interesting to do a survey of the history of the literature of religious disillusionment with an eye toward the implied criteria through which disillusioned writers put this or that religious view to the test. Various Christian revelation claims would not avoid inclusion in such a survey, of course. For instance, Nietzsche reacted strongly against what he considered to be the life-denying or life-repressing character of Christianity because it ran afoul of his experience of and commitment to human vitality.[25] Whether Nietzsche sufficiently understood Christianity is a debatable point—notwithstanding his upbringing as a parson's son—but he found it wanting in the terms in which he understood it.

What tests can we legitimately apply? Most of us would question any blatant self-contradictions or major conflicts with observed experience. Edgar S. Brightman's appeal to coherence as criterion of truth is a useful principle, despite the perhaps excessively rationalistic form of his exposition of it.[26] We judge the truth or error of something not just on the basis of internal consistency but by whether it is coherent with everything we already know or come to know. A truth claim may not be inconsistent within itself nor inconsistent with other things we know. But at the same time we may reject it because it appears to be a bizarre exception to all of our previous knowledge. (Brightman notes, by way of illustration, that it is *conceivable* that there might be a five-legged philosopher living in the fourth dimension. But such a conceivable being does not cohere well with what we already know or think we know about the factual world.)

This is a problem that all philosophers have to deal with sooner or later. Whitehead remarks, for instance, that "the verification of a rationalistic scheme is to be sought in its general success, and not in the peculiar certainty, or initial clarity, of its first principles."[27] He also remarks that "a system of philosophy is never refuted; it is only abandoned," "after criticism, systems do not exhibit mere illogicalities. They suffer from inadequacy and incoherence," and "failure to include some obvious elements in experience in the scope of the system is met by boldly denying the facts."[28] The same can doubtless be said of religious revelation claims, if we also take into account the striking tendency of great religions to change through reinterpretation as earlier formulations of their central doctrines have appeared inadequate or incoherent in face of new perceptions of reality. Einstein notes that the two tests of probability and parsimony establish the adequacy of scientific doctrine. These tests indicate the degrees of likelihood of a particular explanation being the true one and whether it is the simplest plausible explanation available. Fundamentalism, as discussed in the preceding chapter, runs afoul of such tests. But the important point is that since people generally do apply tests of coherence and probability and parsimony in sorting out truth, the improbabilities of a fundamentalist creed have to be adhered to with rigidities of the will more than the clear acceptance of the mind.

There are various ways of stating the philosophical problem of verification, and it is beyond our intention to explore this in technical detail. The main point I have wished to emphasize is that revelation claims must be tested through our whole life experience, even though we know we can never have a final or complete confirmation of their truth since reality is always more than anything we can know. There is, I believe, a kind of rhythm between inherited traditions and lived experience and new insight. We are always putting core beliefs to the test on the basis of whether we can truly live by them. When we can do so at conscious as well as unconscious levels, there is a very deep integrity to our lives. Where we cannot, we are consciously or unconsciously fragmented, disintegrated persons.

To put this differently, there is both a subjective and an objective side to our grasp of truth. We are subjects who experience life (a matter whose significance we shall want to explore in the next chapter), but there is also an objective world to be experienced. Our religious views are not exclusively subjective, for they are always being put to the test of our encounter with objective reality. But they are not purely objective either, for we can never set aside the fact that we are experiencing from our own unique and limited point of view.

What we have said of persons as individuals can never be taken as purely individualistic. We live in community; we are, as Aristotle said, social by nature. Our individuality is always in a social context, which means that we are both individual and social by nature.[29] Therefore, our religious insights are always shared to a very great extent, even though they are also unique to each of us. Our socially shared beliefs are, also to a great extent, inherited from earlier generations—a reminder that the human community exists through history and not just at a given fixed point in time. One of the reasons a great religion like Christianity is so difficult to define with precision is that it represents a vast, complex stream of human cultural history while at the same time it represents individuals organizing their lives on the basis of what they take to be a true representation of reality. Within that great stream, the Bible has peculiar importance as a foundational source—not because it is necessarily believed that it was written or dictated directly by God (as fundamentalists often hold) but because it represented an early consensus within the church as to those writings best preserving the earliest witness of the Christian community about the Christian revelation. Twentieth-century Christianity is also shaped by a vast history of interpretation and reinterpretation of the meaning of that revelation. The question now before us is whether the basic core of meaning any longer suffices.

# 4

## THE CHRISTIAN PERSPECTIVE

We do not have to conclude that all things are equally true, good, or beautiful, nor that our choices of metaphor and revelation are essentially arbitrary and subjective. We do know that some visions of reality contradict ordinary everyday experience and that some religious and philosophical viewpoints even contradict themselves. Every alleged revelation is continually tested by encounter with reality. Inadequate metaphors may persist for a time, but ultimately they must be discarded. The question remains whether Christianity has lost its interpretive power in face of the scientific, social, and moral experience of this new era.

### THE ANTHROPOMORPHIC METAPHOR

For the past two or three centuries, the physical and social sciences have enjoyed high prestige in the Western world as avenues to the whole truth. By any reckoning, science has given us much deeper insight into the physical and social universe. We know much more than people did several centuries ago, and much of this knowledge has also turned out to be very useful when applied through technology to human enterprises. Not surprisingly, many people have concluded that the theories and laws of science are the most dependable basis for understanding reality overall. Such theories and laws are verifiable, at least within their own realms, and they have achieved remarkable results in the transformation of human life—sometimes for ill, but often also for good. Alongside the sophistication of science, the great religious traditions have seemed to many people to be little more than crude anthropomorphism. That is to say, religion has seemed to project human characteristics onto the universe as a whole and thereby to neglect the more rational findings of science.

Beginning with nineteenth-century French positivism, there has been a tendency in some quarters to interpret religion as an earlier stage in human intellectual development, with philosophy and then science depicted as progressively higher stages in human liberation from superstition (just as Greek philosophy could be understood to represent a higher stage than the crude mythologies of the gods and goddesses with their all-too-human characteristics). If the Christian "cup" has been broken decisively, it would appear to be for this reason; and efforts, such as those of Ludwig Feuerbach in the last century and the "death-of-God" theologians in this century, to construct a Christianity without God scarcely conceal the fragmentation. Without God at the center of being, Christianity is scarcely thinkable. And with God it can scarcely escape the charge of anthropomorphism, for belief in God centrally involves interpreting the ultimate nature of the universe in terms of *human* characteristics: thinking, willing, feeling, remembering, judging, forgiving, creating. Is not such anthropomorphism, even in its most sophisticated forms, the crudest kind of reductionism—taking all of the immensities and complexities of space, time, matter, and energy and reducing them to what we know about *ourselves?* Even Albert Einstein, who writes of "the intelligence manifested in nature," strongly rejects the notion of a God "whose purposes are modeled after our own—a God, in short, who is but a reflection of human frailty."[1] Other scientists, most recently including Carl Sagan, have conceived of reality in even more sweepingly nonpersonal terms.

Sagan is an especially interesting case in point because he has so great an appreciation for the grandeur and intricacy of human intelligence. Tracing the evolution of the brain, Sagan marvels at its phenomenal development and capacity. Nevertheless, it remains in his mind a function of material forces. "To me," he writes, "it is not in the least demeaning that consciousness and intelligence are the result of 'mere' matter sufficiently complexly arranged; on the contrary, it is an exalting tribute to the subtlety of matter and the laws of Nature."[2] In the same context, he suggests that machines are now passing over the threshold where "they give the unbiased human being the impression of intelligence," a possibility that, "because of a kind of human chauvinism or anthropocentrism, many humans are reluctant to admit."

The issue, however, is not whether human beings are too chauvinistic about their own intelligence; it is whether they grasp its significance as a clue to understanding reality. For it is arguable that human consciousness represents a reality that is quite other than that of unconscious matter. And if it is, that fact has important implications as we seek to interpret reality as a whole. For if human consciousness is not a purely material phenomenon, then we each have immediate evidence of a fundamental reality that cannot be described in purely material terms.

This has always posed a difficult philosophical problem. The difficulty is that both the material and nonmaterial interpretations of human consciousness are almost self-evidently true! It is possible to attribute every effect to a cause. One can always locate a reason for everything that happens. From that standpoint, all human attitudes and actions can be taken to have causes outside ourselves. We may believe we chose to select ham rather than chicken from the cafeteria line, but our choice of ham can be analyzed into a variety of previous experiences of a quite material sort. We may believe we made the choice of our own free will, but we were actually programmed. A retrospective analysis of human decision making can generally be made in this way if we have sufficient data. Thus, the case for material causation is almost self-evidently clear.

But then, analyzed from the opposite perspective, we cannot deny that experience itself is the most immediate thing about us. We are not simply "things" alongside other things; we are experiencers of reality. We transcend the material realm, the realm of objects and senses, even as we participate in it. While it may seem quite illogical from the standpoint of causal analysis to speak of personal transcendence in this way, it is equally difficult to account for the reliability of knowledge on any other basis. If my consciousness and apparent freedom of mind and will are an illusion, totally caused by natural forces outside my mind and will, then how do I know that anything is false or true? How can I be sure that other things, including my perceptions of material causation, are not also illusions? Must not human consciousness and will, influenced as they doubtless are by natural forces, still be understood to be more than those forces?

It may help, in trying to grasp the character of this nonnatural experiencing of reality, to see it as a problem in grammar. Language almost compels us to treat ourselves as objects (that is, as things) insofar as we name ourselves with a noun. To say that I am a "person" is to give that "thing" a name, and we are then left only with the problem of analyzing and describing that thing. Early twentieth-century sociological analysis in America fruitfully explored the development of the social self, arriving at the conclusion that our self-understanding is derived from other people's reactions to us. No doubt there is much truth in this—enough so that it is not unrealistic for us to refer to our "self" as if it were an object. When we thus refer to ourselves we use the word "me" or its alternate forms. But the word "I" cannot be used grammatically as an object. It is always the subject. I do this, I do that, I think this, I believe this, I see this, and so on. When I say, I am experiencing reality, I refer to that which makes it possible for me to become a self. As Gibson Winter perceptively notes, even the sociological analysis of the emergence of the social self—as portrayed, for example, in the work of George Herbert Mead—presupposes this subjective, experiencing being.[3] But it is very difficult to avoid speaking of our subjective nature without lapsing into objective language, referring to our subjective existence as if it were an object. We are subjects, not objects. We experience. We are not just the things that happen to us.

If that is so, the question remains whether human beings are unique in their being subjects or whether reality as a whole reflects a subject: a center of experience at the center of reality. If that is not the case, then we are left with the situation that human beings are the only known aspect of reality capable of experiencing reality as we do and that we have somehow evolved out of something that is not only less complex than we but out of something that is qualitatively different—for subjects are altogether different from objects, no matter how much they may be dependent upon material objects and processes to sustain their existence. We must acknowledge the possibility that human consciousness is an illusion or, if not altogether illusory, that it is still the highest point in an entirely natural process of evolution. But it is equally possible and, indeed, more probable that our being as subjects is real and that our subjective nature points to an order of reality at the center of all being.

Thus, there is something to be said for anthropomorphism as the basic metaphor for reality, when this is considered alongside the alternatives. For the alternatives, far from going *beyond* the human, turn out to be *less* than human. It comes down to the question whether the capacity to experience reality is not itself more inclusive than any purely objective, but totally unconscious thing or process we can compare it to. Purely scientific metaphors drawn from particular forms of objective data or causal relationships must either explain the human mind and will away as the product of other forces, or they must be subordinated to metaphors treating the mind and will as a realm of transcendence and freedom. "Has our science really come to this," asks F. H. Bradley, "that the beliefs which answer to our highest feelings must be theoretical absurdities?" He goes on to argue that "the mere finitude of the mind is a more difficult thesis to support than its infinity."[4]

The word infinity may have been ill-chosen. Clearly Bradley means the transcendence of the mind beyond those purely natural forces that influence it. He thus points to an intellectual watershed of incalculable importance. Bradley's argument, in which he is joined by personalists of various kinds,[5] is that the fact that we experience a world and that we exercise choice is the most immediate and central fact known to us. To ignore that basic fact of our own being, or to interpret our experiencing of our selfhood as some kind of illusion, places a greater strain upon credulity than taking our capacity to experience life seriously into account. When we do so, we have already accepted a form of supernaturalism. We have acknowledged a realm that transcends nature while still involved in it.

From a natural perspective we are, indeed, puny little specks of nothing much in the vast ocean of the galaxies and over the vast reaches of time; and we are perhaps prone to take ourselves a bit too seriously even here on this limited earth. But we still have to interpret reality in terms of what we experience. And we do not experience anything that is more basic than our capacity to experience! If we are not subjects then we must acknowledge that experience itself is a colossal illusion. When behaviorists like B. F. Skinner attempt to interpret the human psyche entirely in terms of objective, external factors they are engaged in reductionist thinking.[6] They have reduced the experiencing person to something less than he or she really is. They have treated the subject as though he or she were only an object.

This still does not mean that the human subject is necessarily the right clue to the fundamental character of ultimate reality. But is it irrational to believe that reality as a whole is rational, that it reflects rational intent? At least it cannot be irrational to say that reality itself is rational at its center. If we are prepared to accept ourselves as transcendent, rational beings, it is not an impossible further step to suppose that being-itself is transcendent and rational? That is not a *proof* of God. But it is a reminder that the first step of freeing human personhood from being regarded as a wholly natural phenomenon may be a more decisive step than the further argument for the reality of God.

Belief in God makes more sense out of the totality of our experience than does belief that the universe is essentially only blind, unconscious matter and energy. When Bertrand Russell writes about "omnipotent matter rolling on its relentless way,"[7] one may be excused for finding that a less than persuasive picture of a world containing thinking, feeling, loving, and purposing beings. It may not even be a very good account of a world containing brutal, selfish, and hateful beings, insofar as such self-centered behavior is also willful. If reality does not have thinking and purposing at its center, then somehow the emergence of subjective being must always be explained away as an accidental occurrence of no lasting consequence.

But if reality does have intelligent purpose at its center, then the emergence of all things can be seen as part of an ultimately rational intention. Of course, the ultimate character of reality remains enshrouded in mystery for all of us. But it is not irrational to say that that character is itself rational.

## THE COVENANTAL TRADITION

Another advantage of the anthropomorphic metaphor is that it allows people who interpret reality in this way to have a frame of reference that permits almost unlimited growth in their moral, religious, and intellectual lives. Each new insight contributes further illumination to their understanding of God and of God's purposes. The Hebrew covenantal tradition is particularly instructive at this point.

This tradition depicts God as the Creator of all the wonders and beauties and mysteries of the universe while also understanding God to have a direct relationship (or covenant) with the Hebrew people. Yahweh, the God of the covenant, was utterly committed to that people and they, in turn, were expected to respond obediently to the will of God.

We cannot be certain exactly how this tradition began, but it is well to remember that the tendency to personalize everything appears very early in most cultures. Rocks and trees and mountains and stars and rivers are taken to represent spirit beings of one kind or another to the peoples of early and prescientific societies. Such spirit beings are felt to harbor good or evil intentions, and the purpose of religious exercises is to maximize the first and minimize the second. Here and there in the Old Testament there are reflections of primitive animism of this kind, but the basic tradition is that for the Hebrew people there is to be but one God, Yahweh, and that they must be loyal to Yahweh as Yahweh will be faithful to them: "I will take you for my people, and I will be your God" (Exod. 6:7).

If the usual dating of Moses at around 1300 B.C. is correct, the Hebrew traditions developed for at least a thousand years before the last of the Old Testament writings were finally written. Through that very long period of time, we find exhibited a variety of conceptions of God, ranging from a Yahweh who is attached only to this one people to the grander view of a universal God, Creator of the whole known cosmos. Corresponding changes occur in the perceived ethical character and demand of this God, from the sometimes brutal warrior-God of Joshua and the Song of Deborah to the God of Isaiah's Prince of Peace. Yahweh is also depicted in terms ranging from the tribal deity of Joshua or Ezra to the deity of the whole human family, as suggested by the greatest of the prophets and Jonah or

Ruth. Moral demands are variously depicted in the Hebrew tradition from the most trivial of ceremonial rituals to sublime conceptions of social justice. The covenantal metaphor was flexible enough to accommodate the deeper visions and broader insights of the Hebrews as these developed historically.

In this respect, it is interesting to compare the Hebrew covenantal tradition to Greek religious conceptions. Original Greek mythology was crudely anthropomorphic, having a variety of gods and goddesses displaying all-too-human characteristics. But at the mythological stage of its cultural development, Greek religion did not center upon one deity as focal point for its identity and worship. With the development of greater rational sophistication and moral sensibilities, there came a time when the Greek mind had to choose between further intellectual and moral progress and the inherited mythological perspective. The break was made, beginning with the nature philosophers to whom we have already referred and extending to the loftier visions of Plato and Aristotle. Werner Jaeger characterizes the break in these words: "The lofty speculations of the early Ionians were not intended to educate Greece; yet they were, in the midst of the chaotic growth of a new society, and the collapse of the old mythical conception of the universe, a fresh attempt to solve the deepest problem of life, the problem of Being itself."[8] So the original Greek "cup" was shattered; but it was replaced by the great philosophical traditions and new popular movements based partly upon them.

By contrast, Hebrew religion was, virtually from the beginning, a basis for maturing experience, unified as it was around the covenantal tradition. Yahweh had brought the tribes into unified peoplehood, delivered them from captivity in Egypt, given them the law, led them to the promised land, defended them, instructed them, punished them. Regardless of one's view of the evolution of the Hebrews' understanding of God, there is no doubt that the earliest expressions of Hebrew faith were fairly crude. (The "Song of Deborah" in Judges 5, one of the earliest writings in the Bible, illustrates the point, as do some of the mythological materials in Genesis.) But the covenant provided a frame of reference for further and deeper interpretation. Even the catastrophe of the destruction of Jerusalem and the Babylonian captivity of the early sixth century B.C. became the basis for deeper understanding of the meaning of God and of suffering and of human responsibility and, indeed, for a more sophisticated cosmic understanding than that of most of the rest of the Old Testament. So the Hebrew "cup" was never shattered in quite the way the Greek cup was. It was never necessary to choose between deeper perceptions of reality and the existing basic metaphors for interpreting reality. Each new understanding of existence became a new commentary on God's ways with the people of God. Without thinking the matter through philosophically, the Hebrew people were attracted by the basic general metaphor of personhood. It was their revelation of the nature of reality. Sallie McFague comments on the many-faceted imagery opened up by use of the personal metaphor:

> Personal, relational images are central in a metaphorical theology—images of God as father, mother, lover, friend, savior, ruler, governor, servant, companion, comrade, liberator, and so on. The Judeo-Christian tradition has always been personalistic and relational in its religious languages. This need not be seen as crude anthropomorphism, but as foundational language. . . . In any case, a metaphorical theology will insist that *many* metaphors and models are necessary, that a piling up of images is essential, both to avoid idolatry and to attempt to express the richness and variety of the divine-human relationship.[9]

Before dealing with Christian faith in particular, we should note that each of the covenantal religions (Hebrew, Christian, Moslem) has been remarkably resilient. Each has been challenged to new levels of moral awareness and intellectual sophistication, not to mention vast historical vicissitudes over a period of many centuries; but the basic frame of reference has held up remarkably well. Is it not because the transcendental character of human personhood, taken as the basic metaphor for ultimate reality, is continuously open to new experience and moral sensitivity, while at the same time remaining fundamentally rational? The divine-human relationship can be seen as a continually unfolding one, just as human relationships unfold. The relationship itself is the basic revelation; but within that relationship there is room for an infinity of continuing revelations. The cup can essentially accommodate the "water" of life in successive and radically different eras of human history; the wineskin can contain new wine. The only time it cannot is when the personhood of God is subordinated to concepts about God. Covenantal faith relates to the center of being as personal, not as conceptual; just as in a deeply personal human relationship one relates to the other person, not to an idea about the other person.[10] But the covenantal view depicts reality as centered, creative, purposeful—not diffuse and random. So each new understanding or reality can be taken as a new disclosure of the character and purpose of God.

## WHAT CHRISTIANS SEE IN CHRIST

These general considerations—the importance of the personal description of ultimate reality and the Hebrew covenantal tradition—are important background, even indispensable background, to the Christian under-standing. But Christian faith presses beyond this background. One way or another, the Christian faith finally holds that Jesus Christ himself is the best clue into the mystery of this universe into which we were all born. The classic creeds of the church speak to us awkwardly because they were framed in the philosophical and cultural language of a time long past. When the Nicene Creed speaks of Jesus Christ as "the only begotten Son of God: begotten of the Father before all worlds, God of God, Light of Light, very God of very God, begotten, not made, being of one substance with the Father, through whom all things were made," the words ring awkwardly to those not already anesthetized by habitual repetition. But even words like these can be translated meaningfully into a contemporary idiom if one grasps first the main point. What they are saying at bottom is at least that when you confront the reality of Jesus Christ you are on the right track to understanding God. God is more than anything we can know, but the essential character of God is revealed in Jesus Christ. Christ is the key to the puzzle. The Colossians passage puts this claim in suggestive language: "He is the image of the invisible God. . . ." The invisible is revealed in the visible; the character of God, whom we do not see, is revealed in the Christ whom we do see. Everything has its center of being in this God whose character we best understand through Christ. "In him all things were created . . . and in him all things hold together." It is not that this human being, Jesus of Nazareth, is to be taken as himself creating the universe; rather, the point is that this person has revealed the essential nature of the God who is the center and source of all being.

Is this further step by Christians irrational nonsense?

Indeed, if the Colossians passage is interpreted to mean that the man Jesus was himself literally "before all things" and that literally "all things were created through (this man) and for (this man)," then we must grant that such a claim is on the outer reaches of rational experience. But if it means that the nature of the invisible God who is at the center of all being and is the creator of all things is decisively revealed in Jesus Christ, then this is not necessarily nonsense. We must interpret the unknown by the known; and it is reasonable to interpret the center and source of reality on the basis of the best that we know. For Christians, that is Christ. So the question for Christians really comes down to whether Christ can bear the weight of such a claim.

A random sampling of those who have "found Christ" would doubtless reveal that the Christ who has been found varies considerably from person to person—just as the portraits of Jesus vary with time and culture to represent idealizations that are relative to the circumstances and conceptions of particular artists. Yet many speak of "Christ" as though the meaning were self-evident to all. For some, Christ is sanctifier of the status quo; for others, the goad to radical change. For some, he is the basis of pacifism; for others, it is "onward Christian soldiers" (some Christian students of the 1970s even had an organization called "Karate for Christ"!). For some he is a sturdy individualist; for others he is the basis of cooperation in community. Is the meaning of Christ, then, an entirely arbitrary, subjective choice, dependent upon the inclination of the believer? The believer finally does her or his own believing, of course; but the meaning of Christ is given real substance by the New Testament and Christian tradition. The decisive question is, what did this man do to and for the believers? We already know that Jesus was not received as a revelation of God by everybody who encountered him. He was no revelation to the Sanhedrin or to Caiaphas the high priest. He made scarcely any impact at all upon Roman authorities during his lifetime. For these people he was not taken as a revelation of anything important about the nature of being. For them, he was either an irrelevance or an obstacle to be gotten rid of.

But for the little band of Christians and for the explosively growing community of faith, the church of the second, third, fourth, and subsequent generations, Christ opened up reality itself. The New Testament points to that impact upon the earliest followers. The accounts of Jesus' own life and teachings are exasperatingly sparse if our interest is primarily biographical. We know very little of the circumstances of his childhood and youth, and the account of his birth is now immersed in mythology. These stories do indicate humble origins, expressive of common humanity, and they impart the sense of divine destiny which the believing Christian community attributed to that singular life. Later stories of his calling and baptism emphasize his own emerging response to God's special purposes for him. The narratives of his teaching and healing emphasize God's boundless caring for everyone and the fullness of life through faithful response. God is referred to as *Abba*—Aramaic for "papa" or "daddy"—a metaphor drawn from human relationships of great intimacy and love. In parables like the lost sheep, Jesus emphasized God's concern for every single person, no matter how estranged from God and God's purposes. In the parable of the prodigal son, it is made clear that God's response to human rebelliousness is one of grieving love and that God's forgiveness is utterly dependable. A number of parables and teachings, including especially that of the good Samaritan, emphasize that the moral community extends beyond every chauvinistic definition: we are all "neighbors." Jesus' teachings were not devoid of harsh moral judgment, but the most scathing criticisms were reserved not for traditional sinners or even routinely unjust oppressors but for self-righteous hypocrites—that is, for those whose pretensions of moral superiority stood between them and the life of faith and love and whose arrogance laid a terrible burden of inferiority upon others. His message for poor people, the humble "people of the land," was that they were the "salt of the earth" and that the God who notes even the death of individual sparrows cares inexhaustibly for them.

In his interactions with people of all kinds, Jesus is revealed as a witty debater as well as an imaginative teacher, but above all as a commanding personality to whom followers dedicated themselves almost without reservation. The individual teachings and actions are important in establishing the quality of his character and the content of his message; but it is the personality as a whole that made the decisive impression. Again, not everybody reacted to Jesus in that way. But those who did found their whole conception of life turned inside out in the very brief time (perhaps somewhere between one and three years) he was with them.

The narratives about Jesus give special emphasis to the drama of his last week and to his arrest, trial, and crucifixion. The quality of Jesus' faithfulness to the mission of God's love, despite public humiliation and tortured death, brought into stark contrast the power of loveless evil (as garbed in the mantles of public and religious authority) and the power of love. The cross itself came to be understood by Jesus' followers, most notably by Paul, as symbol of God's love in its encounter with human evil. Humanity is always attracted by the nobility of heroic martyrdom, and even an unworthy cause can gain new life if people are willing to die for it. But the cross is not simple martyrdom; it is seen as a gift of love.

Even so, it might also be taken as a symbol of the futility of love were it not also accompanied by the resurrection faith. The narrative accounts of each of the four New Testament Gospels lead up to Jesus' resurrection from the dead, with variations of agreement and disagreement on matters of detail. The historicity of such accounts is important enough and troubling enough to warrant further discussion, and I shall return to that theme below. But the important thing to say about the resurrection narrative, literal fact aside, is that the earliest followers found themselves swept up in the faith that the cross was not the last word and that God had absolutely set its verdict aside. Utter defeat was replaced, on Easter, by total victory. Through the resurrection, God was understood to have affirmed the life of Jesus as the Word, the authentic truth about reality.

Matters of historical detail will be interpreted by different people in different ways; some, perhaps most people in our time, will find it difficult to accept the literal accounts of physical appearances by the postresurrection Christ and by angels. I do not believe one should quarrel over that nor that Christians should insist upon literal belief in such accounts. But the faith itself—that God has affirmed Christ—remains central. It is noteworthy from a factual standpoint that the Christian church which grew out of that faith and acted on the basis of that faith was itself a message of love to the Roman world. Our interpretation of the resurrection event needs to be influenced substantially by the quality of the human response to it. Certainly, the hypothesis of mere fraud would not be consistent with what in fact came to be. Whatever else it was, the resurrection event was such that it could evoke loving sincerity and deep courage among many who formed the church and sent it on its way.

How, then, can we summarize the question of what Christians have seen in Jesus Christ? What is the meaning of that life? What is it in particular about Christ that engages our attention as a revelation of the character of God?

Clearly it is not all of the little accidents of time and place and culture. Nor is it the particular excellencies of mind and spirit, added up to constitute an exceptionally attractive human being. Rather, it is in the way Christ committed himself unreservedly to the whole human condition and interpreted this as a consequence of God's own unbounded caring. Christians believe that God has said "yes" to each of us. Their central belief is that we are all loved by the God who created and sustains the whole of reality. We matter to a caring God. Thus, the Christian's overall orientation is one of profound trust in the goodness of reality, a trust that leads to joyous participation in the venture of life. The overall attitude is affirmative. It is one of *hopeful love*. It knows and appreciates the facts and laws and processes of nature, but its ultimate vision is one of a personal reality that includes but transcends nature. It also knows suffering, but it is deeply creative in its response to suffering. Suffering ultimately is overcome in this attitude, not by denial but by trusting response. This overall attitude also suggests a profounder account of the basis of community than is to be found elsewhere. Community, based upon the covenant of God with humanity, includes all people, and it is community in which all are valued from the very center of their individual being. Thus the ideological contradictions between the individual and social aspects of human existence in our time are overcome at a level affirming the depth and importance of each.

In sum, one may say that the revelation of reality in Jesus Christ is such that we are led to be profoundly optimistic. Reality is ultimately and finally good and good for us.

## CHRIST AS GOD'S SELF-DISCLOSURE

The metaphors chosen to characterize Christ, both in popular Christian speech and in theological writings, emphasize that Christ is not only to be understood as human access to God but also as God's own self-disclosure to humanity. To H. Richard Niebuhr, for instance, revelation itself is in our new awareness that it is God who is seeking us out:

Revelation means God, God who discloses himself to us through our history as our knower, our author, our judge and our only savior. . . . Revelation means the moment in our history through which we know ourselves to be known from beginning to end, in which we are apprehended by the knower; it means the self-disclosing of that eternal knower. . . . [And] when we find out that we are no longer thinking him, but that he first thought us, that is revelation.[11]

That understanding of revelation is consistent with our view of revelation as awareness of God's special caring.

But it also raises problems when expressed in biblical and traditional Christian language such as that of the Fourth Gospel: "God so loved the world that he gave his only Son, that whoever believes in him should not perish but have eternal life" (John 3:16). What does it mean to characterize Christ as "Son of God" and, indeed, as the *only* son of God? How, literally, are we to think of God as having "sent" Christ to earth?

Some theologians, particularly in the Barthian tradition, emphasize that if we do not think of revelation as divine self-disclosure we are left with a religion of our own making. Barth himself insists that "God's revelation has its reality and truth wholly and in every respect—i.e., ontically and noetically—within itself."[12] It is God's breaking into history; it is not the sum of historical wisdom. It must be in history for us to understand it; but it must be from beyond history for it to be more than human. In an illuminating discussion of the meaning of the Christ event in relation to the philosophical problems of space and time, T. F. Torrance points to the fact that the horizontal plane of space and time—now thoroughly relativized by advanced physics—must have a source that transcends space and time. For humanity to escape captivity to the relative world of space and time there must be a point of breaking in which humanity cannot itself initiate. God's act in Jesus Christ is seen to be exactly that:

It is penetration of the horizontal by the vertical that gives man his true place, for it relates his place in space and time to its ultimate ontological ground so that it is not submerged in the endless relativities of what is merely horizontal. Without this vertical relation to God man has no authentic place on earth, no meaning and no purpose, but with this vertical relation to God his place is given meaning and purpose. . . . Unless the eternal breaks into the temporal and the boundless being of God breaks into the spatial existence of man and takes up dwelling within it, the vertical dimension vanishes out of man's life and becomes quite strange to him—and man loses his place under the sun.[13]

Jesus Christ is thus constituted as "the one place where man on earth and in history may really know the Father because that is the place where God Himself has elected to dwell among us."[14] Torrance goes on to argue the point that the theme of God's action in Christ cannot be treated as only metaphorical; it is actual and establishes a new historical reality. It is in light of this that the factual questions concerning Jesus' life on earth need to be surveyed, for any "construct of Christ that has no rooting in actual history can only be a vehicle of our fantasies."[15] For God must use the medium of time and space in communicating to humanity from beyond it.

Some other Christian thinkers address the relationship between God's self-disclosure and the special character of Christ more simply: If God is God, then God is not limited by the observable constraints of natural law and natural process. God has the power to break through those constraints to communicate decisively and unmistakably.

Such talk, even in its more sophisticated forms, is credible mainly to people who already have a predisposition to accept it. A literal notion of Christ's preexistence and of specific divine intention to invade earth at a particular time and place and in a particular way is not disprovable; but neither would most reasonable people, not otherwise committed to the belief, find it very probable.

A group of British scholars addressed the problem of special incarnation in a widely read book published in 1977.[16] While the seven contributors to the volume hold somewhat divergent views, they are united in viewing the idea of special incarnation—of Christ being sent to earth, with miraculous interventions in natural process—as mythological. In their judgment, it is very important for the church to face up to this if it does not wish to undermine the credibility of the essential Christian message among those who cannot accept the myth as literal fact. In particular, the data assembled by Frances Young on the special miracles associated mythologically with other great religious and political figures from around the time of Christ is most compelling. The fact that divine birth and resurrection and ascension narratives are associated with other figures does not in itself establish that claims of this kind made for Jesus are untrue; but it does show that the cultural setting was highly conducive to the unfolding of such beliefs. Moreover, it reminds us that faith in God does not come through such stories—else we might be equally tempted to believe in the divinity of some of the great Caesars and philosophers around whom such mythologies also developed. The fact that special miracle stories attach to very different religious and even political viewpoints does not disprove those stories. But it does lead to serious doubts about them. An unbiased person is strongly tempted to attribute them to the cultural climate and credulities of the times. Despite this, even if we abandon special claims for Jesus that set aside the normal workings of natural process, the heart of Christian revelation remains, probably enhanced by virtue of no longer being dependent upon special effects. As Maurice Wiles remarks, the demythologizing of such special claims for Jesus does not abolish "the truth of God's self-giving love and the role of Jesus in bringing that vision to life in the world." Even the traditional language of incarnation might remain, Wiles believes, "as a pictorial way of expressing these truths."[17]

What, then, about the problem posed by Torrance? How can God communicate with humanity except through use of the medium of space/time? If nature is entirely predictable, then how, so to speak, can God "get through" to humanity? People communicate to one another by means of the material world, with gestures and sounds, pictures and words. These involve interventions in nature. Does not God also have to intervene in nature, at least once, in order to communicate from beyond the realm of space and time?

The meaning of incarnation is that God's message is through humanity. The Hebrew covenant, as we have seen, supposes God to be "like" humanity at least in the sense that God is personal being. Hebrew Scriptures are full of angelic appearances and such special effects as the sun standing still and waters parting to make a path for the liberated Israelites. But the same writings are generally very reticent about actual visualizations of God or, for that matter, even about pronouncing the divine name. Perception of divine communication is generally an act of faith; and that being the case, it is no surprise that the announcement of new perceptions of God's will (as by the prophets) was often greeted with derision and persecution.

So it was with Christ. Christ was the "word of God" to believers because through his being the depth of their own being was spoken to; and both Christ and his followers understood that to be God. God was "in Christ" in a special way, but not through any disruption of natural order and process; rather, God was present in that which transcends the natural order of things. The human spirit, while expressed through physical beings who are bound by time and space, also transcends those bounds. To be human is to be subject, and not object only. When Christ speaks to us as subjects concerning the Subject who is at the center of all being, there is no need for special interventions in nature. Indeed, literal narratives of virgin birth and bodily resurrection do more to change the subject (the pun is intended) than anything one could imagine. Such special effects, occurring entirely within the phenomenal realm, suggest that it is in that realm that God's being is manifested. And thus, miraculous physical happenings diminish God's transcendence. The revelation in Christ is both a revelation of the significance of what we already are and a revelation of what God is. Both call us into a covenant of love in a universe where hopeful love is now a real possibility. But our perceptions of the reality of that covenant are grounded in faith.

Is God disclosed *only* through Christ? Some scriptural passages appear to make such a claim—as in the Fourth Gospel's "I am the way, and the truth, and the life; no one comes to the Father, but by me" (John 14:6). Torrance echoes this claim in speaking of Christ as "the one place where man on earth and in history may really know the Father because that is the place where God Himself has elected to dwell among us."[18] In one sense, Christians may be bound to make such a claim if by it they mean that God's essential character is most fully disclosed through Christ. But that is to put the matter relatively and to recognize that everything about the world is in some sense a self-disclosure. I take this to be an important truth suggested by the sometimes puzzling Christian doctrine of the Trinity. For that doctrine speaks of God's revelation through the whole creative process and through the indwelling spirit as well as through Christ. Surely no Christian would want to deny the revelation of God through Hebrew history and tradition and many Christians of our time have expressed a new openness to God's self-revelation through other religions, other traditions, and other cultures. But, all the same, Christians take the revelation of God in Christ to be the most profound and to test all others by it.

## TOWARD CHRISTIAN REINTEGRATION
## OF CONTEMPORARY LIFE

The prospects for the basic Christian perspective in contemporary world culture hinge upon its capacity to bring knowledge and life into creative focus. And so we have to ask the question yet again: Is the Christian cup broken? Is it possible for those who have experienced the currents of our time most widely and deeply to contain this experience in this vessel without distortion or dishonesty? Or, as the Tom Robbins character put it, is it "all over"?

Those interested in the question will tend to put the faith perspective to the test in different ways. But for all of us, the testing occurs as we experience different dimensions of life in the light of this perspective. Does Christian faith break reality into fragments, requiring us to compartmentalize our life, with Christianity as but one of those compartments? Or does it integrate reality for us? Does it blind us or does it illuminate things for us? Does it help "make sense" out of everything?

It finally has to be tried. Christian faith is no mere intellectual exercise. The existentialists are right in saying that the deepest truths come through commitment in existence and not through abstract speculation. But still, it may help us to reflect upon segments of human experience where any faith perspective must be tested. Such reflection, while it cannot create faith nor substitute for life, can at least help identify obstacles. Bernard Lonergan understood this very well when he characterized the task of the Christian apologist:

> The apologist's task is neither to produce in others nor to justify for them God's gift of his love. Only God can give that gift, and the gift itself is self-justifying. People in love have not reasoned themselves into being in love. The apologist's task is to aid others in integrating God's gift with the rest of their living. Any significant event on any level of consciousness calls for adjustments elsewhere. Religious conversion is an extremely significant event and the adjustments it calls for may be both large and numerous. . . . For commonly needed information, interpretation, the formulation of new and the dropping of mistaken judgments of fact and of value, one reads the apologists. They cannot be efficacious, for they do not bestow God's grace. They must be accurate, illuminating, cogent. Otherwise they offer a stone to one asking for bread, and a serpent to one asking for fish.[19]

The question is how (or whether) Christian faith can be integrated with the rest of our living. In order to address that question we may now explore four main areas of human knowledge and experience where Christian faith is decisively put to the test in our time.

# 5

## CHRISTIAN FAITH AND
## COSMIC VISION

When the Big Bang blew, in 19 billion B.C.,
   was God there?

When the plasma began to swell, 100,000,000° hot,
   all the universe sweltering hydrogen,
   where was He?

When, 3 billion years ago, the cosmic dust
   collected, swishing around and around the sun,
   made the bare, atmosphereless earth,
   what was God's place
   in the scheme of things?

            William Pettit, "In His Image"

These questions, posed by a contemporary Christian poet, point to a very important problem: Does Christian faith bring the emerging scientific conceptions of the cosmos into meaningful focus, or is there a fatal contradiction between the two? We have already agreed that the Christian "cup" is broken if it can no longer "contain" all of our life experience. If any part of experience—certainly any important part—cannot fit inside the faith perspective, then that perspective is already fragmented. If the cosmic view of well-informed people in our time is fundamentally in conflict with Christian faith, then the cup is broken.

### THE OBSOLETE COSMOLOGY

This is no small problem for Christianity in our time because Christian faith began in a very different cultural setting with very different views of the cosmos. The question is whether Christians can abandon the ancient cosmology without abandoning Christian faith at the same time. The ancient cosmology pictured a flat world at the center of the firmament. The stars were fixed in a domelike canopy covering the earth. The sun traversed the skies from east to west, crossing under the earth through the night to continue its rounds the following morning. Similarly the moon coursed across the night skies. A nether region existed beneath the earth, popularly regarded as the habitation place of the dead. Christians thought of heaven as a distinct place, the dwelling place of God and of those chosen for eternal salvation. Christ could therefore "ascend" to that place, just as Moses and Elijah had been pictured as doing long before, and angels could "descend" from that place as heavenly emissaries of God. The earth was the center of God's creative attention; it was the stage of the divine-human drama. Hell was a distinct place beneath the earth, peopled with the damned, whose eternal torments were thought just recompense for temporal sins. As late as Dante this basic cosmological vision provided a frame of reference for his picturing of the drama of salvation and damnation. And even today it is not unusual for people to refer to God as "the Man up there" or to heaven as the "place up there," although the obsolete cosmology such language refers to may coexist in the mind alongside current scientific perspectives.

But that is exactly the problem. The obsolete cosmology cannot serve any longer; it must necessarily be in conflict with informed views. If Christian faith is necessarily tied to the older view, the faith will also be discarded.

There have been several Copernican revolutions in the past few centuries, including the one bearing that name. The ancient cosmology of flat earth, domelike canopy, and sun orbiting the earth has been superseded for centuries. It has been known for centuries that the earth is but one of many celestial bodies, that even the sun has many heavenly peers. The conception of a universe governed by laws that can be known with great precision is not a twentieth-century innovation; it has long been known that the earth's core is molten minerals, not the dwelling place of the dead. The effect of Enlightenment cosmological thinking upon religion was in itself quite considerable, producing, among other things, deistic theological tendencies. Since the universe operated so clearly in accordance with wholly predictable laws, it was not farfetched to think of it as a great clock and to think of God as the divine clockmaker and clockwinder. Already there was the difficulty of reconciling this, however, with faith in God's personal caring. The very dependability of the universe, plainly evident to competent scientists, appeared to exclude divine interventions in the cosmic order of things, and God became remote. It was not illogical for some in the eighteenth century and many in the nineteenth to conclude that the clock could function without the clockmaker and clockwinder.

## NEW IMAGES OF THE COSMOS

Twentieth-century science has developed fantastic new insights into cosmological time and space. One is of the sheer immensity of the universe. There are, it now appears, more than 100 billion stars in our own Milky Way galaxy, and this is evidently only an average-sized galaxy. Besides this one, there appear to be at least 100 billion other galaxies, which yields a total of at least 100 billion times 100 billion stars. Astronomer Carl Sagan has put the total number of stars in the universe in a striking way:

> A handful of sand contains about 10,000 grains, more than the number of stars we can see with the naked eye on a clear night. But the number of stars we can *see* is only the tiniest fraction of the number of stars that *are*. What we see at night is the merest smattering of the nearest stars. Meanwhile the Cosmos is rich beyond measure: the total number of stars in the universe is greater than all the grains of sand on all the beaches of the planet Earth.[1]

The immensity of space also defies conceptualization. The farthest distant galaxies are 10 or 12 billion light-years away. (In miles, that comes to about 48,656,960,000,000,000,000,000,000—which compares to the mere 250,000 miles the astronauts had to travel to reach the moon.) In age, the universe appears to be 18–20 billion years old. The currently dominant, though not altogether uncontested, theory of the origin of the universe sees its beginning some 18–20 billion years ago in a cosmic explosion— the Big Bang—from an incredibly tiny point of beginning. All matter and energy, all galaxies and stars and planets, are understood to have come from an explosion beginning at a point billions of times *smaller* than a single proton. Beautifully simple in its origin, prior even to the appearance of molecular structures, the universe in its vast expansion developed its present incredible complexity. The expansion of the universe continues even now, which means that the heavenly bodies are continuing to move apart. No longer is it meaningful to speak of any location as the "center" of this expanding universe. Nor is it possible to know whether it will end or continue infinitely to expand. Contrasting theories suggest either (*a*) that when the force of the Big Bang has been exhausted it will fall back in upon itself, returning to that same tiny point of origin, or (*b*) that the force of the Big Bang will continue infinitely, with all matter and energy dissipating into the smallest possible particles, out into the endless void. The first

theory suggests the possibility that the universe might continue to oscil-
late from Big Bang to expansion, to contraction, to another Big Bang, and
so on in endless cycles. The second theory sees the Big Bang as a unique
event, with all matter and energy eventually running down like an unre-
chargeable battery. Neither theory appears very friendly to the actual
contents of the universe! Everything would be destroyed in the first, as all
matter and energy eventually plunge back into the single small dot of
reality. While a new Big Bang would create another vast, complex universe, no trace of the previous universe could possibly remain. In the
second theory, all meaningful units of reality would be utterly disintegrated into the endless void. So, by either account every aspect of the
present universe will be erased more thoroughly than a sand castle in a
tidal wave. *Nothing* could possibly remain.

Both of these theories obviously move from the relatively small base of
what can be known into speculations about the far greater unknown. The
fact that they are so very different reminds us that ultimate questions
relating to the origin and destiny of the cosmos are very far from being
settled. As if to underscore that point, Sagan adds what he describes as
"one of the most exquisite conjectures of science or religion," the idea that
the smallest atomic structure would, if deeply probed, be seen to be
another universe—complete with stars, planets, and so on—and that our
own universe is an atom in an incomprehensibly larger one, with still
further universes upward and downward in "an infinite hierarchy of
universes."[2] While noting that this conjecture "stirs the blood," Sagan
does not offer it as having any degree of probability. Still, it is the kind of
freewheeling conjecture that marks the frontiers of exploration in physics
and astronomy. And it is a further reminder that cosmic space and time are
very far from being fully understood. We may be sure that the cosmological
views of science will continue to change, sometimes dramatically, as
scientists continue to probe the unknown. Advances in science over the
next few centuries may be as great or greater than those marking the
progress of knowledge from Newton to Einstein. But that does not mean
that the Newtons and Einsteins have not made enduring contributions to
our understanding of the cosmos. Even the most sophisticated knowledge
today may appear quite elementary a thousand years from now. But even
then, the state of today's knowledge will clearly be seen as a quantum leap
beyond the cosmology of the biblical era. We shall never be able to return to
the flat earth, the domed sky, the nether world, nor even to the heavenly
dwelling place of God.

There is, in Einstein's theory of relativity, even the prospect that our concept of space and time will never again be the same. The revolution implied by his conclusions extends to our very categories of thinking. No longer is it possible to accept common-sense perceptions of distance, velocity, and time literally. None has a fixed point of reference upon which the observer can depend for absolute measurements. Physicist Russell Stannard illustrates the way our common-sense perceptions have to be set aside by observing that if a person were to travel through space at nearly the speed of light, he or she would age thirty times slower than people remaining on earth. Yet, at the same time, that person would not experience any slowing down of mental or bodily processes, and any clocks or watches on board the spacecraft would similarly move that much slower than similar timepieces on earth.[3] Thus, were it possible for a person to take a ten-year trip in a spacecraft at such a speed, as measured from the craft itself, it would take three hundred years as measured from the earth. So the astronaut would have aged ten years, but upon return to earth the astronaut would arrive three hundred years later in earth time! Such claims are difficult to prove empirically, but insofar as physical tests can be arranged, they do seem to confirm Einstein's conclusions. For example, an extremely precise clock flown in a high-speed aircraft is found to have lagged behind an identical clock left behind by the amount of time Einstein's theory would have predicted. Speculating on the meaning of relativity, Stannard raises the question whether there may be a clue here that the universe itself cannot be subjected to the category of time, so that it has no beginning or ending.

Relativity does not mean that there can be no measurements of things nor that dependable relationships between objects in the universe cannot be found. We have already noted Einstein's own sense of wonderment at the rationality of the universe. But relativity does mean that common-sense perceptions of that universe no longer provide a dependable matrix for our cosmological view. Our view of the universe is necessarily less secure, insofar as security has been derived from more comfortable, inherited conceptions.

## IS THERE ROOM FOR GOD IN THE COSMOS?

One tempting way to relate God to the emerging scientific views of the cosmos is to locate God in the areas yet unknown by science (which, as we have seen, are extensive). Without disputing the scientifically corroborated findings of physicists and astronomers, it can be said that God is needed to account for what is still unknown. The "God of the gaps" typifies this approach. Christians using this approach may be in luck now that contemporary physics and astronomy have transformed the more fixed, Newtonian conceptions of the cosmos. The clock-work universe really didn't need God, except perhaps as the celestial clockwinder. Everything could be accounted for without God. But now, happily, there appears to be more that cannot be accounted for. Some Christians have taken comfort in the Heisenberg Uncertainty Principle. According to this principle, subatomic particles behave in entirely random, unpredictable ways when viewed one by one. It is only when viewed statistically that laws of probability can be constructed to predict their behavior. (This is a bit like the actuarial tables developed by insurance companies to predict the number of claims per year in particular age categories. The tables cannot predict which individuals will die, but if a large enough population is surveyed for a long enough period of time, the tables can be astonishingly accurate in predicting how many deaths there will be.) So the Heisenberg principle appears to open the way for reaffirmation of human freedom and an active role for God. But of course the only freedom in the Heisenberg scheme as such is at the totally unconscious subatomic particle level; and it is difficult to see how that affects either human freedom or the question of God. And even that bit of indeterminacy in the universe might disappear if further study of subatomic particles later reveals principles of causation not detectable at the present time.

Similarly one could argue that the Big Bang theory now opens the door for a conception of divine causation. And indeed, the notion that this vast universe began with a total "space" a billion times smaller than a single subatomic particle comes very close to the classical theological principle that the world was created entirely *ex nihilo*. The universe before the Big Bang is revealed as being as close to nothing at all as one could possibly come. But if God is to be affirmed on the basis of this piece of empirical data (or allegedly empirical data, since we are dealing with theory several stages removed from direct observation), what are we to do if a better theory comes along tomorrow to dispose of the Big Bang once and for all? Is there anything in physics that *requires* us to believe in God?

Sagan, who writes with appreciation for the inherited body of religious myths and traditions, still finds himself compelled to dispense with literal belief in God as source of the cosmos. His line of argument is worth quoting:

> If the general picture of an expanding universe and a Big Bang is correct, we must then confront still more difficult questions. What were conditions like at the time of the Big Bang? What happened before that? Was there a tiny

universe, devoid of all matter, and then the matter suddenly created from nothing? How does *that* happen? In many cultures it is customary to answer that God created the universe out of nothing. But this is mere temporizing. If we wish courageously to pursue the question, we must, of course, ask next where God comes from. And if we decide this to be unanswerable, why not save a step and decide that the origin of the universe is an unanswerable question? Or, if we say that God has always existed, why not save a step and conclude that the universe has always existed?[4]

Here, Sagan acknowledges the nearly insuperable intellectual problem of ultimate origins. There is difficulty either in conceiving of the universe as having a distinct point of beginning, before which there was nothing, or as having always existed. To invoke God at either point, far from solving the problem, appears only to complicate it. For then we must account not only for the origin or eternity of the material universe but also for the origin or eternity of God. Unstated, but implied here, is the scientific working principle that the simplest explanation of any phenomenon should be treated as most probable (the principle of parsimony). As applied in this context, the principle acknowledges that God *may* exist as the ultimate source of things, but that it is more probable that the universe exists on its own.

In responding to Sagan at this point, only naive Christians would fail to recognize the intellectual impasse to which he has called attention. How, indeed, can we conceive of the beginning of the universe or God entirely out of nothing? But how also can we conceive of reality as being without beginning? The problem appears to be quite impenetrable when put this way. New knowledge may contribute richer insight into the origin of the universe. I suspect that further progress in the sciences will, without conclusively answering the ultimate problem of causation, help us to see it in radically new ways—perhaps evoking more of Einstein's sense of awe at how elegantly rational yet how far beyond us the receding horizon continues to be. Even so, Christians should be cautious about using God simply to plug the gaps of our knowledge.

At the same time, however, the models of cosmic reality that are currently most prominent among scientists and educated laypersons are very far from disproving God. In a cosmos that may have begun from virtually zero—if the current Big Bang account is correct—one could scarcely rule out a creative force transcending the purely material. So one can at least maintain that the case for metaphysical atheism has not been made, even if some—like Sagan—regard atheism as more probable than theistic belief. In other words, one cannot regard the intellectual case for or against God as open and shut either way.

But to leave the question of God in that honest but minimalist way is to say that Christian faith does *not* serve to bring the cosmic perspective of our age into focus. Since the cosmic question helps set the stage for everything else, this would mean that the Christian cup is at least badly cracked. Even to invoke Occam's razor by separating the empirical knowledge of cosmic truth from our faith in God's transcendence over the natural realm compromises the wholeness of vision that a religious perspective must provide if we are finally to live by it. This does not mean that a religious perspective becomes a substitute for science; it does mean that our perspective is fragmented if the authentic contributions of science, honestly arrived at, cannot be "located" in a religious frame of meaning without compromising the one or the other. So the cosmic problem is scarcely to be dealt with by mere agnosticism or mutual neutrality between science and religion.

Several points contribute to the resolution of this problem. The first is contributed by Paul Tillich. Tillich developed a rather neat rejoinder to the question of God's existence by saying that of course God does not exist. For to say that God exists is to identify God alongside other *things,* and God is not a thing. Rather, God is the source of all things. Tillich's valid point is that if God is real it must be in a very different sense from our identification of other things as real. His own way of identifying this reality, which some have found helpful and others puzzling, was to speak of God as "Being itself" or as the "ground of being."[5] Part of the confusion in such a way of speaking of God is that it conveyed an impression of pantheism, which directly identifies everything that exists with God. Tillich disavowed pantheism, but at the same time he rejected a personal conception of God. Taken literally (which, above all else, one should be wary of doing with Tillich!) this appeared to result in a curious new form of naturalism; for nature, in the depth of its being, still appeared to be quite unconscious. And real atheists might be inclined to reply to Tillich that they would just as soon take their naturalism straight without the halo effect of a God who is no God at the "depth of being."

Still, Tillich's real point is worth lingering over even if one does not want to be committed to its full ramifications. What Tillich has done is to say that "being itself" is the proper starting point if one wants to deal with the cosmic implications of God. If God is indeed the source and sustainer of all being—which orthodox Christian theology has always affirmed—then empirical facts as such could not possibly either prove or disprove the reality of God. That God exists (here I depart from Tillich by using that verb) is an issue of faith. It comes down to whether one finds it possible to trust that the reality underlying everything else is God. When one holds this faith one's view of the scientific portrait of the cosmos is transformed—not in detail, for faith is not a substitute for observable facts, but in the new regard one has for the facts as an expression of God through creation. To identify the cosmos as creation is to attribute ultimate purpose to the phenomena discovered through honest scientific toil, not by treating God as a specific scientific hypothesis to account for particular phenomena, but by attributing the whole of creation with all of its possibilities to God's intention. The only general scientific finding that could disprove this kind of faith would be a scientific finding that reality is profoundly irrational.[6] But that would be a strange thing for science to discover, inasmuch as science could not function in an irrational universe. This is not, to be sure, the same thing as the traditional proof of God's existence on the basis of "design." The rationality of the universe is itself unprovable, and it is conceivable that a rational universe could exist without God. But my point is that faith in God is thoroughly coherent with the rationality of the universe; and, as we struggle to come to terms with the cosmos in our era, faith in God helps us more than it hinders us to keep faith with honest scientific work.

This point is underscored all the more if we note that science must be more than analytical in its effort to arrive at cosmic truth. By analysis we attempt to break reality down into its simplest parts. Thus Sagan appears to regard hydrogen as the fundamental building block upon which the physical universe is constructed; so in a sense, for him, reality ultimately *is* hydrogen. Others trace the simplest subatomic (which also means subhydrogen) reality back to the millisecond prior to the Big Bang, although efforts to analyze this reality at the exact moment of origin have thus far been frustrated. Such an analytical task is important, and I do not wish to denigrate its significance. But there is another point that can be overlooked if one focuses upon it exclusively. Whatever the ultimate building blocks of the cosmos turn out to be, everything in the universe is somehow potentially contained within them. One cannot say that the incredible immensity and diversity of the universe is "only" this or that designated elemental particle without at the same time saying that somehow this or that particle is capable of becoming all of the immensity and diversity. In other words, one cannot explain away everything with an elegantly simple explanation without noting that the basis of the explanation is complex beyond comprehension in its possibilities. In fact, the simpler the ultimate account becomes, the more difficult it may be to sustain (thus reversing the normally valid canon of scientific truth). For one must account for the pre-

cipitant that made things happen in a particular way if there is not sufficient complexity within the ultimate building blocks of reality to account
for it. An oak tree can be reduced to an acorn; but other things have to
happen to the acorn to make its potentiality of becoming an oak tree into
actuality. In this case even other building blocks, such as nutrient soil and
water and solar energy, are needed to create the final product, the oak tree.

We are driven beyond any one simple element even by our analysis itself
as we struggle to grasp the synthetic truth about the universe as it is
actually encountered. A Marxist metaphysics can deal with this by speaking of an ultimate dialectic of matter and energy and seeking to establish
that it is in the dynamic of the opposition of these two that differentiation
and complexity can occur. Still, even that account of things leaves dan-
gling the question whether matter and energy are fundamentally different
realities—and, if so, how they got together to form the universe and, if not,
how they are finally related so that a true dialectic can occur

The reality that most needs accounting for, and which every thoroughly
materialistic conception has greatest difficulty with, is conscious personhood. We have already spoken of this in chapter 4; but in the context of a
discussion of the cosmos it may need to be reiterated that we cannot
consistently reduce our own personhood to purely unconscious forces of
matter and energy. Something radically different enters into the material
stream of things with the arrival of the personal subject, a being with
awareness transcending unconscious forces. I speak of this as radically
new. Yet that is an even more difficult belief to sustain—that personal,
subjective experience is only an emergent reality in a universe that in its
origin was utterly without any form of consciousness. Could this reality, so
categorically different from the purely objective, have simply arisen from
*things*? I strongly suspect not. To be sure, we have little evidence of
personal, subjective being apart from sustaining material bodies and envi-
ronments. But that does not mean that we can reduce personal being
to material factors without also meaning that the material factors somehow contain this exciting possibility and somehow had it from the very
beginning.

We cannot allow ourselves to forget that the cosmos is not simply
material. It contains subjects as well as objects. The astronomer, while
contemplating the stars, must not overlook the astronomer! If the cosmos
has room for the astronomer, then it is not unthinkable that it also reflects
the reality of God. Without God it is more difficult, not easier, to make sense
out of the fact of ourselves. Belief in God makes it easier to conceive of a
universe in which subject and object, people and things, both exist.

## CHRIST AND COSMOS

Belief in God helps bring the cosmos into meaningful focus without distorting the pursuit of further knowledge by the various sciences. Indeed, it is a positive impetus to science inasmuch as true knowledge of the cosmos affords deeper insight into the character of the creator.

But Christian faith is not simply belief in the existence of God nor a reflection of the latest findings of science. This faith also has important things to say about the character of God and the place of humanity. The basic Christian claim is quite extraordinary: The God of the cosmos who is the source of all creation is authentically revealed in the human person Jesus Christ. We have already noted the fundamental optimism contained in this faith, that the God revealed in Christ cares profoundly for each of us and that our overall attitude toward God is one of hopeful love. How well will this faith serve in bringing the cosmos into focus? We remember here that Einstein, while believing that the universe manifests the hand of a consummate intelligence, still found the belief in a personal God—not to say a loving one—to be a piece of superstition.

The New Testament Book of Colossians sets forth the basic claim as it relates to the cosmos:

> He [Christ] is the image of the invisible God, the first-born of all creation; for in him all things were created; in heaven and on earth, visible and invisible, whether thrones or dominions or principalities or authorities—all things were created through him and for him. He is before all things, and in him all things hold together. . . . In him all the fullness of God was pleased to dwell, and through him to reconcile to himself all things, whether on earth or in heaven, making peace by the blood of his cross. (Col. 1:15–17, 19–20)

There are elements in this passage that almost appear to have been written with a deliberate intent to offend the twentieth-century mind—for example, the implication that 100 billion times 100 billion stars were created "in" Jesus Christ, or that he was "before all things," or that "in him all things hold together." The "blood of the cross" reference adds very little to our comprehension of the vast reaches of cosmic space and time. That Jesus Christ, whom we know first as a historical person, literally predated or caused creation in the way this passage seems to suggest seems highly doubtful.

But before the passage is discarded as a piece of superstition more needs to be said about it. In the first place, the words were apparently written in response to an early form of Gnosticism. The Gnostics, many of whom became involved with the primitive Christian church, believed that the material world was fundamentally evil in contrast to the spirit world, which they conceived to be the source of good. Early Christianity was tempted to adopt this dualism and to think of Christ as a kind of spirit manifestation of God, opposed to the world of material objects and physical senses. Read with an eye toward that controversy, the passage is an affirmation of the positive place of the world of things and of God as creator of things. Translated into our world view, the Colossians passage is an affirmation of the goodness of the cosmos. The writer of the passage may indeed have believed quite literally that Christ was before all things, and so on. But the more general point of enduring importance is that the character of the God who created all things is revealed in the character of Jesus Christ. God is, we may and must say, vastly more than Jesus. But the fundamental goodness we see in Jesus is a reflection of the fundamental goodness of God. Thus, the passage affirms that the source of creation is God, whose goodness is no less than that of Jesus Christ. The cosmos, then, is a reflection of this goodness.

The personal relationship of God to each human being, understood now in a cosmic setting, remains troublesome. We have noted Einstein's problems with this. Even James Gustafson, whose theological ethics are grounded in the concept of God, finds it difficult to sustain belief in a *personal* God.[7] I am not sure that the essential problem here has changed much over the past two millenniums, but knowledge of the cosmos today certainly affects our mood in approaching it. We find it difficult to believe in divine interventions in the processes of nature, partly because we understand the dependability of those processes better and partly because we know more about the basis of mythologies of divine intervention in all cultures. We also find it difficult to think of insignificant men and women personally claiming the attention of the God of 100 billion times 100 billion stars. If God's personal attention and caring exist, it is difficult to see how they operate in such a cosmos.

It is to the credit of an Einstein or a Gustafson that they can be as serious as they are about God, cosmos, and moral responsibility even while discarding the tradition of personal relationship. But I am not so sure that the cosmic perspective on God requires us to abandon a very personal conception of God's relationship to individuals. If God is the source and sustainer of all being, then no aspect of being can be considered remote from God. It is impossible for human minds to focus upon more than a few things at once, but then, we are not God. To speak of any aspect of reality as being outside God's awareness is to raise again the question whether God exists. For any aspect of reality that is not so related to God has an independent existence. And if God is extraneous to any aspect of reality, what can it mean to speak of God's relationship to the *whole* of reality?

Communication from human beings to God is thus not the problem. God may be taken to know our thoughts and actions as intimately as anything else in the cosmos. A more serious problem is how do we know when God is communicating to us? That problem has already been addressed to some extent in chapter 4, where the point was registered that our knowledge of ultimate reality is mediated through our faith that certain experiences are an authentic reflection of what we cannot know directly. We can always be wrong; but faith in the presence and character of God also creates intimations of God's response to us in our own personal existence. This is why Christians have so often framed prayer as relationship to Christ. For Christ is known historically and it is not as difficult to extrapolate from our "picture" of Christ how Christ would respond to particular questions. Every generation of Christians does this, and then each subsequent generation has to criticize and correct the results.[8] But the ultimate point of faith is that God's nature is revealed in Christ, so that the visualization of Christ leads one toward, not away from God.

There is another point in the Colossians passage that bears upon our relation to the cosmos. That is the line "and through him [Christ] to reconcile to himself all things, whether on earth or in heaven. . . ." Again, we must not be detained about whether Christ in some literal way brought reconciliation to the contents of the cosmos as a whole. The key point here is what is now—that is, after we have seen the reality of God through Christ—our relationship with the cosmos. The passage has already proclaimed the unity of all things; now it asserts that alienation from the realm of things has been overcome. That bears directly upon the question raised by this chapter as a whole.

For after all else has been said, the real question we human beings must raise about the cosmos is whether we are "at home" here. Do we belong to the cosmos in some fundamental way? Or are we merely guests or, perhaps, a hostile army of occupation, here but for a day? When we contemplate the world of nature—the mountains and forests and deserts and seas—do we see this in some basic way as our home? Do the vast reaches of interstellar space communicate beauty and love in their distant grandeur, or do they remind us only of our cold isolation? Are we alienated within the cosmos or, in some fundamental way, are we a part of it? These are not, of course, scientific questions. They go beyond objective description to the deeper sense of who we are and what the cosmos means to us. In this sense, a Christian conception of reality overcomes our alienation by locating the cosmos in the power and purposes of God while at the same time identifying God's attitude toward us as one of boundless love.

One of the immediate implications of our coming to terms with the cosmos is that we no longer think of the material environment as nothing more than a facility for our selfish use. Use the environment we must, of course; but a Christian vision of the cosmos also leads us to respect it as an expression of God's nature and purposes. At home in this cosmos, we cannot treat the natural world exploitatively or disrespectfully. One of the finer insights of H. Richard Niebuhr's *Radical Monotheism and Western Culture*,[9] which so remarkably anticipated the attitude of the ecology movement, was that monotheistic faith identifies the center of value with the source of being. All of being is included in the value frame of reference. Niebuhr specifically noted that humanism falls short of this, not because it mistakenly values the human but because it excludes the nonhuman from the sphere of valuation. So he considered humanism to be a form of "henotheism," which identifies the center of value just with one's own group. Humanity may be a rather large group, but it is still far less than being as a whole. Christian faith links one with the cosmos in this way, making it possible to find value in all things.

There is yet another biblical theme that is relevant as we contemplate the cosmos. Paul's letter to the Romans speaks of the whole creation as "groaning in travail together until now" and of the "eager longing" with which the creation awaits "the revealing of the sons of God" (Rom. 8:22, 19). Though it certainly could not have presupposed a modern cosmology, this passage suggests a conception of the cosmos as being alienated from God and that in the human release from alienation the rest of creation will also find release. Most intriguing is that it is through humanity (and perhaps other conscious beings elsewhere in the universe) that the cosmos is able to respond to the creator. We are that aspect of creation that is capable of universal awareness and the contemplation and celebration of God. As our own alienation from God is overcome in faith, we bring the cosmos itself into a new kind of relationship with God. The Christian vision of the cosmos sees in it the reflection of God's loving purpose. Whether as scientist or artist or simple, awestruck observer, the Christian is able to perceive the creative work of God in the endless reaches and intricacies and beauties of the cosmos. Every new human vision of this limitless treasure is at the same time cause for celebration of its creative, loving source.

The Christian perspective thus brings new wholeness to our vision of cosmic reality, overcoming the fragmentations of so much contemporary experiencing of the material universe. The immensities of time and space no longer threaten to engulf consciousness, for they are grounded in a transcendent point of reference. Nor is it necessary any longer to reduce the conscious life of humanity to purely unconscious material forces, for consciousness is itself to be found at the center of being. Thus, the Christian "cup" integrates our cosmic vision.

But what about the problem of *evil*? That is a deeper problem, deeper than any challenge of contemporary science. The Christian cup must be able to contain that too. But we shall defer the question of evil until we have had a better look at whether Christian faith can also bring perspective to the personal life and social existence of human beings.

# 6

## CHRISTIAN PERSPECTIVE
## ON THE SELF

We live in a fragmented age. But we yearn for a sense of wholeness. Granted that our access to final truth is always on the basis of some aspects of human experience and never a result of absolute knowledge of all that is, we have asked ourselves whether the Christian faith can truly put the world together for people in our time. The question is partially tested by our view of the cosmos, as we have seen. Here the issue we faced was whether it is possible to think of the cosmos in positive terms as the expression of intelligence and purpose and love.

Our ability to answer such a question positively does not necessarily mean that we have overcome the fragmentary character of human life itself. Cosmic questions can be ignored. But all human beings face the question of their own humanness, and they are on remarkably similar footing. Intelligence and knowledge per se do not seem to matter all that much when it comes to the problem of living with ourselves. In one way or another we all have to face the problem of what enables us to be all that we can be as persons. What leads to authentic fulfillment? What constitutes our personal humanness? What brings focus to our personal problems?

### CHRISTIANITY AND SELF-DECEPTION

Our humanness and personal fulfillment cannot ultimately be based upon self-deception. We may be deceived by the universe and by other people, but we cannot afford to deceive ourselves. Self-deception is self-contradiction; it is "living a lie." As the existentialists say, we must be "authentic" persons; we must live in "good faith." To deceive oneself is to suppress a part of oneself; it is to become disintegrated. An authentic, integrated personality is one that is not at war within itself. Its mind, will, and feeling are unified in a wholeness of personal integrity. Therefore, if the Christian viewpoint is false and we believe it to be false, we must not live on the pretense that it is true. Morever, if the Christian viewpoint requires us to suppress our minds or our feelings, then Christian faith cannot be wholeness for us.

One remembers in this connection Nietzsche's bitter rejection of Christianity as the negation of all human passion. "The church," he writes,

fights passion with excision in every sense; its practice, its "cure," is *castratism*. It never asks: "How can one spiritualize, beautify, deify a craving?" It has at all times laid the stress of discipline on extirpation (of sensuality, of pride, of the lust to rule, of avarice, of vengefulness). But an attack on the roots of passion means an attack on the roots of life: the practice of the church is *hostile to life*.[1]

There is, in Nietzsche's own work taken as a whole, much that is itself hostile to life. Yet in this outburst of a troubled and passionate soul there may be some legitimate judgment against equating Christ with the suppression of the vitalities of life. If Christian faith is still the "good news," then contemporary men and women must find themselves, their honest feelings and thoughts, their creativities, wholly affirmed. Christianity must not alienate people from their authentic selfhood.

Some of Christianity's severest critics over the past century or so have homed in on exactly that point. When Karl Marx attacked religion it was because he perceived it to be a narcotic to prevent oppressed people from experiencing the pain of oppression (while also perceiving religion as an ideology to justify the oppression). His term for religion as "opiate" of the people has sometimes been misunderstood as a purely pejorative term. Actually, he saw the need for oppressed people to have such a narcotic during periods of history when change was not a realistic possibility— better illusory happiness than none at all:

[Religion] is *the fantastic realization* of the human being inasmuch as the *human being* possesses no true reality. The struggle against religion is, therefore, indirectly a struggle against *that world* whose spiritual *aroma* is religion.

*Religious* suffering is at the same time an *expression* of real suffering and a *protest* against real suffering. Religion is the sigh of the oppressed creature, the sentiment of a heartless world, and the soul of soulless conditions. It is the *opium* of the people.[2]

It is better, according to this, to have the fantasy of humanness than no humanness at all. Marx believed, however, that with the overcoming of class oppression there would no longer be need for such fantasy.

Marx's views on religion were greatly influenced by the nineteenth-century theologian Ludwig Feuerbach, who also saw much in Christianity that expressed self-deception. Feuerbach understood the true essence of Christianity to be love. But he viewed God as an abstraction from the human reality of love. The worship of God substitutes the abstraction for the reality; it "alienates" us from our true essence, our true humanity, the reality of which is love. The *idea* of love has thus been substituted for its reality, and we are no longer really human. Feuerbach continued to regard himself as a Christian, but he found it necessary to abandon that part of Christianity (namely God) that distorts our humanity.[3] Marx, while greatly influenced by this theological development, rejected any semblance of Christianity. Religion, even in Feuerbach's very humanistic form, can only confuse the human reality. Moreover, Marx believed that Feuerbach's version of humanism failed to grasp the critical reality of class oppression and hence, also, to understand the full truth about human self-alienation.

Among other nineteenth- and twentieth-century critics of religion as self-deception, Sigmund Freud has had the greatest influence. Relentlessly committed to scientific truth about the human self, Freud analyzed the contents of the psyche through years of clinical observation and generated a new vocabulary of psychological language. Two points emerge from this work that are relevant here.

First, he understood authentic humanness to consist in our becoming consciously aware of the forces within our subconscious that determine our feelings. We may be dominated by early childhood trauma, by suppressed feelings toward father- or mother-figures, or other subconscious attitudes that create crippling conflicts in our emotional life until they are brought to the surface and dealt with. We can scarcely be fully human until liberated from the tyranny of these conflicts. Our selfhood thus depends upon confronting head-on the suppressed reality of our subconscious mind.

The other point is that religion is an illusion that generally contributes to the suppression of reality about ourselves. It is an expression of our desire, in the midst of life's difficulties and uncertainties, to experience again the intimacy and support of our father's love. Belief in the Father God is an illusion, not because it is necessarily false (though Freud clearly believes it to be so) but because it is born out of wish fulfillment and not out of the scientific quest for knowledge about external reality. We believe such religious doctrine to be true, not because we have weighed its claims as reality but because we *want* it to be true: "We say to ourselves: it would indeed be very nice if there were a God, who was both creator of the world and a benevolent providence, if there were a moral world order and a future life, but at the same time it is very odd that this is all just as we should wish it ourselves."[4] Personal maturity requires that we outgrow the need for such illusions.

The most troublesome thing about these views is that there is so much truth in them. People *do* believe things for no better reason than to make themselves feel good in the face of unacceptable reality. Sometimes their religious faith is an escape from the cruelties of human oppression, from psychological conflicts, or from some combination of social and psychological pain. Sometimes the object of religious faith is an abstract symbol, the worship of which dries up the vitalities of life and alienates us from loving relationships. Sometimes it is clearly a form of wish fulfillment. When that is so, we are like the victims of catastrophe who, having lost the will to overcome circumstances with heroic struggle, give way to pleasant daydreams denying the unacceptable reality. Religion, when it prevents us from coping with reality, may be our adversary, no matter how pleasant it seems.

But is that the last word on what Christian faith means to the self? Is it only a form of self-deception?

Acknowledging that religion can be "a cosmic projection of the child's experience of the protective order of parental love," Peter Berger suggests that "what is projected is, however, itself a reflection, an imitation, of ultimate reality."[5] We learn something about the ultimate reality of protective order from our experience in the human setting. That does not prove anything about God, of course, and Berger does not claim that such an inductive approach to religion validates ultimate claims. But it does suggest that the fact that people see a relationship between their human needs and the character of ultimate reality does not in itself invalidate faith in a supportive ultimate reality. Rather, we can find in the human plane what Berger calls "signals of transcendence," which he defines as "phenomena that are to be found within the domain of our 'natural' reality but that appear to point beyond that reality."[6] We may be wrong. But if we are, it is not because there is a connection between our feelings and experiences and our faith. Indeed, Berger's point is that a faith is partly tested by whether or not it helps us confront reality.

## CHRISTIAN FAITH AND SELF-ACCEPTANCE

The ringing challenge of Nietzsche makes Christianity appear to be a very repressive form of religion, as he no doubt experienced it himself.[7]

There are some biblical themes that seem to confirm Nietzsche's judgment. For example, "if your right hand causes you to sin, cut it off and throw it away; it is better that you lose one of your members than that your whole body go into hell" (Matt. 5:30), or "It is well for a man not to touch a woman. But because of the temptation to immorality, each man should have his own wife and each woman her own husband" (1 Cor. 7:1b–2, which thus suggests that the sex drive is a regrettable fact which marriage is designed only to remedy). Other passages might lead one to severe self-condemnation for experiencing anger or fear or envy.

Such biblical materials have done a good deal of psychological harm when they have been used moralistically. When Christianity is reduced to a series of moralistic requirements—as it may well have been in the experience of Nietzsche and in the lives of many of Freud's patients and clients—it often leads away from self-acceptance. The net result can be a crippling of the self.

But there is a deep sense in which such moralism is what even Christian faith is *against*—although that point needs to be understood carefully. Christian faith is about love; about God's love for us and our love for one another and God. The distortion occurs when the commandment to love is put before the faith that God loves us. The problem is that if we cannot feel at the root of our being that we are loved ourselves, we find it almost impossible to respond to the command to love. We may acknowledge intellectually that we ought to love. We may resolve to obey that command. But we may not finally be able to do so. Paul, who gave a good deal of thought to this problem, spoke of his utter inability to do the thing he acknowledged to be morally binding upon him: "I can will what is right, but I cannot do it. For I do not do the good I want, but the evil I do not want is what I do. . . . Wretched man that I am!" (Rom. 8:18b–19, 24a). But this is why Paul emphasized so much the importance of grace. The word "grace" is itself a metaphor taken from Roman jurisprudence. It means a setting aside of the requirements of the law in order to give mercy to the accused. As applied theologically in the writings of Paul and in the work of many subsequent theologians such as Luther, grace is a very rich concept. It is taken to mean that we are fully accepted by God in spite of our imperfections. We can, as Tillich put it, accept the fact that we are accepted (although in Tillich's theology there really is no personal One by whom we are accepted). The God who is the very source and center of all being, who knows all that is to be known about each of us, knowing all still accepts us. No flaw, no fault, no imperfection, or imagined imperfection bulks large enough to set aside God's love. As revealed in Jesus Christ, God has simply and finally said yes to us, and there is no way for us to turn God's yes into a no. We do not have to do anything to *earn* this love of God. So the Christian doctrine of grace, interpreted in this way, means that the affirmation of our selfhood is not something we earn or deserve. It is simply and freely given, from the very center of all being.

Sometimes Christians have overlooked, even reversed, this most central tenet of their faith. Sometimes they have been so anxious to improve upon one another's morality and have been so anxious about their own that they have forgotten the main point that we are, as Paul put it, saved by grace and not by works. We do not have to do anything to make God love us. When we most truly come to our senses it is with the awareness that God is pure love. Jesus' parable of the prodigal son strongly emphasized this theme. This central point in Christian theology means we are not homeless waifs in a hostile universe; we really are at home here!

The psychological *consequences* of this attitude are indescribably important. To feel accepted is to have an integrated center of being. It is to possess the basis for mature growth and extending dimensions of creativity. One sees the point most clearly, perhaps, when this sense of acceptance is *not* present in somebody's life. Occasionally we read of a great tragedy when a supposedly model young person runs amuck in a sudden outburst of violence. Friends, neighbors, teachers are overcome by surprise. But perhaps they need not be. The "model" behavior was possibly conformist behavior, resulting from an anxious but futile drive to feel accepted. Finally, it has to crack.

People who have a difficult time believing they are really valued have a difficult time placing much value upon either their own lives or those of others. Life for them can have a superficial connectedness, but it is generally a conventional kind of wholeness. It is a matter of conforming to what one perceives the demands of one's associates and one's culture to be. Can this be authentic humanness? I suspect that the truly demonic behavior of most of the great villains of human history has such rootage. The struggle to be loved may be at the root of what appears to be a completely free choice of wrong. The callous face of evil masks the pathos of an inability to receive love. This may seem too charitable an interpretation of the spiritual life of history's most demonic figures—the Genghis Khans, the Attilas, the Hitlers—but I believe it to be a true one. Faced with the need to create one's own meaning and salvation, some will work at it conventionally, striving for the approval of fellow humanity in the culturally sanctioned ways. Others will grasp the larger meaning of their lives on the wide canvas of history with no regard for customary restraints or sensitive fellow feelings. At the root of both is a sense that one is not valued unconditionally. In the final analysis, life that is not rooted in love lacks an integrating center. Instead, it is a jumbled pattern of disconnected episodes in which one strives to build something that cannot be created in that way. For if we are not loved unconditionally from outside ourselves we know instinctively that we cannot manufacture the value of our own lives.

Paul recognized the dilemma. The more we struggle to "earn" our salvation, the farther we drift away from it, because salvation consists in the life of love, and our self-centered struggle makes it ever more difficult to give or receive love. If the essence of moral law is the "law of love," then it is impossible to set out to obey that law for selfish reasons. "The greatest treason," wrote T. S. Eliot, "is to do the right deed for the wrong reason."[8] The only motivation for love is an unselfish one. We can do loving things for unloving reasons, that is, for selfish reasons; but then those things are not an expression of love but of our alienation from love. Compounding the dilemma, when we feel that the love we receive from other people or from God is something we have earned we cannot think of it as real love. It is not an affirmation of our inner being, but only of our outer actions.

A deep sense of being loved unconditionally makes it possible to accept our own selfhood and to build a constructive life in response. I am very far from thinking this can only happen to Christians. The theme may have parallels in some other religious systems. Deep expression of human love is to be found among people throughout the world, and that is at least an intimation of the religious grounding. Human love—the love of parents for children, of spouses for each other, of trusted friends—may be incomplete in that it cannot by itself be a basis for trust in the ultimate significance of one's life. But it is a foundation for an integrated sense of wholeness at the level of human society. My guess is that there are a great many people who are more "Christian" as a consequence of loving human relationships than others are who spend their days struggling to please a God whom they perceive to be wholly judgmental.

Putting this in a different way, is it not a very important test of all religions and philosophies of life whether they recognize with Paul the importance of the divide between a religion based upon grace (or some equivalent) and one based upon what Paul called "works"? Seen in this perspective, it may be that the deepest point of vulnerability of Marxism is not its atheism (although that is a serious flaw from the Christian standpoint) but its characteristic moralism. A Christian acquaintance currently living in Eastern Europe remarked that the biggest theological problem she had with the orthodox Marxism of her own country was its unforgiving demand. Even within the Party, loyal Communist cadres could not find or experience forgiveness when, inevitably, they felt themselves falling short of the demand to live by revolutionary and socialist principle. Similar criticism could be registered at Shiite Islam and some forms of Buddhism, Hinduism, and Judaism, but we have also acknowledged that a great deal of Christianity also fails to pass the test. Moralistic Christianity defines the faith in terms of rules to be obeyed or "sins" to be avoided; rationalistic Christianity defines its "works" in terms of articles of belief which must be accepted without deviation. Both presuppose a God who is less than unconditionally loving; both make self-acceptance very difficult. For we cannot fully accept ourselves until we believe ourselves to be fully accepted.

## THE MORAL DEMAND AND "CHEAP GRACE"

There are two possible problems with the sweeping vision of grace given here as the basis of authentic humanness. One is the question whether this means abandoning the claims of the moral life. Are we to exclaim with Voltaire, "Oh, God will forgive—that is his business!"? Faced with what he considered to be an excessively amoral or nonmoral (or even immoral) interpretation of grace, Dietrich Bonhoeffer coined the term "cheap grace" to refer to grace that lays no demand upon us for obedience to Christ, disciplined life, and moral behavior. Cheap grace, he wrote, "means grace sold on the market like cheapjacks' wares."

> The sacraments, the forgiveness of sins, and the consolations of religion are thrown away at cut prices. Grace is represented as the Church's inexhaustible treasury, from which she showers blessings with generous hands, without asking questions or fixing limits. Grace without price; grace without cost. . . . I can go and sin as much as I like, and rely on this grace to forgive me, for after all the world is justified in principle by grace. . . . The upshot of it all is that my only duty as a Christian is to leave the world for an hour or so on a Sunday morning and go to church to be assured that my sins are all forgiven.[9]

The Germany of 1937, when Bonhoeffer wrote these biting words, provided an unusually vivid combination of a complacent Christianity and an increasingly demonic social order. But in any social setting the problem would still have to be faced: Does God's grace excuse us from obedience to the claims of justice and righteousness? Is the thundering judgment of the Most High against inhumanity to be subordinated altogether to the relaxations of easy grace? Are the Nazis to be consoled by the sweet elixirs of abundant love, even while stuffing people in gas chambers? Are the interrogators for repressive governments the world over today to be encouraged to take a moment's respite from the rigors of extracting confessions from innocent people, long enough to be soothed by divine love? Is grace to calm the perturbations of cutthroat business entrepreneurs lest they soften the absolute priority of material gain over every instinct of human compassion? Should Amos moderate his conception of the demand of God?

> Take away from me the noise of your songs;
>    to the melody of your harps I will not listen.
> But let justice roll down like waters,
>    and righteousness like an everflowing stream.

> (5:23–24)

Preaching grace in an unjust world can be a dangerous thing!

The balancing of grace with moral demand is very difficult. To say that God loves you, but that to please God means you must behave in a certain way, appears to limit God's love. And if God's love is limited, then it must be earned. If it must be earned, then it does not reach to the center of our being, but it remains at the point of our external acting. But to say that God loves you regardless of what you do appears to dissipate moral sensitivities and ultimately the life of love itself. So Christians can sway uneasily between excessive moralism and uncaring complacency. Both are wrong, both unfaithful to the deeper meaning of Christian faith.

As a matter of fact, the deeper meaning of Christian faith is that grace is neither "cheap" nor "costly." Grace is absolutely *free*. There is no cost at all. It is strictly and absolutely *given*. There is nothing about it that is earned or could be earned; nothing that could give rise to attitudes of self-righteousness among those who feel they have somehow earned it, nor to feelings of self-deprecation among those who are all too aware of their moral failures. It is simply free. .

The problem of deciding between the grace of God and the judgment of God is a problem only if we confuse the giving with the receiving. For grace to be the basis of positive self-identity it must be given without reservation. Much religion consists of a divine-human transaction in the course of which some indication is given of what humanity must do to please the gods. Subsequently, the price is paid or not and, depending upon that, the gods are pleased or not. But Christian faith breaks through that transaction, whether the transaction is portrayed in traditionally religious or secular form. There could be no breakthrough without an unqualified sense of being accepted by the Power in charge of things. That part must be very secure for it to function psychologically in the way we have indicated.

But then there is the question of how we shall respond to grace. Here we must not forget that a selfish response to grace amounts to a rejection of grace. For how can we receive love unlovingly? To treat the gift of love as a selfish possession is to insulate our inner being from the only authentic message the gift can convey—that we are ourselves a center of goodness and love. The grace of God means that God's love for us is unlimited, but the concept of God's judgment symbolizes the truth that if we reject that love it cannot transform us into the loving, creative persons God intends us to be. Is our response, then, a disguised "work" in the sense Paul meant when he contrasted "work" with "faith"? Have we brought the earning of God's favor in through the back door?

We must take equally seriously both God's profound caring and human freedom. God's caring is an unshakable ground of ultimate security. It means that we *can* be loving, creative human beings whose lives develop as a symphony of gratitude and praise. We do not *have* to be loveless, alienated people. The biblical symbol "fear of God" is not, then, to be understood as fear of God's hostility, for God is not hostile toward us, nor as anxiety about whether God intends good or evil for us, for God intends only good and not evil. It can be understood as fear of the objective consequences of allowing ourselves to slide into self-centered living.

It is in this way that we can also find the relationship between love and spiritual discipline. Spiritual discipline is altogether sterile and dehumanizing when it takes the form of an effort to become righteous before God and fellow humanity, to earn the approval if not the moral envy of others. But it need not take that form. It can be a creative response to God's gift, a conscious effort to become what God has given us the power to become. John Wesley's use of "justification" and "sanctification" is suggestive at this point. Justification is our realization of the complete sufficiency of God's love for us; sanctification is working out the implications through growth to maturity in love. Without justification, there would be no basis, no foundation of security on which to grow. With that foundation we are able to take the sometimes painful steps, knowing that we will be encouraged in our efforts, not condemned for our failures. The classical tradition of virtue and character formation in Christian ethics needs to be seen in similar light. Virtue and character can never simply be the result of our own effort—pulling ourselves up by our own bootstraps, as it were. At the same time, the classical virtues define habits of mind and will that can be developed on a foundation of grace. One does not strive to develop greater patience or sobriety or courage or hopefulness, for instance, in order to become an acceptable human being. But having experienced acceptance, one recognizes these and other virtues as marks of the full humanness that grace has now made possible. Moral and spiritual discipline thus has a positive, not a negative, foundation and character can be real, not simulated.

Some may still wonder whether this portrait of the central role of grace is sound psychology. Does it sufficiently attend to the realities of guilt and the need to explore its basis? It is beyond the scope of the present work to survey this problem thoroughly in light of the various schools of psychology. But if anything, the different schools tend to converge in their understanding of the need to accept the reality of the patient or client in his or her present state of being and to work patiently with him or her in locating the psychological resources to make growth possible. Sometimes, as in Thomas A. Harris's best-selling *I'm OK, You're OK*,[10] the importance of total self-acceptance is made very explicit. Those who derided the book title by reasserting the reality of guilt and sin seem to me to have missed Harris's central point. He seems well aware of the reality of sin and guilt. To say I'm OK does not mean I'm morally perfect, nor does it mean that moral imperfections are matters of small importance. What it means is that we have to accept ourselves before we can begin to work on those problems or, as the second half of the title suggests, before we can truly accept other people. Other approaches to psychology emphasize the importance of listening to the client or patient and encouraging him or her to lay out all of the painful, crippling thoughts and feelings in a setting of full acceptance. Certainly a counselor or therapist who does not communicate personal acceptance will not enable most emotionally troubled people to face their problems.

Then, does Christian faith finally add anything to secular psychology? The limitation of secular psychology is that it cannot convey anything about the ultimate ground of our acceptance. Still, it is a mark of the failure of some Christian pastors and congregations that there are those who feel they have to go to a secular counselor in order to find a sympathetic and understanding ear. Where pastors understand themselves to be channels of God's grace—as is the case of many Catholic priests in the confessional, so far as that is not mechanically legalistic—the results can be very impressive.[11]

## CREATIVITY AND VOCATION

There is another possible problem with the Christian vision of grace: It may seem to be contrary to the creative drive in human beings. Do we not, after all, have to be a little bit neurotic in order to be productive? Do we not create out of the tensions within our selfhood? Does not creation consist precisely in the overcoming of those tensions? Is there not, in fact, a certain sense that it really *is* by our works that we are "saved"? Those who think so might respond favorably to the title of a book by the philosopher Peter Bertocci, *Religion as Creative Insecurity,* even though the contents of that book include a good deal of affirmation of the unmerited love of God.[12] The title suggests the point that creativity may have its roots in our feelings of insecurity, not in the kind of security to which the idea of grace seems to point.

Of course creativity is a complex thing, and it may appear in different forms with different people. Sometimes it is a response to a problem. Often there is some need that it is designed to fill, or a tension between good and evil to be overcome. Sometimes it is playful. Sometimes—as in the case of many scientists—it is the pursuit of curiosity; sometimes it is the celebration of an inner experience of beauty by means of some kind of outward form. But I question whether creativity can develop out of profound insecurity. In all of these cases one cannot be genuinely creative if one is finally preoccupied only with oneself. One can reproduce fragments and perhaps express something of the brokenness of one's existence. But it is not easy to recognize accurately the claims of truth if one's own ego is too closely engaged. And some of the more narcissistic tendencies in twentieth-century art forms may have more rootage in preoccupation with personal ego than with real creativity. Security in love is not the enemy of creativity; it is more often its foundation.

Still, when creativity is interpreted as pursuing a vocation or "calling" from God or as "doing the will of God" there may be a potential problem. It is partly a problem of knowing what the "will of God" is. Many people have justified questionable decisions as coming from the will of God, and sometimes people have dedicated their lives to the pursuit of pure folly on the assumption that this reflected God's purposes. Mental hospitals house large numbers of troubled people who hear divine voices summoning them to messianic missions. Divine calling is not always clear! But even if it were, there is the problem of relating creativity to obedience. The Bible is full of summonses to obey God's will. But if one must always be asking whether this or that proposed project is truly God's will, how is one to find the freedom necessary for real creativity? One's own creativity can take on a curiously lifeless, abstract quality if it expresses conformity to the will of another. That is true on the human plane, where doing something to fulfill somebody else's specifications seems to be the very antithesis of creativity, and it seems even more so, when one is conforming to an abstract conception of God. One wonders whether creativity in service of the will of God may not be a kind of painting by number: God lays out the design; we fill in the colors, first taking care that we use precisely the numbers we are instructed to use. The question is whether creativity in obedience to God may not be too inhibited.

Sometimes, no doubt, it is. Such inhibition, however, is a reflection of fragmentation, not an expression of the source of all goodness and being. A fragmented, conventional religion will lead to superficial, conventional creation. Christian faith points beyond superficiality to the heart of things.

God is God of all reality. No aspect of reality is irrelevant to God. None of the things we encounter in living are foreign to God. But God's love is precisely what frees us to respond without external inhibition, to do constructive things, not slavishly but for the sake of the good that is there to be accomplished. We are free to do good things for their own sake, which finally also means for God's sake. The "secular theologians" were right in saying that Christian faith frees us up to deal with the world in its own terms.[13] That does not mean that the world with which we deal is now devoid of theological significance; it does mean that God, in whose grace we find freedom, is the basis of all that is. When we are most attuned to God we are also most alive to the contents of the world; and when we are most alive to the world we are also most receptive to God. This is why Luther could revise the medieval concept of vocation away from the view that religious orders are the higher "calling" to the view that God's will is equally fulfilled by pursuit of any constructive good: "A cobbler, a smith, a farmer, each has the work of his trade, and yet they are all alike consecrated priests and bishops."[14]

Hegel and Marx powerfully projected into the modern world the notion that we actualize ourselves through our work. But the underlying proposition is biblical before it is Hegelian or Marxist. The biblical understanding of the establishment of the meaning of our lives through the work of our hands suggests that life is active and not merely passive. The psalmist, conscious of the fleeting brevity of life, pleaded with God: "Establish thou the work of our hands upon us, yea, the work of our hands establish thou it" (Ps. 90:17b). To that ancient poet of Israel, the "work of our hands" is the remaining tangible deposit to register the significance of our lives after they pass away. For what we accomplish that is constructively good has enduring importance.

Again, this could appear as a neurotic and futile struggle to enhance the meaning of our selfhood if it were detached from trust in God. Some of history's most demonic happenings have been the result of efforts by megalomaniacs to "establish" the work of their hands. Real vocation is founded on love, expressing our creative conception of possibilities. Secure in love, we can seek to do good things with our lives for the sake of the good. We discover then that the promise of our lives is given substance and actuality. Human purpose then merges with the divine intention; for the Christian understanding of God's purpose is that we should be creative selves.

The creative agenda of each of us must be somewhat unique. We all have unique capabilities and personal histories and situational possibilities. Most of us have the luxury and pain of choosing among possibilities, knowing that some of the possibilities can never be realized if we are to attend to the others that we consider more important. Most of us still have ample scope to be creative about a variety of things. In the modern world, even the idea of a lifework is undergoing rapid transformation, and many women and men find themselves shifting from one career pattern to another, while still pursuing a variety of other projects not considered to be a part of a career. Some of the purposes about which we focus our energies represent attempts to deal with material and institutional needs while others are an endeavor to express meaning and beauty and still others are simply playful. To the Christian, all are freely chosen out of the security of God's love.

An important clue to the character of Christian vocation is that it does not have to be competitive. We do not have to gain our significance at the expense of others. The value of our creative accomplishments is not measured by its superiority or inferiority to that of others. Such relative judgments sometimes have to be made for pragmatic reasons when we decide to appoint this teacher rather than that one, to employ this electrician rather than another, to read this book or listen to this music rather than alternative possibilities. But there is a place for all honest creativity, and we do not measure our worth by competitive standards.

## THE TRANSFORMATION OF THE SELF

Since the days of the first Great Awakening in England and Colonial America, a good deal of Protestant Christian rhetoric has been devoted to the importance of conversion. Earlier, the Anabaptist movement emphasized adult religious decision, rather than infant baptism, as the true entry point into the church. The theme of spiritual rebirth and the new life in Christ belongs to the very earliest interpretations of the meaning of Christian faith. The term "born again Christian" carries both positive and negative connotations in our time, depending upon whether one is an evangelical Christian or not. Those who are not are prone to regard that as a symbol for anti-intellectual religious fanaticism. Those who are evangelical Christians tend to regard this as the test of authentic Christian faith—whether one has had the experience of being "born again." Some speak of this as the "personal gospel" of salvation and contrast it with the heretical "social gospel." Those who stress this personal gospel of spiritual rebirth often think of it as a definite event, occurring at one time and place. They may recite for years thereafter exactly how they "found Christ." The stock in trade of Christian evangelists like Billy Graham has been to preach for a "decision," seeking to lead the unconverted listeners to make a commitment to abandon their previous sinful existence and to embrace Christ. The setting in which the preaching occurs is often designed to encourage such decision making, with opportunity for the sinner to come forward, kneel at the altar, and receive counsel from designated assistants. The intrinsic appeal of the gospel can be greatly supplemented by psychological and sociological inducements or pressures, and the whole experience may be repulsive to many people due to the shallow representation of Christian faith and the manipulative character of the presentation.

But the idea of spiritual rebirth is planted deeply enough in Christian tradition to compel a second look. We have throughout this volume emphasized the importance of Christian faith as an overall attitude toward reality. We have understood it to be a profoundly positive trust in the goodness of reality, capable of bringing the whole of one's experience into coherent focus. Nobody is born with that. Early socialization can contribute powerfully to it by providing one with a human sense of being loved. But finally one must conclude somehow for oneself that one will live one's life on the basis of this attitude. It no doubt distorts reality to think of such a "decision" as though it were always or even usually a sudden thing, and it is not at all unusual for even deeply committed Christians to experience periods of doubt and anxiety. But whether the transformation of the self is sudden or gradual, one event or a long process, the place of one's own personal commitment should not be underestimated. Ultimate reality is beyond final comprehension. We live by intimations, by what we take to be revelations of the reality that is beyond our human power finally to grasp in its entirety. Our choice of which kind of revelations to live by is not, therefore, simply a rational one. It is greatly influenced by our socialization and the general character of our life experiences. But we also make personal decisions that shape all of our subsequent experience. The existentialists are right in emphasizing the risks in our decisions, although they may underestimate the extent to which rational resources contribute to intelligence in decision making. The fact that there are risks points to the uncertainties; the uncertainties point to the role played by our own commitment.

Our basic commitment shapes the course of our whole moral life. Elsewhere I have cautioned against the tendency to treat moral commitment and moral judgment as the same thing.[15] People of good will can make (intellectual) mistakes of judgment, while people who are thoroughly self-centered can choose the moral high road for all the wrong reasons. Even saints can disagree about the best way to achieve good results in a complex world. One should never assume, as some evangelicals do, that all we need to do to make this a good world is to convert everybody. The transformation of the self does not by itself guarantee that one will know what should be done. Intelligence and experience, research and consultation also play a role.

But after one has registered that point sufficiently, it remains to be said that the character of our will makes a very great difference. If knowledge of the good is basic to wise moral judgment, then commitment to the good is even more fundamental. To know the good and to will the good are not the same thing; but the first is almost pointless without the second. A person of good will is likely to make honest mistakes, but that person is also more likely to correct them when they become known. The person of good will is not as likely to make those mistakes stemming from egotistic distortions of the real world. Those Christian moralists who emphasize the transformation of character through commitment and moral growth may sometimes neglect the broader issues of social justice facing human society; but they are clearly right in identifying the moral self as the starting point.[16]

It is also well to remember that the Christian faith perspective cannot put the world together for people—to become the "cup" to which we have referred—unless somehow they are gripped at the center of their being by the claim of love upon them. Important religious traditions are not begun by being laid out rationally and subscribed to dispassionately. They blend mind and heart in the profound appeal of a great, typically charismatic, leader. Enduring faith traditions are based upon more than personal commitment, but they cannot endure long if they are incapable of enlisting that commitment.

Victor Hugo tells the story of Jean Valjean who was imprisoned for stealing bread for his family in hard times. Finally released, he was deeply embittered, alienated from fellow humanity, completely unable to recognize and deal with human kindness. Finally befriended by a saintly old country bishop, he is caught off guard and unable to comprehend his good fortune. After stealing one of the bishop's few valuable possessions, some silver, he is caught by the police. They return him to the bishop's simple house. The bishop, recognizing that this could result in a return to prison for life, asks Jean Valjean why he has returned the silver the bishop had *given* him and why he had forgotten to take a silver candleholder as well. The police depart, leaving a thunderstruck Jean Valjean. The bishop's words penetrate the silence and Jean Valjean's crumbling hostilities: "Jean Valjean, my brother, I have bought your soul of you. I withdraw it now from dark thoughts and the spirit of utter ruin, and give it to God." In Hugo's novel, this is the turning point, the point of transformation. Now it is possible for Jean Valjean to be a self, to begin to put his world back together. The remainder of the novel, *Les Miserables,* does not portray human perfection, but it explores how this character could become a real person, spreading that same loving acceptance to others.[17]

Hugo's story is a parable of what Christian faith means about the transformation of the self. Its point of origin must necessarily be a profound sense of being accepted at the root of one's being. The rest is a response of faith and a commitment to the good.

# 7

## CHRISTIAN PERSPECTIVE
## ON SOCIETY

In a word, what the soul is to the body Christians are to the world. . . . It is they
who hold the world together.

*Letter to Diognetus*, c. 130 A.D.

The Christian view of life was not designed to fulfill requirements of any
particular school of psychology. But it is profoundly in harmony with what
has been discovered about psychological integration and the human quest
for meaning and purpose. People cannot accept others until they accept
themselves. They cannot accept themselves until they find acceptance.
The deeper the roots of that acceptance, the more effective it can be and
the more it can evoke loving responses and broader life purposes. Ultimately, psychological integration is religious.

But we do not live solely for ourselves. A religious account of human life
must also bring the whole fabric of social existence into focus. It must
provide a grounding for the meaning and values that inform the common
life. The Indian chief whose "cup" was broken was pointing to the breakdown of a whole cultural frame of reference. That happens when one's
religious orientation no longer provides a basis for understanding the
actual facts of social existence and a source of direction for one's own
action in society. The claim of the *Letter to Diognetus* at the head of this
chapter was not that Christians were in political control of their world (as,
after Constantine, they were to become); it was that their faith com-
prehended the meaning of the world and constituted its hope. But the
twentieth-century world is very different from the world of the second
century. Fractured by murderous conflict, riven with oppression, con-
fused with complexity and change on a scale previously unknown in
human history, humanity does not have any sure foundation on which to

reorder its common life. Can Christian faith contribute such a foundation for this troubled epoch of human history?

## THE BASIS OF SOCIAL EXISTENCE

It was Aristotle who made the point that we are social "by nature," and that is a doctrine for which there is every empirical evidence. From earliest infancy we are dependent upon one another. The very modes of our thought are formed, through language, out of social interaction so that our very thoughts are always, to some extent, derived from others and shared with others. Incurably gregarious, we experience loneliness when we are unable to share our experiences with others. Our concept of ourselves is largely derived from the impressions of us that are conveyed to us by others. Social psychologists have shown conclusively that our values and our perceptions of reality are largely derived from the "reference groups" with which we most closely identify ourselves.[1] We find it very difficult to believe or value things that are not believed or valued by those whose approval and love we prize the most. We are so clearly social "by nature" that it is astonishing to find thinkers, such as Ayn Rand,[2] who have held out a purely individualistic conception of our humanity. Even the relative handful of genuine recluses are usually so disoriented that their individualism tends to support, not to refute, the point that we are social by nature.

Of course, we are also individuals by nature. We could not be social in the human sense if we were not also persons capable of interacting. We share, but we are not identical beings; hence our sharing contributes to growth and creativity. When our individuality is destroyed, our social nature is dissolved along with it; and our individuality also depends upon the fulfillment of our social nature.

These are not particularly Christian insights. But the covenantal tradition shared by Jews and Christians and the specific content of what Christians believe to have been revealed in Christ provide this view of human nature with deep theological foundations. The Hebrew covenant was not simply a relationship between individual Jews and God. It was between the community of Israel and God. In fact, it was the covenant that *formed* that community. Hebrew worship, therefore, was communal worship of Yahweh, the God who brought the community into existence and sustained it through trials and tribulations. Loyalty to Yahweh, obedience to Yahweh, was understood to be communal loyalty—so that when

Jeremiah confessed the sins of the nation he did not excuse himself from the indictment.

In Christian theology our common relationship to the God who loves each of us as a parent is understood to make of us brothers and sisters. The family analogy is almost inescapable. The family, understood in the perspective of Christian theology, is ultimately all of humanity, including past and future as well as present humanity. The immediate family unit, based upon ties of intimate love and biological parenthood, is not to be denigrated. But the moral claim of "family" extends beyond this to the whole of humanity, the vast majority of whose individual members we shall never know personally.

L. Harold DeWolf has made the point that even the concept of love can sometimes convey individualistic overtones if it is defined simply as a transaction between persons doing things for one another—even if this is on an altogether altruistic level. A Christian understanding of love moves the false dichotomy between altruism and egoism to a new plane of mutuality. Thus DeWolf finds the New Testament concept of *koinonia* to be its deepest portrayal of the meaning of Christian love because that term suggests that love is a sharing of life in common.[3] We are so used to thinking of love in individualistic terms that we find it difficult to grasp the sense in which it is an identification of "we" that goes beyond "you and I" or even "I and thou." "We" acknowledges basic kinship, a belonging to one another. Paul Lehmann makes similar points in his characterization of Christian ethics as "ethics of Koinonia,"[4] as does Joseph Haroutunian in his expression of "fellowman."[5] Each of these theologians grasps the central theological point that we are, in God, one people.

The higher forms of humanism, including classical Marxism, make a similar point about our common humanity. But they lack the transcendent basis—that this fellow human being has ontological status as a person of eternal value, one whose life is also rooted in God. They also lack the recognition that all are dependent alike upon the grace that is freely given despite our undeserving. Marxism therefore is able to slip too easily into characterizations of class enemies that imply that there are some people who are outside the bounds of the moral community, although such a conclusion is by no means required in Marxist theory. Any view of community that is not rooted in something beyond the human plane is vulnerable to divisiveness and oppression, for the value one places upon others and even upon oneself cannot be as high.

This is perhaps the place to observe that the theological basis of social existence is also a basis of human equality. Inequalities place a severe burden upon genuine mutuality. When separated by great barriers of status, people may interact in the pursuit of common objectives, but they find it much more difficult to identify with one another as "we." But the Christian valuation of every person transcends the usual bounds of human status and pretension. Our equality is rooted in the fact that we are valued boundlessly by God. Ordinary life requires distinctions based upon differences of function. But in what matters most—our ultimate value—we are all loved unconditionally, and therefore equally, by God. All social pretensions and status competition are accordingly sharply relativized. Human pretensions are also relativized by the recognition that all are sinful, if not equally at least fundamentally. We are equal in our need for God's grace and in our receiving it.

The great visions of social idealism, such as Martin Luther King, Jr.'s idea of the "beloved community,"[6] project the Christian basis of society into a conception of what such a society could be if freed from the distortions of sin and oppression. Whatever one might say about sin and oppression—and we must attend to that shortly—the vision of a loving, caring, and just society reflects the aspiration of the most sensitive ethical spirits of every age. Such a vision is so deeply grounded in Christian faith that one is not surprised when those who do *not* hold that view of the good society are seen to dismiss Christian faith as irrelevant. And while that vision is in tension with much of the lived experience of human civilization, it is profoundly in harmony with what is required to sustain social experience. A society in which people really do relate to one another as sisters and brothers will have problems and tensions, but it will *work*. For its problems can be dealt with as problems "in the family." And within the "family" everybody's humanity is respected and enhanced. Those whose real faith is in their own status, and who enhance that status by cultivating superiority over others, may well feel that Christian faith is not for them. I suspect, though, that this does not represent the brokenness of Christian faith as much as the brokenness of those who have rejected Christian faith.

## THE REALITY OF OPPRESSION

It is nevertheless true that most known societies are very oppressive of some people. Society can be profoundly destructive of our humanity, just as it can be supportive. It is destructive when it enslaves people in mind and body and undermines their sense of the wholeness of life.

The usual account of oppression sees two classes of people: the oppressed and the oppressors. The oppressed are the losers, the oppressors are the winners. But it is a deeper insight that whenever inhumanity occurs, *everybody* loses, oppressors and oppressed alike. Those who are oppressed suffer physically and spiritually: physically because they are denied important material needs or because they are tortured or killed, spiritually because they are led to view themselves as inferior. But the oppressors, meanwhile, also suffer—though unwittingly. By degrading others, they deprive themselves of meaningful affirmation from those whom they despise[7] and reduce the meaning of their own humanity to the pathetic symbols of their supposedly superior status. When we deny our essential kinship with others, we undermine our own sense of worth along with theirs. The deeper versions of Marxism understand this point: the destruction of class oppression will bring liberation to the oppressor as well as the oppressed, for alienation dehumanizes both. The non-Marxist Martin Luther King, Jr. makes that same point clearly in the context of the struggle to overcome racist oppression: "In the final analysis the white man cannot ignore the Negro's problem, because he is a part of the Negro and the Negro is a part of him. The Negro's agony diminishes the white man, and the Negro's salvation enlarges the white man."[8] King understood the Christian roots of this insight; Marx did not. King could relate this to the sense in which we belong to one another because we belong to God; Marx could not. Yet both grasp the fact that when it comes to oppression, there are no "winners," there are only losers.

We may as well admit that Christians have been guilty of every imaginable sin against their fellows, including war and slavery and racism and economic exploitation. But Christian faith itself is profoundly supportive of social integration. As we have said, its social conception is that humanity is the family of God. It envisions a society based upon the mutual love of all.

But Christian tradition also helps one comprehend the realities of sin and oppression. The much-misunderstood doctrine of original sin is presented mythologically through the story of Adam and Eve in the Garden of Eden in the Book of Genesis and has sometimes been treated as a sexually transmitted disposition toward sin, as though sex were itself somehow at fault.[9] The mythical story is not to be taken literally, and the attribution of sin to sex misses the point that it is sin that distorts sexuality—not the reverse. Original sin is also misunderstood if it is taken to mean that people are guilty for evils they did not cause or for misdeeds they could not have avoided. The real question is whether there may be something in human nature that predisposes us to sin, and if so, what that might be.

Reinhold Niebuhr's account of this is especially persuasive.[10] In barest outline, he notes that human beings are uniquely able to transcend their immediate experience and to have a universal perspective, a world view. But having this universal perspective, they also are able to comprehend their own finitude, the fragility of their lives, the fact that they do not finally control their own destiny. Until they find it possible to trust the source of their being they are virtually forced to do everything they can to shore up their lives, to create some kind of universality or permanence for themselves. Having discovered a universe, they are driven to place themselves at its center if they cannot trust what is at its center to be good for them. The essential root of sin, then, is pride (hubris). It is self-centeredness, worship of the self. Being self-centered, we seek to dominate others or, failing that, to abandon meaning for pleasure or lethargy. When we oppress others we are acting out our frustrated sense of meaninglessness.

> Man is insecure and involved in natural contingency; he seeks to overcome his insecurity by a will-to-power which overreaches the limits of human creatureliness. Man is ignorant and involved in the limitations of a finite mind; but he pretends that he is not limited. He assumes that he can gradually transcend finite limitations until his mind becomes identical with universal mind. All of his intellectual and cultural pursuits, therefore, become infected with the sin of pride. Man's pride and will-to-power disturb the harmony of creation. . . . The moral and social dimension of sin is injustice. The ego which falsely makes itself the centre of existence in its pride and will-to-power inevitably subordinates other life to its will and thus does injustice to other life.[11]

In religious terms, this is rebellion against God, but it is born out of a profound anxiety, an inability to trust ultimate reality. The answer to the dilemma is to find a basis for trust. If one can trust the goodness of the source of one's being (that is, if one can entrust one's own well-being to the source of all being), then one need no longer be driven by self-centeredness. One is released from self-centeredness to respond to reality on its own terms. One can find wholeness in the life of community without being threatened by it.

Such a Christian understanding of original sin is relevant to the reality of oppression in two ways: In the first place, it helps save us from illusions about the perfectibility of human nature. Those who are most troubled by social evil may be most susceptible to such illusions. In their search for easy solutions they open themselves up to disillusionment, despair, and finally cynicism. If the doctrine of original sin is a true statement about human nature, one would not expect to abolish it by purely institutional means nor to circumvent it by placing sinless people in charge of human affairs. No institutional solution can, by itself, cure the evil of original sin, although well-devised institutions can mitigate its effects and the wrong kind of institutions can exacerbate them. So far as placing sinless people in charge is concerned, that will prove quite impossible since there are no such people. Christian faith helps bring the reality of oppression into focus by requiring of us a forthright realism about sin.

But the Christian understanding of original sin also helps by pointing to the resources of faith that help move people beyond the need to be self-centered. When those resources are portrayed in too individualistic a way—as conservative Christianity has sometimes done—the effect has sometimes been the ironic one of deepening the self-centeredness. But faith in God's grace has both personal and social dimensions. Personally it means a letting go of self in order to receive the love of God. Socially it means a shared confidence in the centrality of God's loving acceptance. As long as people possess some degree of personal freedom and a universal world view we can expect sin to manifest its reality. But as long as faith and love can be shared we can expect sin to be overcome. So the perspective Christians bring to bear upon social evil is, on the one hand, the need to be realistic in checking its power in institutions, but, on the other hand, a recognition that the power of faith and love can bring release from its grasp.

The most difficult dilemmas in Christian ethics have to do with how to relate the negative restraint of the effects of sin to the positive drawing forth of the best in human faithfulness and love. A Christian strategy toward society that totally neglects either side of this dilemma is doomed to failure and disillusionment.

In assessing other religious or philosophical options, one of the key questions is whether they recognize this kind of dilemma and, if so, how they deal with it.

## LIBERATION AND SOCIAL JUSTICE

It is not surprising, in light of the vast scale of human oppression in the contemporary world, that many Christians have taken up the theme of liberation as the cardinal foundation for interpreting the faith. The God we worship can be portrayed as the God of the exodus, the One who released the captives from Egypt and made of them a new nation. This is the God who "has put down the mighty from their thrones, and exalted those of low degree" (Luke 1:52). As expressed by such theologians as Gustavo Gutierrez and José Míguez Bonino, the theme of liberation also owes much to Marxist analysis.[12] But then, at that point Marxist analysis may really owe more to Hebrew-Christian roots. For human oppression and liberation are major themes in biblical religion. The theme has been picked up powerfully by black theology and feminist theology, especially in North America where it has pointed to two forms of oppression. Liberation theology has grasped a very important part of the truth, as seen through Christian eyes. Human oppression is dehumanizing and utterly contrary to God's loving purposes. It is so central a reality that one can go further, as liberation theology also tends to do, in identifying complacency about oppression as a distorted Christian consciousness. Classical Marxism treats Christianity (and all other religion) as ideology or false consciousness. It considers religion to be a form of moral support for existing forms of oppression, expressing the class interests of the oppressor. But liberation theology can justly argue that Christianity is such false consciousness only when it neglects the gospel of liberation or when it addresses that gospel only in sentimental, pietistic, and individualistic ways.

But theology is also more than liberation. It is an affirmation of ultimate faith in the root of our being and, as such, it cannot be restricted to the sociological plane. Even on the sociological plane it can distort reality for us to identify Christian faith with only the overcoming of existing oppression, for that neglects the root of oppression and the possibilities of new forms of oppression ten times worse than those they replace. History is replete with instances of oppressed people gaining freedom only to institute a new order of oppression. Christian faith offers resources for offsetting that possibility. For instance, those who seek liberation not only for their own sake but for the sake of reconciliation with the oppressor and the deeper humanization of all give evidence of being grounded in faith and love. Liberation, seen as freedom *from* oppression, must be joined with a positive faith in ultimate good and by a positive theory of social relationship. These are a part of the essence of Christian faith.

A biblical understanding of social justice unites the quest for liberation with the deeper grounding of faith and love. The term justice has, of course, been used in many different ways. These uses include Plato's conception of harmony and social classes, Aristotle's theological view of justice as the fulfillment of the ends of human nature, the utilitarian formulation of the greatest good for the largest number of people, the various contract theories, the equation of justice with power in Machiavelli, and contemporary theories like the "justice of fairness" of John Rawls. Most theories of justice contribute something to our understanding of what it is that gives moral force to our claims upon one another through society. But most views of justice lack grounding in a religious conception of reality and lead to the question whether we really do need such a grounding.

The biblical tradition itself displays more than one theory of justice, but the profoundest and in some ways most characteristic one is a religious communitarianism grounded in God's covenant with humankind. The covenant is both radically personal and radically social, and in light of the covenant it is not possible to pit the personal against the social. God's creative and redemptive love affirms each person in the most intimate terms. That same love establishes the unity of humankind and, indeed, of all creation. Human love at its deepest levels is our recognition of that fellow humanity we have with one another. In light of that love, all theories of justice based purely upon deserving or accomplishment must yield to the recognition that we are first of all beneficiaries of God's gifts of creation and grace and that we do not "save ourselves" through "works righteousness." Theories of justice based purely upon contract must yield to the consciousness of a social self, a belonging to one another in the being we have from God that is deeper than the moral reality of transaction and promise keeping. Theories of justice based upon happiness must yield to a reality greater than the state of our feelings and consciousness, important as these are. Theories of justice based upon nature must yield to a conception of personal and social freedom in being that transcends even though it is rooted in nature. And theories of justice based purely upon the interests of the collectivity alone must yield to the more inclusive claims of the personal and the social and to a divine meaning that challenges the notion that it is the collectivity itself that confers meaning.

Even thus expanded beyond the bounds of these partial truths, a Christian conception of justice is not simply the presentation of Christian theology in general. How is it that a Christian conception illuminates the question of what gives moral force to our claims upon one another through society? How can there be conflicting claims in the commonwealth of love such that the issues of justice even have to be raised? Once raised, how can such issues be resolved in meaningful detail?

Two realities are crucial to a Christian understanding of how the community of love needs a theory of justice. First is the reality of sin and oppression, which we have already touched upon. In part, justice is protection against the evil effects of sin and oppression in human community. The other reality is the fact of our being a part of a created, very physical world, in and through which the existence of loving community must be expressed. The fact of this physical world means that material relationships affect the character of loving community. We have physical needs and most of our moral purposes require physical facilities for their expression. Those needs can be frustrated, fulfilled, or surfeited. Moral purposes can be aided or impeded or defeated altogether by the circumstances of our life in this physical world.

The Old Testament conception of justice—*mishpat*—is rich in meaning and includes the notion of justice as divine command. But one level of meaning is especially important to social justice: it is the understanding of justice as the recognition and preservation of one's "portion in Israel"— that is, one's security in the conditions required if one is to exist in the commonwealth of Israel. It represents protection of the institutional and economic rights of vulnerable people, such as widows and orphans and nonproperty-holding foreigners, along with those better able to protect their own interests. So justice (from that angle of vision) can be viewed as whatever is required to protect the right of people to function humanly in the life of the community. The demands of justice will change from one era to another—what was required in ancient Israel or in the Roman Empire or in the medieval world was very different from what may be required in our own time. Christians may have no final word on exactly what justice *does* require in any particular age. But the general perspective can help illuminate the debates currently raging worldwide over social justice. To repeat that general perspective, it is that justice is establishing the material and institutional relationships that best guarantee to every person the right to participate fully in the life of a community of mutual love.

This definition of social justice is often at odds with what may be a more prevailing view, which we can term the "compensatory" conception of justice. By compensatory, I mean the view that justice means giving people what they deserve, as precisely as possible. That view, too, has important biblical roots, even though it does not reflect the central biblical message as profoundly.

The compensatory view can appear either positively or negatively. Negatively, it calls for precision in retribution so that the punishment exactly fits the crime. The biblical roots of that are evident when we recall that "an eye for an eye" is a biblical expression. Positively, a compensatory view calls for rewards exactly commensurate to the contributions people make to life and community. Biblically it is suggested wherever the morally upright are held to be rewarded with prosperity—as in a number of the Psalms and, with a question mark, in the Book of Job. The compensatory view of justice is almost a canon of faith in modern capitalistic societies, rooted as they are in the Lockean view that property is what people have earned or made. But my impression is that most socialist countries are also pretty moralistic about meting out to people what the Party thinks they deserve. The power of the compensatory view is revealed in the sense of outrage most of us feel when somebody gets away with wronging an innocent person or when a law-abiding citizen is shown to have been wrongfully punished for a crime committed by somebody else. That sense of outrage tells us that the compensatory view of justice is partly right.

But the compensatory view does not bring moral reality sufficiently into focus when we rely primarily upon it. For one thing, it is extraordinarily difficult, as a practical matter, to weigh "deserving" accurately. In the great race of life people begin so unevenly and receive assistance or face impediments that are virtually incalculable. But even if such calculations could be worked out with computerlike precision, the compensatory view subtly replaces mutual love with competition and community with individualism. Viewed in the deeper Christian perspective, it replaces joyful creativity grounded in grace with works-righteousness. To be sure, the problem is more complex than this. A society in which selfishness is rewarded and moral heroism punished is hardly conducive to the fuller realization of community of which I speak. The compensatory view has a role to play. But the organizing theme of social justice is still the establishment of conditions making it possible for all people to participate. Christian faith helps bring that reality into focus at every level of community life.

Illustrations can be drawn from every aspect of social existence. I shall refer here to four deeply troubled areas of contemporary social life where the ability of a Christian view of justice to bring things into focus is on trial.

## THE STRUGGLE AGAINST RACISM AND SEXISM

Two of the great continuing struggles in contemporary society have to do with racism and sexism. The former is based upon the alleged inferiority of certain races, the latter upon the subservience of women. Western culture, in particular, has been deeply flawed at both points. Black people and other racial groups have been treated as inferiors and the road to equality and genuine social integration has been long and hard. Women too, from time immemorial and in most cultures, have had inferior social status affecting both their actual opportunities and their own self-image. In the case of women, this inferior status has been reinforced deeply by theological language projecting male characteristics upon the source of all being, a matter to which the churches are just now beginning to attend. Until quite recently, churches also reinforced these social barriers and distinctions by maintaining segregation and by denying equal access to the ordained ministry.

The effect of this upon the victims has been severe. Bearing in mind the fact that our concept of selfhood is largely mediated to us by the response we receive from others, is it any wonder that racially oppressed peoples have often suffered from a profound sense of inferiority? And that women have had this ingrained in them for so long that some find it difficult even to conceive of real equality with men? When we are treated as inferior, we tend to believe that we *are* inferior. But the effect of this difference of status is to drive a wedge through the heart of society, making it difficult for all persons to be fully human.

Notwithstanding the fact that churches have often reinforced these divisions through institutional structures and theological concepts, the Christian faith itself sharply relativizes the biological grounds of human social fragmentation. In Christ there is neither black nor white, red nor yellow—just as there is neither male nor female. Young and old alike belong, as do the strong and weak, the brilliant and the retarded. All distinctions pale in significance before the leveling relationship we all have in covenant with God. Even those Christians who appear most devoted to racial divisions find it difficult to justify their attitudes on theological grounds. While doing research on racism and the churches some years ago, I was astonished to discover that even the Dutch Reformed Churches of South Africa—the very bastion of racist apartheid—had to affirm through its Commission on Race Relations that the unity of the church must take precedence over racial exclusion if put to the test ("We therefore accept the existence of separate churches according to each indigenous group, but as a matter of principle no person will be excluded from corporate worship solely on the grounds of race or colour"[13]). Most other churches have made the point against racism much more emphatically, and in recent years even churches like the South African Dutch Reformed have felt the theological pressure to move further in this direction.

Christians have not been the only voices raised against racism, of course, nor have Christian values been the only ones invoked against it. Values having ultimate roots in the Enlightenment and ancient Stoicism are embedded in the great founding documents of Western democracy, and

these provided splendid ammunition to the American civil rights movement. But that movement was led, for the most part, by articulate Christians such as Martin Luther King, Jr., Ralph Abernathy, Andrew Young,
and Jesse Jackson (all Christian ministers), and they saw the question
finally in a theological light. This is one reason why the method of non-
violent resistance, typically employed by the movement, linked the struggle for liberation with the quest for reconciliation.[14] Racial justice was
understood to be the realization of the beloved community, not simply as
the assertion of long-stifled selfhood nor the defeat of the oppressor.
Neither the racists nor the advocates of a new black identity quite understood how *strong*—socially, psychologically, politically—the attempt to
develop a thoroughly Christian answer to racial discrimination would
prove to be.[15] It could not have had this strength had it not been able to
assert the common humanity of us all in terms that were irrefutable.

The feminist movement has not been as explicitly Christian, although
some of its most articulate leaders have been Christian theologians and
some of its most interesting battle grounds have been within the church
(such as the struggle over the ordination of women and the controversy
over sexist language in the Bible, church liturgy, and hymnody).[16] When
once the question of oppression is raised, there can be but one theological
answer: Women have exactly the same status and rights before God as
men. Women as well as men have all of the attributes of selfhood and, as a
matter of fact, much the same range of talents and abilities. The important
truths are brought directly into focus by the Christian faith. Nevertheless,
the problem of sexism is especially troublesome because the unequal
status of women has been so intimately woven into the fabric of religious
culture and tradition that it is difficult to extricate it from values that are
central to the identity of Christians. A good example is the concept of the
"Fatherhood" of God, a term deeply embedded in the sayings of Jesus and
in much subsequent Christian rhetoric. The term clearly sought to convey
in the deepest possible way the intimate personal relationship of God to all
"his" children. Christians can scarcely abandon that sense of personal
intimacy with God. But "Father" is biologically male imagery, and God is
not a biological entity. Since social inferiority of women is reinforced by
projecting male characteristics upon the center and source of all being, we
cannot treat this as benign symbolism. The fundamental reality is personal intimacy, but without gender. Changes of language to accommodate
this important point will bring Christian faith more clearly into focus by
removing a distortion.[17]

Christian faith, in itself, does not provide answers to all of the complex problems of social role and family structure, but it sets terms on the basis of which these problems can be brought into focus. These terms include the fundamental equality of persons and the mutual kinship we all have in the family of God. They also include the life-fulfilling obligation to be resolutely dependable sources of love in relationship, manifesting in human society something of the dependable love and grace we have in God. Everybody needs such dependable love, but everybody also needs to be a source of such love in order to be fully human. One of the reasons sexism is such an exquisitely difficult problem is that gender roles are also tied up in those familial ties of nurturing love and dependability in relationship upon which every society depends. Oppression in such an intimate context is sometimes very subtle; it is both difficult to identify accurately and difficult to deal with without damaging other important values. But there are also resources peculiar to familial intimacy for addressing these difficulties. A Christian commitment to basic equality and dependability in love is deeply consonant with the enduring values of family life, even though that commitment may not spare us considerable anguish as society shifts from easy assumptions of male dominance to real equality and mutuality.

## THE STRUGGLE FOR POLITICAL JUSTICE

Does Christian faith also bring political justice into focus?

In answering this, it is helpful to establish two very important points about politics: First is the fact that politics has to do with society *acting as a whole*. Robert M. MacIver refers to this in his comment that political power "alone is the organ of the whole community."[18] This is not just an abstract point. It means that the state is in a position to bring all the resources of a society to bear upon particular objectives, whether or not everybody agrees with them. We may even be opposed to something the state proposes to do, but our energies and resources will still be used to further those objectives. During the Vietnam War, singer Joan Baez was strongly opposed to the American involvement and devoted many of her popular concerts to singing antiwar songs. Notwithstanding her strong opposition to the war and even her refusal to pay income taxes to help finance it, the U.S. government had no difficulty in tapping her bank account for those tax revenues—which, owing to her popularity, were quite considerable. Thus, by singing antiwar songs she was engaged in an economic activity helping to finance that very war! It is very difficult to avoid contributing to the pursuit of whatever the state is doing at any time. The moral consequence of this reality is that the state truly represents all of us; we are doing what it is doing, like it or not.

The other point about politics is that it typically represents the power of *influence*. Our will to support particular parties or leaders and our will to obey the laws of the realm reflect a variety of influences. But it is an illusion to think of all political power as sheer coercion. Even coercion is typically best understood as a (negative) form of influence: You do this, or else. . . . Franz Neumann helpfully contrasts this form of power with power over nature. Power over nature can be expressed in purely physical terms. But political power involves influencing decisions that remain partly a matter of free choice.[19] If political power comes down to influence, then it is noteworthy that virtually anything that can influence people can also have political significance. This means that almost anything can be politicized, depending upon what actually does influence behavior in a given cultural setting.

Both these points mean that the political order is bound to be related intimately to the religious life of a society. In the first place, it is not possible to carve out a separate religious sphere unaffected by the state, because the bearers of religion—the people—are also necessarily the political actors, even when they imagine themselves to be aloof from all political contamination. But in the second place, the values to which appeal is made in influencing people to support particular forms of political leadership are often closely related to deeper religious values. People respond to many influences, and some of their values may appear remote from the religion they profess. Indeed, that religion may be only a fragment of their disintegrated existence. But when life is wholly or largely integrated, lesser values presuppose a center of value. The importance of religion as a central, sometimes definitive point of influence upon the human will means that it is often in the interest of politicians to use religion in an effort to manipulate the people. Machiavelli carefully advised the prince always to *appear* to be very religious lest he lose their support. Rousseau rejected French Catholicism, even advocating that it be banned. But he still believed it essential that a civil religion be constructed in its stead to provide a focal point of support for a new regime. The Caesars founded religious cults with themselves as deities, not because they took this literally—though one or two may have—but because they found it politically expedient to have such a common point of cohesion in governing so vast an empire. Virtually every American president and large numbers of lesser officials have found it useful to invoke the deity with sufficient frequency to establish their rapport with the values they perceive to be fundamental to the people they hope to lead. It is the same everywhere. Even Stalin, his back to the wall after the German invasion of 1941, made his peace with the Russian Orthodox Church in order to enlarge his influence over the millions of faithful Orthodox Christians in that officially atheistic country.

In face of these realities about politics, does Christian faith help bring needed perspective or is it only a value system that should be tolerated or manipulated (to the extent of its actual influence upon people), but not taken seriously?

A new form of Christian triumphalism seeks to use the state to ram what are alleged to be Christian values and beliefs down everybody's throats through the power of the state. The so-called Moral Majority in the United States, to which passing reference was made in the second chapter, unblushingly identified a shopping list of positions on a variety of issues as the only Christian view and targeted opposing politicians for defeat. The organization's agenda included opposition to all abortion, the Equal Rights Amendment, rights for homosexuals, sex education, drugs, pornography, ratification of an arms limitation treaty, and the Department of Education in the U.S. government. The group favored free enterprise and voluntary prayer in the public schools; it opposed budget deficits and lower defense expenditures. It favored the defense of Israel. Most people could find some things to support and other things to oppose on such a list. But this organization insisted that the entire list be the agenda of all moral Christians.

In the main, I believe such a phenomenon undermines the credibility of Christian faith among people who know that such organizations have staked out positions on several issues that are opposed to real justice and real moral sensibilities. Opposition to the Equal Rights Amendment lent support to the notion that women really are second-class human beings, whether or not that was the intention. Opposition to all abortion seemed insensitive to the human circumstances out of which many pregnancies are terminated and foreshadowed a heavy-handed state imposing its power in the most intimate areas of human decision making. The attitude on defense issues displayed no sensitivity to the awesome dangers of nuclear holocaust. Opposition to the Department of Education was probably fatuous. The whole thing seemed based more upon defensive reaction than upon positive construction in politics. But the larger point is that people of deep moral sensitivity who disagree with such a "Christian" political agenda may feel forced to think of their own moral experience in non-Christian terms.

Such a political movement forces us to refine our views of how Christian faith does relate to the public order and to social justice issues. When Christianity is construed as a narrow straitjacket to be imposed upon the political process, then one way or another society will burst those bonds and Christian faith will itself be in disrepute. When, on the other hand, Christians in the political process work actively for social justice, liberation of oppressed peoples, protection of the helpless members of the community, opportunity for the young, and world peace, they are being true to the implications of the faith, and they will be respected even by those who disagree concerning particular issues. They will have supported the political integration of the community and helped to prevent its disintegration.

Even so, there are Christian thinkers who have believed that the state is necessarily too evil for the Christian faith to find expression through its normal functioning. A substantial pacifist tradition is among the strands of Christian witness throughout the history of the church, and there is a less prominent, but still noteworthy, tradition of political anarchism. The first recognizes some morally legitimate functions for the state, but not generally its coercive role. The second in principle regards the state as such to be evil. Exemplifying both traditions was Leo Tolstoy, who believed that human sinfulness and injustice are the direct result of repressive political institutions. If we could abolish police, armies, jails, and so on, the innate goodness of human nature could be expected to flower as God intended. Taking Jesus' words "Do not resist one who is evil" (Matt. 5:39) quite literally, Tolstoy believed nonresistance to constitute the heart of true religion.[20] While this would not necessarily rule out purely administrative or service functions of the state, it emphatically denies the necessity or legitimacy of any coercion by political authority. Thus, for instance, forcible levying of taxes would be wrong; but then that would also appear to be unnecessary if human goodness can be relied upon as Tolstoy believed.

More recent Christian thinkers have questioned the legitimacy of state force while nevertheless being less sanguine about human goodness. Jacques Ellul and John Howard Yoder, for instance, both raise serious questions about the state while still holding few illusions about human nature.[21] Both express skepticism that good things can ever come from violence. Yoder strongly affirms the Christian struggle for social justice, while insisting that it can be conducted without breaking faith with Jesus' way of love and nonviolence. Through the resurrection, he writes, God has said yes to Jesus' way. Our responsibility is to follow that way, refusing to cooperate with evil, and recognizing that we do not take responsibility for the management of the course of history. God will use our efforts, but God alone can ultimately bring in the kingdom of love and righteousness. Yoder insists that this is relevant to history (noting that Jesus would not have been crucified had he not been relevant).

It may be that the Christian anarchist and pacifist traditions play directly into the hands of those who consider Christianity to be too "soft" to bring the hard problems of actual political process into focus. A whole tradition of political realism, from Machiavelli to the present, smiles indulgently at Christianity but does not find it helpful in actual political thought and action. We may need to keep the "ideals" of loving decency alive, and we may need the "inspiration" of worship and religious ceremony to impress upon us the solemnity and frailty of life. But the realist tradition is pleased to excuse the chaplain when it is time to get down to the serious work of politics. How could it be otherwise, if the anarchist or pacifist traditions correctly state the Christian position? If political leaders become Christian in that sense they either have to abandon their political post to others or at least refrain thenceforth from all coercive uses of the state's power. No longer could they levy taxes (except, perhaps, as suggested guidelines for voluntary contributions), nor could they employ police to restrain evildoers. They could not act through the power of the state to redistribute economic resources nor to protect the weak or powerless members of society from those who are all too willing to take advantage of the vulnerable. They might believe that God would somehow intervene to preserve justice, but they would have to foreclose the possibility of God acting through their own political leadership in the state.

Realism can itself dissolve into cynicism, of course. The Machiavellian tradition, whatever its contributions (and there are some), tends to make power an end in itself. But is *that* finally relevant to real politics? What are we to *do* with that power? Will any and all methods prescribed by the Machiavellians prove relevant to the ends to be sought for human society? That depends upon what those ends are! Some accounts of human nature, for instance, that of Thomas Hobbes, depict human life as thoroughly self-centered. Political life is then only the scramble of conflicting wills to power in which the weak are constantly exposed to the oppression of the strong and in which the strong are themselves in constant peril lest they encounter others still stronger. In the "war of every man against every man" (Hobbes), life is "solitary, poor, nasty, brutish, and short." In such a world, the best one can hope for is alliances of common self-interest, reposing sufficient power in a common authority to hold predators in check—even though the authority itself is likely to be predatory.

The views underlying this gloomy portrait of political life are, of course, more than political. They confront us with an overall conception of reality that is profoundly pessimistic, so pessimistic that it does not help us at all to understand the political significance of human feelings of kinship, compassion for the helpless, love of art and beauty, yearnings for justice. And it could not bring realism to bear upon political objectives derived from such human feelings and attitudes. The weakness of *Realpolitik* for its own sake was ruthlessly demonstrated by Socrates in the dialogue with Thrasymachos in Plato's *Republic*. To be relevant to actual politics, power must finally have constructive ends in view. These ends may, from a Christian standpoint, appear selfish; but they must have positive content of some kind. But then, do Christians need to apologize for the alleged unrealism of their recommendation that social justice for all should be the overarching objective of every political order? Is such an objective irrelevant to the political order taken as a whole?

Reinhold Niebuhr makes the point that Christian faith is profoundly relevant to politics in general and to democracy in particular, by virtue of its recognition of the contrasting tendencies of sin and goodness in human nature: "Man's capacity for justice makes democracy possible; but man's inclination to injustice makes democracy necessary."[22] Christian insight into the reality of sin is not naive, but it is balanced by recognition of the human capacity for good. Niebuhr insists, correctly, that both are relevant to politics. Any approach to politics that neglects the need for institutions preserving order and justice will prove irrelevant to the hard realities; but so will any approach that is pessimistic or unconcerned about justice. Niebuhr's affirmation of democracy recognizes both its creative possibilities and its protective role in empowering all members of society, and his many writings on political questions illustrate how well this Christian understanding of human nature brings political reality into focus. I have argued elsewhere[23] that this presentation of the political implications of Christian faith would be even more relevant if it included a built-in bias against coercion and other negative methods in political life—thus recognizing that force may sometimes be necessary for the sake of preserving justice, but that negative actions should be required to bear the burden of proof. Christians can participate fully in political life, but they do so not only with a commitment to social justice but also with a bias toward methods of achieving social justice that are also wholly constructive.[24]

Christian faith, while it does not spare us the dilemmas and tensions of political life, does bring into focus what is at stake in politics. It helps bring the realities of politics into harmonious relationship with the positive vision of social justice.

## THE QUEST FOR ECONOMIC JUSTICE

We are also vexed by questions in the economic sphere. Christian faith does not provide detailed answers to all the economic problems in any simple sense. But the basic Christian perspective would surely help us integrate the fractured world economic picture at certain basic points.

The most important of these is helping us clarify the real purpose of economic life. That is not to increase the gross national product of any or all nations. It is not to have a balanced national budget. It is not to make a profit for any business or corporation. It is not to avoid recession or inflation. Such objectives may be important in a given situation, but they are secondary. The real purposes are the deeper ones of providing the material basis for genuine community, undergirding the material well-being of all of the members of the community, and contributing to the self-respect and opportunity of all. The definition of such objectives requires that much more be said. But even this much should tell us that we need to be much more intentional about our economic policies as they relate to economic justice.

Economic justice, like all forms of justice, cannot simply be compensatory, although most societies (even socialist ones) are tempted to treat economic well-being too simply as a reward for productive achievements. Economic justice must be communitarian first, recognizing that the good community requires that some attention be paid to incentives and disincentives. But first things must always come first; and economics must first be designed to serve the more fundamental values. So economics affects more than material things, and economic decision making cannot be considered to be a self-sufficient science.[25] Nor can we trust entirely in market forces (in the manner of trust in Adam Smith's "invisible hand") to fulfill the public good; for sometimes it is pure illusion to expect an unregulated market to yield the highest public good.

This leads to the second point, that Christian faith helps bring focus to economic life by diminishing the effects of human egoism and greed. Self-interest is a powerful engine and it may, to some extent, be needed to power economic life. Writers like Michael Novak and Robert Benne[26] make much of the fact that all objectives for economic life—be they ever so noble—depend upon there being sufficient material wealth to attain them. To some extent, probably exaggerated by these writers and others, inventiveness and productivity are dependent upon self-interested motivations that must be tapped for that purpose. But greed, left unrestrained, can tear economic life apart. For example, inflation is largely rooted in the escalation of demands for economic gain by competing groups.[27] And the cure of inflation, all technical rhetoric aside, is often a matter of persuading individuals and groups to lower their expectations.

The third point is that Christian faith helps clarify true material values and discourage the production of wasteful and harmful commodities. There are some things we simply do not need: electric can openers and large gas-guzzling automobiles and colored contact lenses and electric pencil sharpeners. Some things are not only unnecessary but truly harmful, such as cigarettes and Saturday night special revolvers. Investors make no contribution to an economy when they put their resources into precious metals, jewelry, and other such commodities for speculative reasons. Speculation, in fact, tends to exacerbate economic crisis.

Fourth, Christian faith helps clarify the relationship between economic issues and the conservationist agenda. Patterns of economic development that pollute the environment, decimate other living species, and undermine the long-run future of life on the planet may be seen for what they really are in the light of Christian faith. This is God's world, a beautiful gift in perpetuity, for which we are appointed as stewards for our brief day. Selfish, short-run exploitation of this gift is disintegrative; Christian stewardship is constructive. The response of Christian faith to the impertinent question posed by Robert L. Heilbroner, "What Has Posterity Ever Done for Me?"[28] is to say unequivocally that we are linked to posterity as a part of the family of God. All life everywhere, past, present, and future, is part of that great commonwealth. The incalculable gifts of life and love become truly humanizing when we respond with loving generosity.

Many questions remain unanswered. Thoroughgoing capitalists and Marxists alike are impatient with the notion that economic life should be responsive to moral values. Both are convinced, though in different ways, that economic life is governed by science and not moral values.[29] The one regards the market mechanism, left alone, as the more or less automatic source of societal good. The other regards the scientifically predictable breakdown of capitalism, resulting from its internal contradictions, as the basis of a new socialist future in which humanity will be relieved of social evil. Both overlook the capacity of human beings to transcend economic interest in their fundamental behavior. To focus our attention upon economic life through religious lens is therefore to see its relationship to human values more clearly. When that religious lens is Christian, it comprehends both the nature and extent of human selfishness and the wellsprings of real human creativity and devotion to social good.

## CHRISTIAN FAITH AND
## INTERNATIONAL CRISIS

The late-twentieth-century world is a very dangerous place. Everywhere there are deep fissures in the fabric of human culture, politics, economic life, and religion. There are, in several regions and within many countries, murderous, intractable conflicts. Taken together, these form the tinder that could ignite the vast reservoirs of nuclear destructiveness which have been stockpiled by nations, ironically in search of greater security. The present world crisis is misread as a breakdown of rationalism, although that is part of it. It is also misread as a simple question of struggle for liberation or of economics or of political creativity. The crisis is all these things, to be sure; but at its heart it is the want of a generating center of faith powerful enough to effect the reconciliation of our times and to establish common purpose and identity enough to make humanity a community.

Robert Heilbroner made this point, although pessimistically, in his *An Inquiry into the Human Prospect.* Noting the great accumulation of seemingly unsolvable problems pressing down upon the late-twentieth-century world, he concluded that we must expect great increases in oppressive authoritarian regimes, with consequent losses in civilizing values, as societies attempt to keep pace with the objective problems. Our survival itself seems to be at stake as we blunder toward an Armageddon. Acknowledging that "we know very little about how to convince men by recourse to reason," Heilbroner despairs that we also know "nothing about how to convert them to religion."[30] Religion might help generate the needed "sense of caring"; but religion is in disarray, with many competing faiths.

An ethic that is rooted in a universal center of value—particularly if it is frankly theistic in character—will always have a strong tendency toward world consciousness when it is taken seriously. Other forms of rationalistic ethics tend toward self-interested or group-interested conclusions. Garrett Hardin's celebrated "lifeboat ethics" illustrates the point and so, in a sense, does the work of John Rawls.[31] Whatever the legitimate place and value of personal self-concern and group identity, the present world crisis makes it abundantly clear that humanity needs to find a basis for mutuality in thought and action.

Obviously the Christian perspective upon humanity as a great community of sisters and brothers can be integrative when Christianity does not itself become a source of divisiveness. My own tendencies to make excessive claims for Christian faith as a basis for just and peaceful world integration have been restrained somewhat by such things as a newspaper headline reading "Christian Gunmen Massacre Refugees," which appeared in the wake of atrocities one day in Lebanon. But such events speak more of the looseness of popularly conceived religious identity than they do of the deeper resources of faith to inform life. In a later chapter we will consider the relationship between Christian faith and the pluralism of world religions. But here the point can be made more directly and simply that Christian faith, taken seriously as faith in God's reconciling love, can build community where once there was chaos. The Christian God is beyond the nations—with their anxieties, their pride, their greed—and the Christian definition of community is universal as well as local. Every international conflict is within the wider family. Where international perceptions are touched with a sense of wounded national pride, there is particular need for the wounds to be interpreted at a deeper level, for humiliation easily leads to dangerous policies. National identity needs to be interpreted, not as pride of place, but as service to the cause of a new order of peace with justice for the whole world. Christian faith helps locate the real roots of identity and reveal the basic humanity of those whom we might otherwise treat simply as enemies.

Patient, constructive attempts to fashion a new world order grounded in faith and love were never more critically needed. Apart from the world vision itself, patience may be one of the most important contributions of Christian faith. Many people who are not grounded in a sense of the interconnectedness of history "burn out" too quickly in face of frustration. As Keynes remarked, "in the long run, we are all dead." Those who see only that fact may wonder whether patient effort to construct a new world order is worth the effort, for the achievement of creative institutions securing peace and justice for the whole world as a community is the work of decades, if not centuries. But if one also sees this as the work of the God of the ages, one can more easily endure the hard work and momentary frustrations.

Speaking at the opening of the World Population Conference in Bucharest in 1974, U.N.Secretary General Kurt Waldheim remarked that the conference, along with similar ones dealing with food, environmental issues, housing, and so on, were spelling out the common agenda of humankind "for the rest of this century." That was a good reminder, not only of the enormity of the problems facing the world, but also of the fact that the development of global institutions is largely incremental. Those who dream of establishing world government in one stroke, like the achievement of the American Constitutional Convention of 1787, overlook the seriousness of the divisions that must be overcome, including great differences of cultural perspective and seemingly insurmountable conflicts of interest and ideology. But constructive mutuality can be born out of working together on those problems recognized by all. Foundations can be laid for the larger achievements later. Christians do not have technical blueprints for solutions to all the problems; but their basic perspective is large enough to sustain the task of finding them.

To be sure, this is only a sampling of the difficulties humanity faces today as it seeks to come to terms with social existence. But everywhere one probes, Christian faith holds up well as an integrating perspective. Such faith is not a substitute for actual experience, nor a detailed prescription of solutions to problems. But those who live on the basis of this faith do not have to put the faith aside when they confront the problems. The faith provides the framework of meaning within which the details can find their place. Christian faith is "functional," as the social scientists might say, to the true interests of society, although it also helps define what those interests ultimately are. As the *Letter to Diognetus* suggests, it can "hold the world together."

# 8

---

## THE SHADOW OF EVIL

Tiger! Tiger! burning bright
In the forests of the night,
What immortal hand or eye
Could frame thy fearful symmetry?
. . . . . . . . . . . .
Did he smile his work to see?
Did he who made the Lamb make thee?

—William Blake

Christian faith may provide a basis for holding the strands of life together, but there is a fundamental level at which the basis of that faith is tested: whether it can contain the terrible realities of evil. Having announced Christian faith as the good news, how do Christians propose to deal with the bad news?

That is not exactly a new problem. The Book of Job wrestles with it as profoundly as anybody today could hope to, yet also with what appear in the end to be such inconclusive results. And while the twentieth century may have achieved new evidences of how serious evil can be, it does not appear to have contributed much to further understanding of the problem. The very fact that so many age-old afflictions of humanity have been overcome in the era of the industrial revolution heightens the sense of frustration in face of suffering that will not yield so readily to human engineering.

### THE FUNDAMENTAL PROBLEM

How can we *dare* treat reality as being centered in a loving, caring God in face of the facts about evil and suffering that have exploded in our time? We who live in the century of total war, of nuclear destructiveness, of holocaust and racism and starvation? We who continue to be afflicted by the furies of nature in earthquake, wind, and fire? We who know the dread of cancer, the gnawing of unconquerable disease, the abruptness of accident? Humanity would prefer that its time not be taken with easy answers to those serious problems, although humanity itself seeks easy escape from them often enough—and sometimes with evil compounded as the result.

The problem of evil is in fact a much more serious challenge to Christian thought than is science. I agree with S. Paul Schilling's assessment at this point: "Probably most of those who deny any divine reality today do so more because of the existential impact of the pain and injustice endured by innocent people than because of any theoretical world view, though the two influences often reinforce each other."[1] Science, like Christianity, presupposes an ultimate unity to the cosmos. Like other theoretical world views, it suggests a rational universe; and that, as we have seen, is but a short step from locating rationality at the center of being. But the facts of evil raise serious questions about that unity of being and remind us that such a faith may prove to be superficial. How can we continue to believe that the whole cosmos is centered in loving purpose when there is so much ugliness and suffering? Would the God portrayed by Christian faith have programmed things in such a way? After millions watched the television series "Holocaust" in the United States in 1978, a survivor of Auschwitz was interviewed at his American home. When first imprisoned, he said, he had been devoutly religious. But horrors of his experience forced him to abandon his Christian views: "A hair can't fall from your head unless it is God's will, and here whole families were going to death. I saw whole families being systematically murdered, and whatever I had learned about God, didn't make sense any more."[2] How many parents watching a beloved child's tortured death even under more normal circumstances have wanted to echo those words? How many people suffering from crippling handicaps, from birth or as a result of injuries, have wondered how this could have been if a caring God existed?

The problem as posed by the philosophers is how we can believe in a God who is both perfectly good and totally in control, for if a good God is totally in control such evils surely would not be allowed to exist. We have said that the Christian "cup" is based upon an unconditionally loving God who is the source and center of all reality. But is not evil a reality? Can the Christian "cup" contain this reality and frame a sufficient response to it?

Some of the answers given to how and why God should permit evil are not very helpful. Perhaps the most cruel of all is the belief that people suffer as punishment for their own sin. That is, of course, the view that Job explores. That classic was written in a culture that made too easy connections between moral goodness and human happiness. For example, note the easy faith of Psalm 1: "Blessed is the man who walks not in the counsel of the wicked, nor stands in the way of sinners. . . . In all that he does, he prospers. The wicked are not so, but are like chaff which the wind drives away. . . . The way of the wicked will perish." That was attractive doctrine, particularly, one might suppose, among the prosperous. Job's friends try to explore with him the hidden sinfulness in his life that could account for the wretchedness he is forced to endure; but it will not wash. He is not wicked; the book has made that clear from the beginning. It is all the clearer to us today. Relatively innocent people suffer beyond human endurance, while thoroughly mean-spirited villains live prosperously and die comfortably.

The idea that suffering is only a test is scarcely a better account. Job is framed on that literary premise and, happily, he passed the test. But if wretchedness, sorrow, and suffering are only a divine test of our character and faithfulness to God, it is a curious thing that those chosen for the most difficult tests are chosen so at random—especially, that some are tested so terribly from the very moment of birth before ever there has been time to develop the resources needed to respond to the testing. And there is a similar problem with the notion that evil is there in order to help us develop our character. The world may be constructed as it is with that in view, a possibility to be explored below. But if evil exists for that purpose, we must again ask why the randomness. Why are some chosen for suffering beyond any possibility of creative response, while others are permitted to live easily and naturally? If suffering is designed to develop character, then why isn't this pedagogical opportunity distributed more equitably?

We have already abandoned the notion that God intervenes specifically in the natural order, so we need not be detained by the conception that each piece of evil persons have to suffer has been designed specifically by God for particular reasons. It is well that we have abandoned this notion. For if God had to assume responsibility for many instances of specific evil we should have to think of God as monstrous and not wait for an ultimate unveiling of the inscrutable mystery behind every such occurrence.

Yet another approach is promising but troubling at the same time. It is the notion that evil is something that God cannot control and therefore ought not to be blamed for, thus solving the dilemma of how to relate God's goodness and power to the fact of evil by abandoning God's power. The troubling thing is that while this may relieve God of the moral scandal, it also seems to relieve God of being *God*. One could no longer say with confidence that unbounded love can be trusted at the very center of being, because something else then appears also to be at the center of being. I am not thinking simply of the ancient dualisms, like Zoroastrianism or Manichaeism, but also of some forms of modern personalism and process theology. The latter offers suggestions that need to be taken seriously. But in doing so, one needs to take care lest evil be given a reality independent of God at the center of being.

We also need to be wary of theories of evil that argue the whole thing away with the assertion that evil is but a figment of distorted consciousness. Consciousness can, no doubt, exaggerate evil and magnify its consequences. And some kinds of evil, being a product of mind, can be expected to disappear upon the renewal of wholeness to a troubled spirit. But evil is real. Some kinds of sickness may be a consequence of hypochondria, and faith healing may have an important role to play there. But I have greater difficulty imagining how to heal by faith an utterly crushed leg (or how one could use this method to deal with the persons vaporized in a nuclear holocaust). The distorted consciousness way of dealing with evil only pushes the problem back a step, anyway. For there is the problem of how and why people have distorted consciousnesses, and why some have it so much more than others.

Evil is too serious a thing to be explained away so simply. In framing a deeper account of it we may be helped to remember three forms of evil that are sufficiently distinct to suggest that different accounts must be given for each of them.

## MORAL EVIL

In dealing with human nature, we have already mentioned the reality of human sin, pointing to the suggestive analyses of its source and implications by theologians like Reinhold Niebuhr. We must not be surprised that very much evil is caused directly by human sinfulness. The deeper question is, how could God have set up the human venture in such a way that we could be so murderously cruel to one another?

Two of the most searching criticisms of belief in a personal God in our time come from the pens of theologians who have felt they could no longer believe in such a God in light of the moral evils of this period of history. The first is Richard Rubenstein's *After Auschwitz*,[3] which questions whether Jews can any longer believe in a God who could permit such massive evil as the holocaust to occur. The second is William R. Jones's *Is God a White Racist?*[4] which doubts whether a God who biologically set up black people for racial oppression corresponds at all to the Christian view of providence. Different as well as similar issues are framed by the two thinkers. Both find the massive evil suffered by their respective communities of reference to be inconsistent with the conception of a caring God. Rubenstein's community of reference has a very long tradition of self-understanding as a people specially chosen by God for divine purposes. But here is this community, the Jewish people, made visible in history by God's own action and forced to suffer oppression for century after century culminating in the awesome evil of the holocaust and the death of some six million innocent people. Rubenstein finds no explanation plausible enough to reconcile the stark realities with the traditional faith.

Jones, conscious of the many generations of suffering by black people, with slavery and the most degrading racism destined to be their lot in America, wonders how the God who made this people black could be considered just and benevolent as pictured in the standard Christian view. Jones's own clear preference is to abandon a theistic orientation altogether and to have us choose a creative humanism instead in which everybody will understand that goodness and justice come from human and not divine hands. Both Jones and Rubenstein pose formidable challenges to conventional forms of faith. In particular, they both expose the utter frivolity of treating particular evils as if they were somehow intended by a loving God. Could that possibly be the case with the death camps? Or the evils of American racism? Or the stunted lives of malnourished children in Bangladesh or Bolivia or the Sahel? Could a loving God actually do such things?

While leaping to answer no, we should also explore more deeply than either Jones or Rubenstein lead us to do what is the relationship between God's love and human freedom. To be human is to be a centered self who can value and act, who can experience things and whose response is free even though influenced by many things. To be capable of freely pursuing good purposes, people must also be capable of freely pursuing evil ones—a point made strikingly in the narrative of the Garden of Eden in Genesis.

Then, why should anybody *want* to choose evil? Why should God create people so they will possibly (even probably) prefer evil to good? The serious pursuit of that question has led important Christian thinkers from Augustine to Calvin (arguably including St. Paul himself) to speculate that God creates the capacity in some people (the elect) to respond to good while consigning others to the pursuit of evil. But that solution leaves us with exactly the original question: Why would a good God do such a thing? None of us is helped much by attributing that to God's mysterious inscrutability! Nor would many of us be content to affirm, along with some of the earlier Calvinist clergy, that we are willing to be damned if necessary for the greater glory of God! Why, then, should people be "programmed" in such a way that they might choose evil?

Remembering Niebuhr's analysis, we do not have to lay this on God in quite so definite a way. Humanity exists in a sea of competing values. Sometimes what appears to us as good is not, and our lack of trust in God clouds our judgment and captivates our will. Our sinfulness is based in large part upon our effort to deal with our anxiety. But only by coercing our faith and will could God guarantee that this not occur; only by making us spiritually shallow and psychologically dependent could God provide the constant visible assurances that calm the gnawing acids of doubt which exist in the absence of deep trust.

Ernest Becker's striking account of the same phenomenon is not developed theologically. Indeed, he is of all things careful to avoid theological shortcuts out of the human dilemma that might substitute pleasant illusion for bitter truth.[5] The bitter truth is that *"evil comes from man's urge to heroic victory over evil."* We are fundamentally anxious concerning our own mortality and driven to perpetuate ourselves through culture and society. "The evil that troubles man most is his vulnerability; he seems impotent to guarantee the absolute meaning of his life, its significance in the cosmos. He assures a plenitude of evil, then by trying to make closure on his cosmic heroism *in this life and this world*."[6] To bring this closure requires concrete victories over evil persons and evil societies. Thus Becker accounts for Auschwitz and other atrocities as the rational irrationality of human efforts to extirpate filth and evil by transferring it onto target peoples and then brutally extirpating *them*. A similar analysis could be made of the evil of racism (and in fact has been by earlier sociological studies of American racism) and of other monstrosities of social evil that make it difficult to reconcile reality with God.

Becker offers no real solution other than the hope that clearer exposure of the social lie about such socially based immorality and its relationship to evil will finally prove persuasive to enough people. He acknowledges the thinness of this reed, and his own death cut off the possibility of his offering any further reflections on the problem.

The reason he did not suggest theological answers even to what may finally be theological questions is understandable. There are so many ways that cheap theological answers can only compound the problem. Religion itself so often has been the vehicle for exactly the kind of social scapegoating to which he refers. At present some of the most venomous struggles on earth are being waged under banners of religion, gods of all kinds being defended against their supposed enemies in holy war. That is what the headline "Christian Gunmen Massacre Refugees" finally meant, just as it also helps one understand events in Iran, Northern Ireland, and also wherever Marxist fanaticism confronts anti-Communist fanaticism.

God is not to be blamed for all this, any more than God is to be held accountable for the petty-scale sins and trespasses ascribed to venial motives. To be held responsible, God would have to assume full control; but if God assumed full control humanity would lose whatever margins of moral control it presently possesses. Without the capacity to do evil, humanity would have lost the capacity to do good. Without the possibility of self-centeredness and hatred, there can be no possibility of mutuality and love. The Christian account of the divine-human drama sees the enormity of God's own self-giving risk. God has created humanity with a capacity for self-transcendence and love; but that necessarily means that God has also created the possibility, unique in nature, for self-idolatry and rebellion. The fact that genuinely trusting response to God must be in the face of some anxiety and much uncertainty means that it can also be deeply rooted in our own being and not be a shallow reflection of the obvious or of our own clear self-interest. There are, in the skid-row sections of many American cities, gospel missions doing the laudable work of providing food and shelter for lost, homeless people. Occasionally one of these institutions will require certain religious acts, such as attendance at worship services, as a precondition of receiving physical sustenance. Sometimes, no doubt, that form of imposed discipline does in fact lead to new hope and transformed life. But, more often, it may lead to mechanical conformity or even cynical conformity. That is just the kind of "religion" that God has not programmed us for! We are invited, rather, to say (with one of the hymn writers), "Deepen our spirits for a love like Thine."

Still, an analysis like Becker's leads one to ask whether God is basically impotent in the face of this human monster that has been created on earth. Does Becker's account present us with the fundamental picture about humanity? Is that what the human venture really all adds up to, in spite of everything? Are we, at last, motivated by anxiety, driven to save ourselves through wrong-headed scapegoating of other people, alien societies, whoever gets in the way? Becker himself does not seem to go quite that far, for he also recognizes other, more positive realities at work in human society. And finally I think the realities of grace and trust may run deeper, relatively, in most places and most of the time, then he can quite believe. His analysis does reflect quite intelligently what it means for old mythologies of human salvation to break up into secular equivalents. For it is these equivalents that push us to fight a titanic struggle for good over evil entirely on the horizontal plane of history.

But I must also say that the more one pushes an analysis like Becker's the clearer it is that the only escape from the morass of anxious motivation is the capacity to trust the goodness of the power beyond ourselves. Christian faith again is exactly what brings release from the deadly compulsion to immortalize oneself historically, the compulsion Becker finds at the root of the worst human evils. It is so easy to misstate this truth and to find oneself with a new, even more deadly kind of religious self-righteousness. Virtually the same symbols can, in fact, serve both a deeply trusting faith and loving response to life, on the one hand, and a crusading, vindictive war against God's "enemies" on the other. The symbols therefore need to be used carefully in face of the abyss of moral evil.

How far, indeed, would God let moral evil go? Physical interventions in human history must come from human beings. There does not seem to be any basis for the hope that God would intervene directly even to stop us from annihilating ourselves, if that should be the tragic turn of events. At one time Billy Graham argued that God would act directly to prevent such a catastrophe, but we had better not assume so. Our actions in history, even actions of that magnitude, are neither a test of God's power nor of God's goodness. They are a test of human faith and love—if one wishes to describe them as "tests" at all. God's goodness has been confirmed, not denied, by the creation of life in such a place, with its capacity for freedom and trusting love. The possibility of evil has always and necessarily accompanied such a gift. But the enduring antidote for evil is in trusting love.

## NATURAL EVIL

Of course, there are also forms of evil that are not moral in nature. No person causes hurricanes or earthquakes or volcanic eruptions. In the literature of philosophy, the problem of theodicy was most definitively raised by a work of Gottfried W. Leibniz in 1710. But his characterization of the necessity of natural evil in a finite world and of this as the best of all possible worlds was rudely shaken in Europe by the great Lisbon earthquake of 1755 in which perhaps sixty thousand people lost their lives. Could one really believe that a benevolent and omnipotent deity would cause or permit such a castastrophe? A number of lives were swallowed up in the volcanic explosion of Mt. St. Helen's in 1979. One of the most interesting of these people was an elderly hotel-keeper named Harry Truman who refused to heed the warnings to leave his resort hotel near the summit of the mountain in response to expert advice. His own death was not, therefore, entirely involuntary. But he loved the mountain with almost mystical passion. He trusted it; and in the end it destroyed him. Is that a parable of our lives on earth? We love this earth because we find it good and, perhaps, because we trust its Maker. And then, sometimes when we least expect it, disaster strikes with lightning suddenness. No one who has seen the death masks of those suddenly engulfed at Pompeii, preserved intact for many centuries, can fail to see in the contorted postures and expressions of agony what it means to be the victim of such catastrophe.

The point is that it is God's catastrophe more than it is ours. We can be blamed for nuclear war and lesser moral evils; but we cannot be held responsible for causing the violent convulsions of nature which we have not in fact caused. How does Christian faith bring such facts into focus?

The question Leibniz had to deal with is whether this is the best of all possible worlds. Could God have done it better? I am not sure that anybody knows enough about the material universe to be able to say that it could have been designed better. I am not sure what "better" would mean, since we cannot regard the natural world and universe simply as a resource for human disposal.

But it is obvious that a world in which persons with physical organisms and nervous systems, who have the sensory means of touching, feeling, seeing, hearing, must almost necessarily present a measure of vulnerability. If we are to have senses and if we are to experience so varied and beautiful a world, those very senses become the occasion for injury. A stone on the pathway is not experienced as evil until we stub our toe against it. Volcanic eruptions and earthquakes are natural phenomena reflecting the movements and tensions of the earth's crust—of no particular moral importance until people perish in volcanic gases and the rubble of fallen buildings. Such things are nobody's "fault," in one sense, although one could say that there is a moral obligation to get out of the way and also to help others avoid predictable disasters. There must be room in the vast interplay of genetic life for those handicaps that often are experienced as human tragedy. One cannot argue for the direct utility of genetic malformations or of all God's creatures, great and small. But the harmonies and disharmonies of nature have excited the wonder of sensitive human spirits from the time of Job. Perhaps even the mosquito has some essential part in the great drama of life, or had such at one time, or will have at some time.

Certainly the mosquito has an essential part in the drama of life from the mosquito's own point of view, if not from ours—bearing in mind the particular fact that mosquitos do not *get* malaria!

The problem of natural evil is not to be waved away. The evils we encounter in nature are indeed *evils*. We must presume that they also frustrate God's loving purposes for us. But they pose the question of how faith and faithful action can respond to the perils of catastrophe, physical accident, and the accidents of birth. It would seem that the response of Christian faith would be, on the one hand, to do everything humanly possible to reduce the scale and effect of such evil and, on the other hand, to help one another to respond with courage and deepening of spirit where we cannot otherwise affect the physical outcome. This no doubt means that we have to take an active hand in structuring the circumstances of life. Disciplined by faithful love, there are no grounds for being negative about efforts to regulate population growth, to intervene for the protection of environment, to erect physical protections against floods and earthquakes, to continue the struggle against disease, to engage in responsible genetic research; in effect, to "play God" in respect to the circumstances of our existence. For God's work in such matters must be conducted through the work of responsive human beings.

## "NATURE RED OF TOOTH AND CLAW"

The third form of evil is not always considered because it falls somewhere between moral evil and natural evil, and it is not an easy thing to comprehend theologically. The problem is how we are to account for the conflict of life against life that is not simply a reflection of freedom but rather a necessary part of the survival of biological beings. That problem, curiously enough, first struck me with force one night when I was awakened from a sound sleep by the frantic cry of the pet rabbit belonging to one of my children. The rabbit was being attacked by a dog who was, himself, responding neither to the claims of good or evil but rather to the very nature of his being. As the rabbit's cry pierced the stillness of the night it came to me as the protest of all innocent life against the injustice of the suffering that nature *has written into its very constitution*. Even this would be more acceptable if one could believe that the animal had no feeling, but plainly it had. There can be no doubt that animals experience vividly the terrors of "nature red of tooth and claw." As Becker says,

> Existence, for all organismic life, is a constant struggle to incorporate whatever other organisms they can fit into their mouths and press down their

gullets without choking. Seen in these stark terms, life on this planet is a gory spectacle, a science-fiction nightmare in which digestive tracts fitted with teeth at one end are tearing away at whatever flesh they can reach, and at the other end are piling up the fuming waste excrement as they move along in search of more flesh.[7]

Perhaps there is some ultimate time ahead of us when the Hebrew poet's grand design will find fulfillment, when "the wolf shall dwell with the lamb, and the leopard shall lie down with the kid, and the calf and the lion and the fatling together, and . . . they shall not hurt or destroy in all my holy mountain" (Isa. 11:6, 9). Perhaps the humanizing mission of redeemed humanity will one day construct a world in which sentient being truly no longer consumes sentient being, and then a full dimension of the responsibilities of faith before God become clear to us. Possibly then we shall see our calling to be God's stewards in creation in larger terms as a part of God's loving design. We must not speculate too much about this, especially we who are not vegetarian. But lest we conclude that sentient life depends for its life upon the consumption of sentient life, let us not forget that all of the nutriments ultimately required by sentient beings are to be found in nonsentient life.

In the order of nature as it now exists, the balances between the predators and the creatures who are their food supply are such that the interests of each kind of species tend to be served. Typically, the weaker animals are the vulnerable ones. Overall the size of the population of a particular species is kept in check when the normal balances of nature occur. Interestingly, the U.S. white-tailed deer population appears to have remained stable in recent years, in spite of the vast incursions of industrial civilization upon the original North American wilderness. The deer's natural enemies have been more vulnerable to human intervention than have the deer themselves. It has arguably been in the deer's own best interests as a species to have hunters "prune" the herds. That point would be hard to explain to an individual deer about to be shot or to one who had just lost a mate or a parent. But then,

> Are God and Nature then at strife,
> That Nature lends such evil dreams?
> So careful of the type she seems,
> So careless of the single life. . . . [8]

It remains, however, that even for the hapless victims of nature's cruelties, life is experienced as a good—else death would have no terrors. But that seems to have led us to the deeper problem!

## THE STING OF DEATH

Of course the real evil, for which God (or nature) can clearly be held accountable, is the universal fact of death. Whether in the form of nature "red in tooth and claw" or in the premature loss of human life to disease or accident, or in the serene passing of old age, death comes finally as the termination of all the good that life has afforded. It is a reminder of the profound truth of Paul's words that "the creation was subjected to futility, not of its own will" (Rom. 8:20). Every human life, every human project, vision, desire, relationship finally comes to an end. Therefore, in a manner of speaking, to be human is to be under death sentence or to be terminally ill. Nothing is gained by being morbidly preoccupied with death; but neither can we forget that death presents itself as the ultimate evil. It is at least the cessation of every good we experience in life and the apparent deprivation of every future good. If one is concerned about anything at all, how can one fail to be concerned about this, the quintessential loss of everything else?

The Epicurean response is one that expresses a certain level of wisdom. Death is not painful when it comes, said Epicurus, it is painful only in anticipation. But anticipation is an empty pain:

> So death, the most terrifying of ills, is nothing to us, since so long as we exist death is not with us; but when death comes, then we do not exist. It does not then concern either the living or the dead, since for the former it is not, and the latter are no more.[9]

Death itself cannot be experienced; and how can we describe anything that cannot be experienced as though it were "evil"? There may be a grain of wisdom in this, in face of the terrors of the night. But it betrays a casual attitude toward life. The wise man, Epicurus continues, "seeks to enjoy not the longest period of time, but the most pleasant." There is here no great investment in meaning, no passion for good or truth or beauty; only an acceptance of fate mildly tinged by concern lest life become in any way uncomfortable. It is an answer to the problem of evil based on the supposition that there is nothing that is either particularly good or particularly evil apart from the pleasure or pain of the moment. Applied theologically (which Epicurus of course does not) it would be to say that we should be content, more or less, with things as they are and not blame God for not giving us more. Again, theology taken from this standpoint might say that it is a bit ungrateful of humanity to want more when God has already given us so much. We should accept the gift of our little day and not begrudge its ending.

Some have gone further by affirming death as a good friend which brings us release from suffering, gently rounding out in sleep the fullness of our days. One remembers the old characterization of pneumonia as "the old man's friend." There comes a time when further life seems a burden, and then death is liberation. The point is underscored by the American funeral industry, with its sweet perfumes, gentle music, and cosmetic artistry to present the body of the deceased as though it were quietly asleep. *Requiscat in pacem!* It is as though nothing really important has happened.

But of course, if death is not important, neither is life. Cosmetology aside, the body is dead, and it will soon begin to decay. When death truly does come as a release, as it often does, the true implication is that other evils have overtaken a person to the point that this final evil is only relatively good. Worst of all is the notion that there must come a time when we will want release from the lengthening of days, as though life finally adds up to burden and boredom when one has been through enough of it. Perhaps this is indeed the sum of it. But if so, the great drama of life is itself belittled. God may be relieved of any further responsibility for evil; but then, what is left of God? In proportion to the depth and goodness of life, it seems inconceivable that death is not evil. Better, perhaps, is the defiant admonition, "Do not go gentle into that good night!"[10] Death must come; but it is to be fought against, not welcomed or even tolerated.

Paul, again, saw the meaning of all this. The creation has, according to him, been subjected to *futility*. Every human endeavor, everything we have poured ourselves into and care about, finally goes down the drain. And that is supposed to be a welcome release?!

I will not review again Becker's thesis that a good deal of human evil results from our endeavor to secure secular immortality for ourselves and for our cultures—though that is another, though deeply troubling, answer to the problem. A more benign form of "denial," as the psychologists would term it, is to explore the evidences for personal immortality, finding our reassurances there. Several investigators have recently explored this as a scientific problem. Most noteworthy among them is Raymond A. Moody, who has studied the reports of experiences recounted by patients brought back from death or near-death situations.[11] Moody, who is a physician himself, describes the care with which he attempted to exclude accounts of after-death experiences that could be attributed to other causes. His conclusion is that a body of quite genuine data exists pointing to survival beyond physical death. (For example, reports by patients who were able to describe accurately the contents of hospital rooms their spirits visited during the period of clinical death and before being revived, even though they had never physically been inside those rooms before.)

I frankly do not know what to do with such accounts! I confess to a degree of skepticism. The reports come secondhand: patient to doctor to reader of doctor's book. Possible alternative explanations flood to mind, ranging from fraud, to the exaggeration high hopes tend to feed, to some temporary psychic phenomenon, to genuine, enduring immortality. One should remain open to such things even while remaining skeptical. That openness was illustrated somewhat surprisingly by a committed Marxist scholar participating in a Christian/Marxist dialogue in 1982. While maintaining a properly radical stance on every question of politics and economics, in a textbook rendition of Marxist theory, this man astonished both the Christian and Marxist participants by announcing his belief in the authenticity of these findings of "life after life."

Were the findings as announced by Moody, Elizabeth Kübler-Ross, and others to prove entirely accurate, Christian faith would have little difficulty accommodating that result! This is particularly so because many of the patients seem to have reported how overwhelmed they were by grace and kindness in their "life after life" experience. Possibly even those Christians whose conception of God emphasizes stern vindictiveness might be able to adjust to finding themselves surrounded by healing love!

Meanwhile, it may be better to confront ourselves and the world with the worst-case assessment of death, and not the most credulous. Death we know with great certainty. Our attitude toward its tragedies and evils should not be sweetened cheaply. By any realistic account, death comes as the end of our physical experience here and now. By any account it deprives us of loved ones with all the marks of utter finality. As Paul said, it stamps all creation with the note of futility; for everything under the sun comes to an end (Rom. 8:20). This, surely, is the most fundamental challenge to Christian faith.

But this is also where the strength of the Christian perspective, not its weakness, becomes most evident. The undeniable fact that the whole creation is subjected to futility is a decisive obstacle for most human perspectives on life. Death must be ignored, covered over with illusion, or allowed to destroy creative purpose, or occasion a demonic human reaction against its own ultimate frustration—according to standard attitudes. But the Christian quality of hopeful love stands by us in life's deepest tragedies, so that we are able to look beyond the abyss of suffering and frustration into the reconciling power of good. The God who subjected creation to futility is—also in Paul's words—the God "who subjected it in hope" (Rom. 8:20, 24). And "in this hope we were saved," even though our hope is of something we cannot yet see.

We cannot forget that Christ himself made no effort to gloss over the reality of death nor to evade its claim. His earnest, almost bitter prayer was that, if possible, his own life might be spared in that fateful night of his final encounter with evil. His words from the cross itself were remembered by the church as, "My God, why have you forsaken me?" That was not the last word from the cross; but that was an authentic response to the enormity of its evil. The centrality of the cross in Christian life is a reminder that faith can be equal to the most awesome tragedies.

No Christian can lightly claim factual evidences to prove the ultimate victory of the good over the realities of suffering and death. But it is the nature of Christian faith to believe that we belong to God and that God cares about us ultimately and finally in spite of death. The Christian faith in resurrection can easily be trivialized by factual speculation. It is better for Christians not to base their faith in Christ's resurrection upon physical details referred to in the New Testament Gospel narratives. The world has too many such miracle accounts available to it from the widest array of mutually contradictory religions and cults as it is. Those disinclined to accept Christian faith on the basis of the interior quality of its revelation of life and love will not be turned from their skepticism by yet another miracle story. It is better to acknowledge the tremendous power and goodness generated by that faith itself as it blossomed forth in the life of the early church among people who believed honestly and wholeheartedly that God would not let death destroy their Christ.

It is also best not to structure our faith upon factual assurances concerning life after death, but rather upon simple trust in the caring God who is at the center of all being. It is the nature of things to change and decay. But although we are material things, we also know ourselves to be more than that. Our faith in God finally is our faith that that which is more than material is the better clue to our ultimate destiny since we are loved by God, wholly without reservation. Those who can give over their lives to God trustingly have no difficulty with forms of evil that are less than death. Paul's own summary statement is that "in all things we are more than conquerors through him who loved us" (Rom. 8:37).

# 9

## THE CHURCH: COMMUNITY OF HOPEFUL LOVE

We have to make of the Church in every place a voice for those who have no voice, and a home where every man will be at home. We have to learn afresh together what is the duty of the Christian man or woman in industry, in agriculture, in politics, in the professions and in the home. We have to ask God to teach us together to say "No" and to say "Yes" in truth.
—World Council of Churches, 1948

To speak, as we have done, about how Christian faith can bring the experience of the world into focus is not to engage in purely abstract exercises. It is not possible to believe very deeply in anything that we do not give ourselves to wholeheartedly. We must base our life—our decisions, our values, our goals, our politics, our economics, our recreation, everything—on the hopeful love we find at the center of all being. If we do not, we shall find ourselves only clinging to fragments again. In the world we inhabit, we must bend every energy to creating a society of justice and lovingkindness if we intend the Christian cup to be whole for ourselves and others. This is all very easy, in one sense, because we are dealing here with the very wellsprings of life and vitality. But it is also very difficult in another sense, for the abandonment of hope and the forces of greed and self-centeredness in our time are so great and exert such influence upon us.

The disintegrative currents of the age are obviously too strong for us if we attempt to sustain a solitary faith and to act in a solitary way in the world. We are social beings. We cannot avoid being influenced by others; and our own lives spread influences we can scarcely imagine. If we derive much of our self-conception from our interaction with others, how much more are we going to be affected by the other kinds of values expressed by the people with whom we associate? Nobody can long be a Christian entirely alone. The church is therefore very important as the sustainer of the Christian cup in the contemporary world. Christians are, almost by definition, committed to the church. But to say that is to open up another series of problems that we must address.

## THEOLOGICAL VS. SOCIOLOGICAL PERSPECTIVES
## ON THE CHURCH

Not the least of these problems is the question of what the church *is*. Two sometimes conflicting ways of viewing the church can lead to confusion. On the one hand, the church is itself a theological topic, along with God, Christ, grace, sin, and so on. Theologians speak about their "doctrine of the church" (or their ecclesiology), and the church is even incorporated in certain of the classical Christian creeds. But on the other hand, it is also obvious that the church exists as an empirical fact, as a social institution alongside other social institutions. One does not need to be a Christian to observe this institution in all its variations and complexities. One can study its workings as one would any other kind of institution, such as educational institutions, family structures, government, economic institutions, and so on. It is inevitable that both these perspectives should be involved, the theological and the sociological. The confusion is when they are mistaken for each other. For instance, a theological description of the church may prove to be very difficult to reconcile with what one sees in that building with the cross on it in the center of the city, or across the green suburban lawn, or in the rural village. It can be very difficult to take one's "doctrine of the church" and seek out something that corresponds to it sufficiently to be called the church. Indeed, there are so many mutually contradictory claimants for status as the "one true church" that nothing can be taken entirely at face value. Sometimes, as in the contest between Confessing Church and German Christians during the Hitler period, the question of definition has deadly serious consequences.

By the same token, if we take the social reality of the church as it exists anywhere to be a concrete statement about the meaning of the Christian faith, we may find that difficult to square with the faith as it is generally understood or as we understand it. When a church council proclaims "let the church be the church,"[1] we may wonder how such redundant speech could clarify anything, until we notice that the first use of the word "church" in the sentence refers to the actual social institution and the second to what the church must be if it is to fulfill the theological understanding.

## THE CHURCH, VIEWED THEOLOGICALLY

All of this is, no doubt, puzzling to outsiders—and frequently to church members, too. The puzzlement is only partially abated by the definition of the church in the old Anglican Articles of Religion: "The visible Church of Christ is a congregation of faithful men, in which the pure word of God is preached, and the Sacraments be duly ministered according to Christ's ordinance, in all those things that of necessity are requisite to the same." Where, exactly, is such a congregation to be found? What is "pure" word of God? Of what importance are the sacraments, ultimately? Such a definition, when placed alongside any human reality, suggests that the theological definition of the church always stands above any institutional embodiment, calling it into judgment for its shortcomings. And yet, to be the church is to be an institutional embodiment, not a Platonic abstraction.

That point is driven home by Paul's metaphor for the church, the "body of Christ." As a characterization of the church, that metaphor makes two important points. First, it suggests that the church is a kind of continuation of Christ's own presence in the flesh. The church, as a physically visible entity, continues to make tangible the revelation of Christ. The Christian claim concerning Christ is that he manifests the essential nature of God. He unveils the truth about God, the center and source of all being, but not through abstract concepts. As a person Christ is a compelling key to the riddle of the nature of ultimate reality. He is the "word of God," not the spoken or written word, but the embodiment of the meaning of God in whom the meaning is revealed to those "who have eyes to see." That incarnation is what the church means, too, as the body of Christ. It is a continual manifestation of the visibility of Christ in the world. When the world sees the church, then, it is drawn to the reality of God (that is, if it is really the church, if it is really the "body of Christ").

The other point is that the church is a cooperative community in which all have functions to perform and none are to be accounted superior or inferior. Here the metaphor of "body" takes up the different members and functions of the human body as a way of characterizing how closely coordinated the people of the church are, and how none should think themselves superior to others.

These are things that come to mind when it is proclaimed in the liturgy that "the church is of God." At the same time, such a way of speaking of the church is not free from risk. The risk is that we should assume too readily that God decreed the creation of this particular institution which we also know to contain very fallible human beings and to be structured in ways that are contingent upon particular historical circumstances. The real risk is that people shall be led to believe that the church is itself God's inclusive purpose for humanity. Thereby one would lose sight of the deeper Christian understanding of God's love for all humanity and that God has immediate access to every human being everywhere, as well as to all other aspects of being. It is particularly troublesome to hear it said that there can be no "salvation" outside the church. Sometimes the church's sacraments are described in such a way that God appears to be quite dependent upon them in order to overcome the divine estrangement with humanity. (And sometimes not just the sacraments but particular forms of administering the sacraments can be insisted upon.) So a baby who dies without having received baptism is apparently estranged from God and heroic efforts must be made to get water to scalp before it is too late! And if one does not take communion with sufficient regularity and in the prescribed manner one is placing oneself at risk!

This kind of ecclesiastical narrowness trivializes Christian faith, reducing it to a fragment of the real meaning of God's love. Worse, it becomes an idol, worshiped in place of God.

Still, the church can be what Paul meant by the "body of Christ." It can embody the meaning of the faith in its wholeness, serving as a powerful instrument for God's loving purpose in the world. When it does so it can be understood as fulfilling two functions. First, it is within its own life an embodiment of God's purposes for all humanity. When people look at it they are given a visible sense of what human society as a whole would be if it responded without reservation to God's gracious love. In that sense, the church exemplifies what a community of love and justice can be. It shows what it means to be "a home where every man will be at home." As a demonstration of God's purposes (or as the "kingdom of God") the church is not simply a means to an end. It is also an intrinsic good, an end in itself. One does not ask what a friendship can be *used* for, as though friendship were only to be used for something else. The church in that sense is a community of friendship; it is not simply to be used for something else.

Thus, some correction must be given to the theological cliché that "the church *is* mission," a proposition fashionable in church missionary circles a generation ago. To say that is to obscure the equally important truth that the church is a community where we are accepted for what we are and where we understand more deeply than ever we thought possible what we really are. One of the church's functions is simply to be what God has created human community to be.

But the other function is instrumental. The church is also there to serve

God's purposes in the world. It is a community, but it is not limited to the reality of its own community life. It consciously seeks to be an actor in the world in behalf of God's venture to overcome human alienation from the source of all being. In that sense, the church partly *is* mission. So the church, theologically understood, is both an anticipation of God's purposes within its own life and an instrument of those purposes in the world.

## THE SOCIAL REALITY OF THE CHURCH

I doubt that any institutional church ever perfectly fit that theological description. The church is a human thing; it is full of the imperfections implied by the human material and subject to the usual dynamics of social groups. For instance, it characteristically functions as a reference group—that is, as one of those groups in which we find or seek social acceptance and with whose values we identify ourselves.[2] Such groups help establish our basic identity. We value the approval of other group members more than anything else. Consciously or subconsciously we mold ourselves into their image. Any kind of group can perform this function and, particularly in complex urban societies, people can have more than one reference group loyalty at a time. Our social lives may represent a complicated pattern of group identifications, including family, church, neighborhood, workplace, political association, recreational groups, and so on. While we take on the beliefs and values of those with whom we identify ourselves in such groups, some of our valuations may come from one kind of group, others from another. Nor does the pattern of values always correspond exactly to the publicly recognized function of the group. Within a particular church certain economic or political attitudes may be more important as controlling values than anything that is clearly theological in character. Conservative or liberal or radical economic views may seem more important to the group than attitudes toward any particular tenet of religious faith; similarly, racial or political views may dominate the group's basic sense of identity. During the period of the civil rights movement in the American South there were churches in which outright doctrinal heresy would have been tolerated more readily than deviation from the dominant racial prejudices.[3] Social researchers have also discovered that the perception of unanimity is extraordinarily important in shaping group attitudes. If it is perceived that *everybody*, without exception, holds a particular view of things, it is very difficult for a group member to deviate even on relatively trivial matters.[4]

This phenomenon, readily verifiable in the ordinary experience of most people, is not necessarily a threat to the integrity of Christian faith or any other religious beliefs. Indeed, churches often strive to heighten the reference group identification of members for essentially theological reasons, as when the faithful are encouraged to form such bonds of identification with those Christians of present—or past—who are considered most authentically representative of the faith. But where the immediate attitudes of the present group with whom one is identified in the church are the most important thing, conformity to the group can of course substitute for more ultimate values. The phenomenon of conformity to group values can, in general, inhibit the full expression of personal integrity and creativity if the group does not point beyond itself to the transcendent reality of God.[5] But even where persons have a high degree of interior strength based upon a faith that is more than conformist, the social power of the reference group identification can be very great. It is always a source of illumination to discover what a person's most important reference group identifications are and how they bear upon his or her attitudes.

Sociologists from the time of Max Weber and Ernst Troeltsch have explored the different social forms taken by religious groups. Troeltsch's distinction between "church" and "sect" has proved particularly useful.[6] By "church" Troeltsch referred to the ideal of an ecclesiastical unity of a whole civilization. The church is coextensive with all of society, incorporating everybody within its own institutional framework and attempting to bring the values of the society into conformity with the Christian faith as far as possible. If one is born into such a society one is to be baptized, as soon as possible. After arriving at puberty one is confirmed through what might be called rites of initiation in other settings. Church ceremonies and liturgies mark the high points in the year for the whole community and the significant events in the life of each person, attempting all the while to infuse these times and seasons with distinctively Christian meaning. In its medieval form (perhaps the one period when the Catholic Church could be said to have come close to fulfilling Troeltsch's description of the "church-type") the church was understood to objectify the means of salvation for all through its sacraments.

The "sect-type," on the other hand, referred to the ideal of a community of deeply committed believers.[7] One does not enter the group at infancy (hence the "sect" does not practice infant baptism) but only when one is old enough to make the commitment for oneself. The general attitude of the group is that those who have not made the commitment are evildoers who are alienated from God. Every effort may be made to convert such lost souls, but as long as they resist they are beyond salvation. The world outside the group is utterly corrupt and "fallen."

Troeltsch understood "church" and "sect" to be important tendencies, always present throughout Christian history but rarely to be found in perfect form. Nevertheless, it is interesting to survey the vast panoply of Christian churches and groups through the centuries to discover which tendency is most evident at a particular time and place. Troeltsch avoided placing value judgments on the two tendencies. Examining them theologically, one could argue that both make legitimate points. The one holds that God's gracious love reaches out to incorporate everybody. The other reminds us that personal commitment and belief matter. A theologically defensible doctrine of the church doubtless falls somewhere in between.

Nevertheless, Troeltsch's study contributed another very important insight: The form of church organization tends to express an attitude toward society as a whole. Church organization is not, in that sense, purely neutral, purely utilitarian. For the "church-type," society as a whole is treated as the sphere of God's activity; it is at least redeemable as a whole even though it may be profoundly corrupted and unjust at particular times in history. In other words, to the "church-type" society at large is a proper project for the church at all times and in all places. For the "sect-type," on the other hand, society as a whole is fallen. It cannot, as such, be redeemed. The only hope is to save as many people as possible. Thus, also, the church-type has more investment in the present, while the sect-type is more exclusively future-oriented either in terms of afterlife or in terms of a vision of a time when God will intervene directly to transform history.

These sociological perspectives can. be elaborated endlessly, but we must not pause further in the domain of sociology of religion. The sociological perspective is important, however, in giving us some sense of the social reality of the church we hope to use for theological ends. We must proceed now to highlight the three formative tasks of the church as they relate to the overall theological perspective. I shall speak of these as the three *linkages* that are especially important for the people of faith. The assumption lying behind each of the three is that God's gracious love is the central reality of life and that human embodiment of response to that reality is what brings everything to focus and fulfillment.

### LINKAGE 1: INTERPERSONAL RELATIONSHIPS
### IN A CARING COMMUNITY

We have mentioned already the idea of the church as an anticipation of God's purposes for society. Surely no aspect of that can be more important than for the church to be within itself a community in which the members really care about one another. That should come before questions about doctrine and propriety of worship and efficiency of church government because an uncaring community will undercut everything else. What does it mean to be a caring community? The call of the Message of the First Assembly of the World Council of Churches to make the church "a home where every man will be at home" is a part of it: to be able to identify this community as one's own place, where one is thoroughly and completely accepted for oneself and where one has an opportunity to grow through interpersonal relationships. A little church I belonged to as a boy in an obscure town of southern Arizona had the right idea. The building where most of the activities of the church were conducted was called *Su Casa*. In Spanish that means "Your Home," and that is the way I remember that little church. Its members were ordinary people, the usual collection of saints and sinners (the latter doubtless outnumbering the former). But it really was "home" because people cared about other people. A church that is really a home deeply undergirds the integrity of Christian faith, even among those sorely troubled by intellectual and moral doubts. Its nurturing of children and youth is such that they can feel free to express all of their questions openly and clearly within the fellowship, never fearing that they will shock anybody. Such a church takes people seriously in the integrity of their being and responds lovingly in the moment of their need. It knows no enemies, only the children of God.

In its own life, such a church makes the point about God's grace. People who have actually experienced the accepting, unconditional love of other people—imperfect and somewhat conditional as it is almost bound to be—are far better able to grasp what it means to have faith in that same quality of love at the center of reality. Such love is not sentimental, nor is it indifferent to the claims of justice and to the destructiveness of human sin. It is fully consistent with calling one another to account within the life of the church. But that calling to account is rooted in grace, not in condemnation.

When the church fully exists as a fellowship of caring Christians it does not depend solely upon professional clergy to serve the pastoral function. Everyone is a pastor to everyone else. Real Christian leadership works very hard at building up the church in this way. It gives that very high priority. The capacity to lead a church in the development of a caring community may be the single most important mark of competence in ordained ministry. It certainly is to be preferred to the flash of the pulpit prima donna or the pseudoprofessionalism of the amateur psychiatrist. A caring community of faith builds us all up in freedom and love.

Any number of silly and even dangerous cult groups have gotten a free ride at the expense of the church because they have made a home for the homeless and really seemed to care about those incorporated into their fellowship. A religious group can fulfill purely social functions as an accepting, enhancing fellowship while being grossly inadequate as a source of ultimate meaning. The communal experience of people in groups as diverse as the Latter-day Saints, the Unification Church, the Jehovah's Witnesses, and even Rev. Jones's Peoples' Temple has often been very caring, even though aspects of their theologies are subject to serious question. (I feel safe in characterizing the theologies of these groups pejoratively because they are so absolute in their claims and so diametrically opposed to one another that no more than one of them could possibly be correct in its central claims. But they are still life-enhancing communities in many ways, except of course for the Jonestown group.) It is a great tribute to the importance of communal life that so many people will overlook absurd beliefs in order to participate in it!

## LINKAGE 2: INTEGRITY IN MEANING

What we believe and what we worship still matter very much. It is a wonderful thing when a caring community is also a place of high moral and intellectual integrity and when the God it worships is also credible. The church must also be a place of intellectual engagement, with encouragement for serious study and discussion and with a high premium placed upon honesty in face of the most difficult issues. Those issues include the kinds of cosmological and moral issues this book has been concerned about, recognizing that the Christian faith gains its greatest integrative power when its relevance to the hardest problems becomes clear. It should be possible to confront the hardest problems without breaking the fellowship of love. It should be possible for Christians to disagree on intellectual issues without rejecting one another.

It also matters very much what and how we worship as a church. There is no need to be detained over the liturgical niceties, the proper little rules of order and the fads and fashions of passing aesthetic taste. What must interest us very much is what we *worship;* that is, what we ultimately *value.* The liturgy is the language of our shared faith. It conveys our attitude toward things. The theologian and the ethicist need to attend very closely to what is being said and believed and celebrated in corporate worship. The world is being put together or torn apart in the liturgy. We had better pay attention.

Note, for example, the subliminal message in this "Prayer for Enemies," found in the *Book of Worship for United States Forces*.

> Have mercy, Father, upon those who live to enslave the world rather than let
> men live in freedom. Bring light to their darkened minds, peace to their
> warring hearts, and sanity to their warped designs. Hasten the day when
> international enemies are won to friendship by those who have the power of
> your love.[8]

There is much more, almost all of it in this same vein of self-righteous
judgment of adversaries. Are we here invited to join the enemy, as brother
or sister, in the reality of grace, humbly seeking forgiveness and reconciliation? How would the listed enemies respond to such a prayer if they heard
it said?

And when we give thanks for our many blessings, do we word this in
such a way as to imply that God has made us rich and other people poor as a
matter of divine intention? Could the hungry people of the world take heart
and join us in our prayer of thanksgiving? And when we confess our sins,
do we concentrate on the little immaturities that God might even find
amusing, and ignore the great sources of our alienation from ourselves, our
fellows, and God?

Worship can never touch accurately upon life until it finds its base in the
affirmation and reaffirmation of grace. Everything has its significance
from the fact that we have been accepted at the core of our being by God,
the source of all being. Everything else flows from that. So that is the heart
of worship. In light of that, confession is healing and the caring of the
community is reinforced. In light of that our worship is driven to undergird
the common cause of justice for the whole human family. Worship can no
longer be treated as a specialized fragment of life but more as a summary of
the whole.

In recent years, Protestant churches have begun to recover the importance of Eucharist and Baptism as central to the life of the community.
Both provide opportunity to celebrate the wholeness of the faith.[9] Through
Eucharist we celebrate God's gift and the unity and redemption evoked by
Christ's passion. It is a fragmenting experience for people if it is reduced to
esoteric formulas or treated as an entirely individualistic transaction
between God and the believer. It is a community celebration and it is based
upon actual events that are remembered in the life of the church along
with the implications of those events for faith.

Baptism, as symbol of new life in Christ and incorporation into the
church, depends very largely on how we define the difference between the
old life and the new. Through preparation for baptism and through the
liturgical act itself, there is occasion for reaffirmation of the Christian's

whole new orientation upon things, centering in hopeful love. It is a peculiar kind of scandal that these sacramental observances of the church have so often been occasions for division among the various denominations. It need not be so.

The church is also a center of educational enterprise. It nurtures us all, so we help one another along in the faith. It clarifies the connections between faith and the realities we encounter in the present age. It preserves the traditions of faith, passing them from generation to generation. It nurtures the young in the tradition and in a growing sense of their own self-confidence in faith and life. I will not comment at length on the educational task beyond saying that the educational ministry of the church is absolutely critical to the health of a Christian faith perspective for our time. Lay education should be prepared to take people as far as they are able to go in comprehending the backgrounds of Christian faith and the applicability of Christian faith in the contemporary world. It must always have integrity, meaning that it cannot bypass hard questions or varnish the truth.

In one sense, it is amazing that there are still battles being fought over the verbal inerrancy of Scripture and that some people are still led to believe that the Bible must be accepted in every detail or not at all. Too many Christian pastors, even today, are afraid to share frankly and clearly the findings of the past century or so of biblical scholarship and to explore honestly the implications of a scientific perspective on miracle stories. The price we pay for this neglect is the wholeness of faith of the people and the attractiveness of the truth of the gospel to our times. Perhaps we need to reflect more upon Paul's words, "In your thinking be mature" (1 Cor. 14:20).

## LINKAGE 3: THE CHURCH AS
## AGENT FOR CHANGE

We come, then, to the role of the church as an actor on the stage of history, as a center of redemptive purposes. The church cannot evade the task of seeking to restructure life, to re-form civilization in harmony with the gospel. There is a sense in which the task is altogether beyond the capacity of the church while yet still being within the reach of faith. By faith we can "move mountains." Empowered by God, people do what nobody thought could be done. Sometimes a handful of Christians has made a very great difference. Instinctively one thinks of the little band of people who gave impetus to the civil rights movement in the U.S. Compelled by great faith and great love for both the oppressed and the oppressor, they really did move mountains. One could never have predicted what in fact was done. People of faith can sometimes discern realities that escape the more hardheaded. They can see the possibilities of human responsiveness, the constructive impulses waiting to be unleashed. They are not so bound by personal egoism and self-interest as to arrest their own creative imaginations. Those who really care must not allow the present entrenchments of injustice to weaken their resolve.

There is much at stake. Being a center of purpose in human history is not merely one of the side activities of the church, a specialized ministry to be committed to a few overzealous activists while the rest of us deal with more substantial or "spiritual" things. Historical purpose is God's agenda. It is seeking to know God's purposes and to bring them to fruition.

Something else is also at stake for the church. Social engagement involves the further question whether people can even find it possible to believe in and live the Christian life. A profoundly unjust world undermines Christian life. It forces Christians to live in a perpetual state of self-contradiction. An unjust world makes it impossible for them to live in accordance with their beliefs and values as Christians. Walter Rauschenbusch, the most notable leader of the Social Gospel Movement, expressed the point vividly in his definition of what makes a social order Christian or unchristian. Speaking of an unchristian social order, he wrote that it is one where good men are compelled to do bad things. A Christian order, by contrast, is one where bad men have to do good things.[10] The last line is oversimplified, but the first one may not be. An unchristian social order is one where good people are forced to do bad things in order to live normal lives. That is a reminder to us that we live in a world of institutions and systems. Acting normally, we contribute to the institutions' and systems' well-being and effectiveness. If the corporation we work for is doing bad things, anything we do to be effective on the job will contribute to evil. One did not have to be a racist in one's personal attitudes to help racism along in a society where segregation prevailed, nor, if one were white, could one help benefiting by that racism—even if one totally despised it! This is even more clearly true of the political order. It is almost impossible to avoid lending our support to actions and policies by our government, whether we believe in them or not. Whatever the government is doing, we are there, like it or not, as a part of the enterprise. We are all caught up in systems and carried along by systems. The conflict between our values and our social existence is a profoundly important source of spiritual lethargy, cynicism, and despair.

For this reason, if for no other, social injustice is a very important *pastoral* problem for the church. Inhuman conditions stand between people and the fulfillment of their lives in God. These conditions have to be addressed or the church fails as a church. It is unlikely that the church will be able to create perfect social institutions, so the tension will continue to exist. But the church can link people to the forms of social witness and action that further the process of change toward justice and social well-being. To be acting in behalf of God's purposes is at least to be relieved of lethargy, cynicism, and despair, even when the fruits of that action fall short of our hopes.

## THE CHURCH AS PROCLAMATION
## TO THE WORLD

In all of this the church is (to paraphrase Marshall McLuhan's expression) the medium that is the message. It is the city set on a hill that cannot be hid. It is inextricably identified with the Christian faith as it actually exists in the world. Bearer of the Christian hope, its life and actions contribute either to hope for the whole world or to deeper despair and cynicism. It cannot escape its visibility.

Paul A. Carter makes this point strikingly in his interpretation of the rise of secularism in American life during the period between the two world wars.[11] His thesis is that it was the churches' insensitivity to human suffering more than any conflict with science that made it difficult for people to identify with Christianity. He cites two points of particularly conspicuous failure by the church. One was the way in which churches treated the First World War as a noble crusade—when in fact that war was a catastrophic bloodbath, an unspeakable tragedy. The other was the way in which the churches rammed Prohibition down the throats of the American people. Even though the latter movement began out of a real moral concern over the human suffering caused by excessive consumption of alcoholic beverages, it degenerated into an arrogant, moralistic vendetta against all who stood in the way. In both cases, the churches appeared blind to the real human condition. Consequently, the emerging cultural leaders of the 1920s—including the most sensitive artists and writers—found it quite impossible to repair to Christian faith as a beacon of hope for the age. Even the exceptions to this, such as T. S. Eliot, were prone to express the mood of disintegration and decadence that hung heavily over the times. Whether the church could have been otherwise in that era is one question; whether it can be sensitive enough and provide the necessary leadership in our age is yet another. Certainly it makes a great cultural difference when the church is engaged in that way, as its involvements in the civil rights movement clearly suggest.

By all that it is and says and does, the church is an "evangelical" community; its life and message come down to "evangelism" if that term can be rescued from its unhappier connotations and restored to its original sense of proclaiming the "good news." For the Christian perspective is above all and for everybody truly good news. I can see how some people cannot bring themselves to adopt this perspective or to live by it. But I cannot see how anybody could be led to think that it would be anything other than good for them, if true. For the heart of it is faith that God, from the very center of all being, has said yes to each of us and that we can trust and give ourselves over to the life of love. It is also good news that this perspective brings everything into focus: our personal life, our social existence, our creative impulses, our scientific pursuits, even our encounters with tragedy.

But again, much depends upon how the church defines its evangelistic task. Is it merely a matter of mouthing pieties and recording "decisions for Christ"? No, it is real *conversion*. It is transformation of the human perspective and remaking the vision of an age. Efforts that often pass for evangelism in the church—efforts like the "Key-73" and "I Found It" campaigns in the U.S. in the 1970s—usually deal in fragments. Paraphrasing Jeremiah, they touch over the "wound of the people" lightly. They substitute advertising techniques for serious communication with people that takes people themselves seriously. They appear to be satisfied with superficial results, as recorded in institutional statistics and not in the transformation of life. And the irony of it all is that they usually do not even effect very much long-run statistical success! We should not be surprised. People know when they are being manipulated and when they are confronted with fragments and not invited to the real cup of life!

But the human hungering remains very deep. In the biblical expression, the fields appear to be "white for the harvest." Never has there been a more widespread yearning for exactly those treasures of mind and spirit that Christians have to share. But never have Christians been held to more exacting requirements of honesty and integrity and humanness.

A critically important test, which we have postponed until now, is whether the Christian claim can be made in such a way as to respect the world's religious pluralism. How does the Christian cup relate to the other cups?

# 10

## MISSION AND IMPERIALISM

All men need the Gospel. For the human sickness there is one specific remedy, and this is it. There is no other. The Church cannot compromise on its missionary task without ceasing to be the Church.
> —Stephen Neill, *Christian Faith and Other Faiths*

The missionary enterprise of the last one hundred and fifty years is closely related to and interwoven with the expansion of the economic, political, and cultural influence of the Anglo-Saxon world. We from the Third World call this expansion neocolonialism or imperialism.
> —José Míguez Bonino, in Anderson and Stansky, *Mission Trends No. 1*

There remains the question how the church can approach its mission of evangelism without engaging in cultural imperialism. The words "mission" and "evangelism," in fact, have an ominous ring. They smack of disrespect for the views of other people and of insensitivity to cultures other than one's own. When one reflects seriously upon the vast number of people in the contemporary world who are *not* Christian, and when one considers the various proud cultures and religions they represent, one is a little more hesitant to make exclusive claims in behalf of the gospel of Jesus Christ as the organizing principle for the *whole world*.

Yet, that clearly seems to be what we are doing when we speak of the power of the Christian metaphor to bring reality into focus in its wholeness. If Christian faith cannot do that, then it is a "broken cup." But to claim that a particular faith perspective can bring all of human experience into focus is to make a universal claim. It is to say not only that this faith perspective is valid for whatever we ourselves might experience but also that it is valid for everybody. How can one say that without being culturally arrogant or imperialistic?

## WHAT'S WRONG WITH IMPERIALISM?

"Imperialism" has become a decidedly pejorative term, a code word for various forms of human oppression. The reality it symbolizes is indeed negative in light of the increased moral sensitivities of recent years. But loaded terms, such as this has now become, sometimes lead us to close off discussion before we have fully understood what we are discussing. In this case, to dismiss anything that can be labeled "imperialistic" risks losing sight of an important moral dilemma that should not be oversimplified.

As a political term, imperialism refers to the attempt by a state to assert power and dominion over others, both in order to enhance its own security and to improve its economic well-being by stripping subject peoples of their own resources. Ancient empires (Assyrian, Babylonian, Roman, etc.) often began as small city-states or tribes, conquered their immediate neighbors, and then progressively expanded the area of conquest to include most of the accessible world. The empire was able to use the human-power resources of the captive peoples for further military conquest and to exact tribute and taxes to sustain the power and glory of the imperial center. Sometimes, but not always, the empire contributed relative peace and stability to the subject peoples and to overall cultural development. Imperialism has generally been rationalized (by its practitioners) as a benefit to subject peoples, as in Rudyard Kipling's lines,

> Take up the White Man's burden—
> Send forth the best ye breed—
> Go bind your sons to exile
> To serve your captives' need. . . .

> Take up the White Man's burden—
> And reap his old reward:
> The blame of those ye better,
> The hate of those ye guard—[1]

Kipling acknowledged that imperial rule would not be popular among the "newcaught, sullen peoples." But he had no doubts about the benefits that would accrue to "those ye better." Of course it is easy for Romans, Britons, and Americans to overestimate the relative respective benefits of the Pax Romana, Pax Britannica, and Pax Americana. Convinced of the superiority of its culture, an imperial power is bound to regard the increased contact of subject peoples to that culture to be an unblemished kindness to them. Even the resultant economic exploitation may appear to be a relative benefit if, overall, the dominated group is better off materially than it was before.

There is no question but that the great missionary expansion of Christianity in the nineteenth and twentieth centuries has been deeply implicated in the political and economic imperialism of the sending countries of Europe and North America. The degree to which missionaries have consciously abetted military conquest and political dominance is subject to much debate. The truth no doubt lies between the most cynical and most naive characterizations, with many available illustrations at both extremes. Certainly, however, imperialistic dominance played a major role in opening up foreign territories and providing relatively safe conditions in which the missionaries could do their work. Equally certainly, the success of missionaries provided increasing numbers of indigenous peoples better disposed to cooperate with the alien rulers—although in the long run the work of missionaries can also be credited with awakening subject peoples to the moral urgency of revolt. The cross and the flag often did accompany each other in the lonely outreaches of mission and imperialism, even though their relationship was not an unambiguous one.

The moral flaws of imperialism include the temptations it always affords for gross brutality and exploitation. But they also include the greater subtleties of paternalism, social dominance, and inequality. Even when the material benefits of imperialism have been great—and arguably they sometimes have been—the loss of autonomy and the heightened sense of inferiority are deeply offensive to subject peoples. The point was made vividly by a leader of the Coptic Evangelical Church of Egypt: "We would like to go to heaven with the help of brothers. But if you want to send us to heaven by being our masters, we prefer to go to hell."[2] A Philippine church leader added that the missionary has become "a symbol of the universality of Western imperialism among the rising generations of the Third World. . . . The most *missionary* service a missionary under the present system can do today in Asia is to go home."[3] The big debate over a proposed moratorium on the sending of missionaries (proposed by the Lusaka Assembly of the All-Africa Conference of Churches in 1974) may have had most of its rootage in this sense of lost autonomy and the imposition of inferiority. Nevertheless, the strongest case against imperialism is probably one mounted on the basis of Christian faith itself. For Christian faith uniquely values the integrity of the self, subordinate only to God in whom the self finds both affirmation and freedom. And Christian faith provides a remarkably firm foundation for human equality, based finally upon the belief that all are equally valued by God. The irony is that the faith implicitly containing the harshest judgment against imperialism was spread partly under the protection of imperialistic power.

The era of outright colonialism has largely passed away. Its demise was incredibly rapid, viewed in the long historical perspective. Within two decades of the end of the Second World War more than a billion people of Africa and Asia had changed their political status from colonial dependency to formal political autonomy. Some of this occurred as a result of violent military upheaval, some was relatively pacific. All of it was greatly influenced by widespread belief both in the centers of empire and in their farthest reaches that political imperialism was fundamentally wrong.

But imperialism in this new era has a different connotation, in large part derived from Lenin and other Marxists. That is the notion that Western capitalism is dependent upon the exploitation of Third World territories for raw materials, cheap labor, and growing markets. In its Marxist form, this view makes connection with a whole doctrine of exploitation. Behind this doctrine of exploitation, in turn, there lies a definite conception of human nature and even a negative understanding of the role of religion. Many who do not subscribe to the Marxist views of religion are still persuaded by its economic analysis and particularly by the doctrine of imperialism.[4] It is debatable among economists whether the doctrine of imperialism is accurate in its most sweeping forms,[5] but the reality of great economic power and influence being directed to underdeveloped countries from the industrialized economic giants is beyond dispute. The tendency is to create dependent economies and with them new forms of political and cultural domination. Third World societies have found themselves undergoing rapid transformation in directions heavily influenced by external economic power, in spite of their formal political independence. Where this has fostered the old paternalism and inequality, the moral objections to the old imperialisms can be repeated. Again, ironically, the Christian mission has sometimes been the beneficiary even though the moral objections are also largely Christian in origin. Liberation theologians have been especially vocal in condemning the oppression derived from new forms of imperialism.

It does need to be remembered that imperialism can sometimes be a lesser problem than more localized forms of economic or political oppression. Some present-day countries appear to be vastly more oppressive than the more benevolent empires were. (Albania and Paraguay might fit that description at this time of writing.) And sometimes local business enterprises can be less enlightened than vast multinational corporations, partly because the former may be less exposed than the latter to responsible criticism. Moreover, Western forms of development may be exactly what is wanted by Third World people in many countries.

Linkages between the Christian faith mission and "imperialistic" social power may not invariably be bad. Nevertheless, such linkages are at least suspect insofar as they entail uses of power that are not accountable to the people who are most affected by it.

## CHRISTIAN FAITH AND CULTURAL PLURALISM

The morally questionable thing about imperialism, thus, is its creation of patterns of unilateral dependency and inequality. Again, we must acknowledge that Christians, acting out of what they perceived Christian faith to require, have been deeply implicated in these offenses of imperialism. But is such behavior an outgrowth of Christian faith? Or is it a violation of Christian faith? In 1961 the staff member of the Methodist Division of World Missions responsible for liaison with Africa remarked that half the missionaries in Africa were doing more harm than good. Behind that comment was the fact that Africa was undergoing sweeping transformation from colonial status to independent nationhood. Many of the missionaries were so tied to the old order, so committed to colonialism, that they were unable to adjust to the new situation. Some still insisted that indigenous Africans come to the back door at the mission homes and in other ways persisted in treating Africans as second-class human beings. That was by no means true of all missionaries, however. And the same mission executive noted that, while half the missionaries may have been doing more harm than good, the other half more than made up for them by the ways in which they welcomed the new day.

So one must be cautious about generalizations as long as it is agreed that respect for the equality and worth of all peoples is a value of universal importance. But does this mean that all cultural values are equally valid, equally to be approved? A certain kind of cultural relativism would say so. What right, it may be asked, do we have to ram our culture down other peoples' throats? Indeed, we may not have a right to ram anything down anybody's throat! Everybody is worthy of respect as a fellow human being. But that is not the same thing as saying that all cultural patterns are equally worthy of approval.

Cultural relativism itself is an untenable position. If all cultural perspectives and values were equally good, then how could we deal with direct contradictions among them? One culture defines women as inferior, assigning them the most menial tasks, making them entirely dependent upon their husbands or fathers, and not allowing them to hold positions of honor or leadership in the community. Another culture is structured on the basis of the complete equality of women and men. Which culture is right? The problem of polygamy is closely associated with this question. A number of African and Middle Eastern societies still practice polygamy, thus occasioning no little tension between Western missionaries and indigenous leadership (even within the same church).[6] Sometimes the missionaries have been very insensitive, for example, by requiring the breakup of plural marriages in which older women have invested every shred of their life meaning and economic security as a precondition of their admission into the church. But such heavy-handedness aside, the issue of polygamy is, at bottom, the issue of equality for women. The institution of polygamy almost invariably entails subservient status for women. So, is it well for the representatives of Western cultures in which women are held in more nearly equal status to seek the elimination of polygamy? Or was it proper for Western missionaries and others to seek the elimination of the Indian caste system or the practice of suttee whereby widows felt compelled to hurl themselves upon their deceased husbands' funeral pyres? Was it a good thing for Americans in northern states to work vigorously to end the practice of racial segregation enshrined in the culture of southern states? Where such direct contradictions exist, one is pressed to make a value judgment between cultures—or one is left only to say that it just does not matter (which would also be to disagree with the cultures, since these are points at which cultures make very strong value judgments themselves).

As a matter of fact, every moral evil known to humanity represents somebody's cultural viewpoint! Indeed, if all cultural viewpoints are equally good, then what is wrong with a frankly chauvinistic cultural viewpoint? Why should we complain about the cultural perspective that sends some narrowminded missionaries out to proselytize the "heathen" if that is what they feel compelled to do? Why should we complain about racism or sexism or imperialistic nationalism? If all cultural viewpoints are equally valid, why should one be disturbed about fascism or totalitarian communism or the Ayatollah Khomeini's brand of Islamic fundamentalism? If cultural relativism is to be affirmed, then are we not bound to equate the People's Temple cult of the Rev. Jones to the Unification Church of the Rev. Moon, and each of them to the World Council of Churches and Roman Catholicism—and all of these to Tibetan Buddhism? By the same logic, would the Ku Klux Klan then turn out to be the same thing as the NAACP and the Anti-Defamation League? If we reflect seriously on the matter, we are forced to conclude that total cultural relativism is the same thing as treating everything as having no importance. In which case, cultural bigotry is just as good as cultural tolerance! But we know better.

There are in fact serious theological reasons for affirming cultural pluralism, but there are equally important theological reasons for making value judgments about particular patterns and practices.

Here we may note a paradoxical fact about Hebrew-Christian tradition. As a monotheistic covenantal faith, this tradition has sometimes been held responsible for the spirit of intolerance in Western culture. The thesis was advanced early in this century by the Italian legal scholar Francesco Ruffini in words that have been echoed by others:

> When the idea of a single and universal God was set, first by the Hebrews and then by the Christians, against the ancient polytheism, there arose a new form of religious exclusivism, contrary to the old not less in its basis than in its effects. The gods of the other peoples were said to be false and fallen, and religion lost its national and public character, and became on the one side cosmopolitan and on the other proper to each individual. From this followed not only an inextinguishable spirit of proselytism, but also the principle that he only could be saved who worshiped the true God; that is to say, the principle of absolute intolerance.[7]

Ruffini's point was that if there is but one true God, those who do not worship this God are manifestly in error and may need to be coerced a bit into seeing the error of their ways or at least to prevent them from corrupting others. The case for such intolerance can be made biblically (see, for example, Deuteronomy 13 or the books of Ezra and Nehemiah) and in other writings of Hebrew, Christian, and Moslem traditions. Thus, in the Old Testament we find Israelites exhorted to stone to death those who entice them to worship foreign gods and Hebrew men strongly urged to put away their foreign wives after the return from the great exile. We have the awful spectacle of Christian crusades and Moslem wars of religious conquest and the pogroms directed against the Jews. We have the Inquisition. We have the principled statements of St. Thomas Aquinas and John Calvin justifying the killing of heretics. We have the religiously principled crusades of even this present century, with God invoked in support of the Allied war against the Germans and the *Gott mit uns* of the Germans themselves. And we have the righteous condemnation heaped upon the godless communists. Monotheism leaves little room for deviation, it would appear; for if God is "with us," then God must be enemy to our enemies. We, as God's servants, can faithfully execute God's wrath upon them. At the least we are wholly justified in pressing as hard as we can for their absolute conversion. That at least *appears* to be the implication of covenantal monotheism.

But it is very interesting that there is an exactly contrary implication to be drawn from this very same faith, and at a more profound level. It is that if there is but one God, who is the center and source of all being, then nobody can claim to know enough about the mind of God to warrant absolute claims for one's own way of looking at things. God's transcendence beyond the human sphere becomes, then, the basis of principled tolerance. This view also has important rootage in Hebrew-Christian faith traditions. Thus, we encounter in Jonah a compassion for the hated Ninevites and in Ruth a receptiveness to the foreigner. Thus we have the breadth and mystery of Job, magnificent Psalms of nature, Hosea's compassion, the openness and love of Jesus himself. Thus also Francis of Assisi, the Quakers, and others who have experienced God as the foundation for humility and love, not arrogance and intolerance.

The profound love of God for every person and God's immediate access to all is also an important implication of Christian faith, as understood in this book. One must be open to the possibility of God's acting in and through persons in ways that may prove fresh and creative and unexpected. An affirmative attitude toward cultural pluralism gives expression to the faith that God is present in the positive aspects of all cultures. When we summarily reject any cultural perspective because it is not explicitly Christian we may thereby deny a very important implication of Christian faith itself. That such an irony should be reenacted frequently throughout Christian history must not, however, lead us to substitute intolerance for Christianity.

Again, all this is not to imply that cultures are equal and that all values within a given culture have the same validity. Christian faith entails a critical principle as well as an affirmative one.[8] The critical principle is against idolatries that make absolutes out of relatives and against all that is against love for people and for God's creation. The critical principle leads us into prophetic discernment of the subtle dangers of chauvinism in all its forms and an exposure of self-righteousness. It leads us into rejection of the legalism that stands against grace. Affirmatively, it leads us to embrace the love of God and to affirm that love in the positive currents of human history and in the harmonies and rhythms of nature. It leads us to respect the equality of persons and into greater understanding of the fulfillments possible in the life of community. It leads us to seek and value structures of justice undergirding the participation of all in human society.

Thus, Christian faith provides a deep grounding for openness to cultural pluralism without requiring us to consider all cultures or cultural patterns to be equally good or valid. God is profoundly at work everywhere, not just in Western cultures (and not just in non-Western cultures, either). Sin and error are present everywhere as well. We must be prepared to criticize error and evil wherever we find them while remaining open to the redeeming power of God's love wherever it too is to be found. Perhaps this means that we should abandon some of our broad generalizations about whole cultures and come down to specifics, always being prepared to interact with the world as we find it, in all its particularities. Some things need to be accepted, other things rejected. If we are honest about ourselves we will find ourselves rejecting everything within the life of the church that is a denial of hopeful love, just as we will affirm that quality wherever we find it outside the church.

## THE ATTRACTIVE DANGERS OF SYNCRETISM

One possibility might then occur to those who noted carefully the lines attributed to the old Indian chief by Ruth Benedict: "In the beginning God gave to every people a cup, a cup of clay, and from this cup they drank their life. They all dipped in the water, but their cups were different. . . ." To say that one perspective brings everything into focus is not necessarily to say that other perspectives cannot *also* do the same. While the faith perspective that is distinctive to Christians is universal in its applicability, could not the same be true of other faiths—such as Buddhism, Islam, and Hinduism (due allowances being made for the large number of subcultures within each of these great religious systems)? Could not the faith system based around Jesus Christ be "true" without that based upon Buddha or Muhammed necessarily being "false"?

The famous Laymen's Foreign Missions Inquiry of 1933 arrived at such a conclusion when it suggested that other universal religions have profound insights which are also worthy of human allegiance. All are working toward the same goal, all are paths to the same destination. The real adversary, if there be such, is not the other great world religions; it is the spirit of secularism and materialism. It is therefore time for the great religions to enter into serious dialogue and, where possible, to make common cause. Christian faith may prove to have more satisfactory answers in the long run, but that does not negate the validity of the other faiths. In the final analysis, the Laymen's Inquiry report concluded, "The Christian will . . . regard himself as a co-worker with the forces within each such religious system which are making for righteousness."[9] The importance of such a view of other non-Christian religions is underscored when we remember that the great world religions have been remarkably unsuccessful in their efforts to defeat one another through proselytism. They may influence one another in various ways, but they have not been very successful in gaining actual converts from among those who are convinced adherents of other faiths. Many Christians would say that the perspective outlined by the Laymen's Inquiry half a century ago is the sound one.

But this has also been disputed hotly by Christian thinkers who criticize its syncretistic tendencies. Stephen Neill's flat statement is indicative: "All men need the Gospel. For the human sickness there is one specific remedy, and this is it. There is no other."[10] Hendrik Kraemer's response to the Laymen's Inquiry wholly rejected its relativism. All religions are, according to Kraemer, expressions of human quest for the divine; they are human creations. That is even true of Christianity, seen as a *religion*. But Christian faith is response to God's immeasurable gift of grace through Jesus Christ. Seen in the dichotomy of faith and works of St. Paul, religions are "works." They are attempts by humanity to save itself, to please God or the gods.[11] Characterizations of all religions as roads leading to the same destination only seem to make this point for Kraemer. For, in Jesus Christ, the destination has come to us!

Kraemer here voices the Barthian theme—but not only Barthian—that Jesus Christ is God's one decisive Word to humanity. God has chosen to speak through Jesus Christ. To equate Christ—or nearly to equate him—with Buddha or Muhammed or Confucius or any other great religious or philosophical figure is to miss the central point that Christ is uniquely God's own chosen Word to humanity. The proclamation of this fact to other religions need not be insensitive, but it is still the central missionary responsibility.

Recent Roman Catholic teaching has appeared to be somewhat more moderate in its expression of central Christian claims. In the important document *Nostra Aetate* (Declaration on the Relationship of the Church to Non-Christian Religions), the Second Vatican Council went out of its way to affirm the values to be found in other world religions while continuing to voice the ultimate claim for Christian faith:

> The Catholic Church rejects nothing which is true and holy in these religions. She looks with sincere respect upon those ways of conduct and of life, those rules and teachings which, though differing in many particulars from what she holds and sets forth, nevertheless often reflect a ray of that Truth which

enlightens all men. Indeed, she proclaims and must ever proclaim Christ, "the way, the truth, and the life" (John 14:6), in whom men find fullness of religious life, and in whom God has reconciled all things to Himself (cf. 2 Cor. 5:18–19).

The Church therefore has this exhortation for her sons: prudently and lovingly, through dialogue and collaboration with the followers of other religions, and in witness of Christian faith and life, acknowledge, preserve, and promote the spiritual and moral goods found among these men, as well as the values in their society and culture.[12]

Arnulf Camps, a Dutch Franciscan priest who has taken up this call for dialogue with other religions in a serious way, has emphasized that true dialogue requires that one spend more time listening than talking and that one strive to locate the points of common ground on the basis of which one can then speak of one's own faith in the hope of being heard. He challenges the missionary "to find the salvific work of God as Creator always present and operative in every religion." Then, he continues, the missionary may "escort" this value in other religions "to its fulness in the Church, in the name of Christ the Redeemer."[13] There is here an acknowledgment of the work of God in other religions, combined with a judgment that it is incomplete until perfected in the Church. Representatives of other religions might well resent the suggestion that the values of their faiths have to be "escorted" into the Christian Church in order to find their fulfillment. Camps obviously does not wish to be arrogant or to suggest a new triumphalism for the church. The dialogical process "demands a real conversion on the part of the missionary: no imposition of self, humble invitation, positive listening, and acceptance of all that is good in the other party." At the same time, however, the process "also requires conversion on the part of non-Christians. Sin has affected them too, and they may all too quickly be convinced that they have already given a complete and perfect answer to God's revelation."[14]

This general perspective certainly appears more defensible than the arrogance of limiting the expression of God's gracious love in human history only to the "salvation history" associated with Jesus Christ. Even the Christian tradition itself, taken as a whole, does not compel one to such exclusivism, and the empirical evidence of gracious love at work in all parts of the world must be acknowledged honestly and appreciatively. The case for Christian faith as the organizing perspective for human life does not rest on denigrating values to be found in other religions. As a matter of fact, the Christian understanding of God is more confirmed than threatened by such evidences. If God is truly God, what else would one expect? That there would be no evidence of profound love and trust outside the Christian church?

The real character of God is what matters here. The Christian revelation, perceived joyfully and in faith by Christians, is a perception of the nature of reality. Jesus Christ is vehicle of that revelation, enough so that Christians can proclaim that "God was in Christ" without reservation. No value discerned in another religion can shake that proclamation, and insofar as one finds values that confirm it one should not feel threatened.

The real issue posed by syncretism is different. Syncretism is the joining together of elements of different faiths and defining one's own faith by the sum total of the elements joined together. It is an eclectic faith, which means that the end result is not an integrated whole but a porridge of the most widely disparate elements. The truly syncretistic spirit is one that regards all religious claims as equally valid, all assertions as equally true, all values as equally good. I do not even want to be placed in the position of having to affirm everything connected with Christian history and tradition as true and good, much less affirming everything about other religious histories and traditions concerning which I know much less! The critical spirit must also be at work, sorting out the true from the false, the good from the bad, the important from the trivial. True openness is not, in that sense, syncretistic. It seeks out the true and good wherever it can be found, but it also acknowledges a perspective about the center of being.

In the long run, the real question at stake in the encounter of Christian faith with other religions is not which is totally true or good and which is totally false or evil; it is not which is the "true religion" as fundamentalists often put it. It is, instead, which can best provide a profound understanding of the others. Which religious perspective, seen from its center, best brings the others into meaningful focus? An honest person, no matter how committed to any particular religious faith, must always be open to the possibility that another faith may at last speak more profoundly of the meaning of the central deep. A Christian can be open in that way because the Christian faith is such "good news" that anything better could only come as better news.[15]

## THE WORLD CHURCH AND WORLD RELIGIONS

Should Christians, then, seek to proselytize the adherents of other world religions? Should their ultimate objective, beyond all the dialogue and sensitivity to others, be to baptize non-Christians into the church?

In response, let it first be noted that the Christian church now exists in virtually every part of the world. When one speaks of the spread of the church among nonbelievers in predominantly non-Christian countries, one no longer thinks of this as a task for missionaries from Western countries. Indeed, the problem of "imperialism" is now raised *within* the world church: Should Western missionaries be allowed to dominate the church as it exists in Third World countries? While nineteenth- and early twentieth-century missionaries were sometimes very effective evangelists, the present work of spreading Christian faith and building up the church is primarily in the hands of indigenous Christians. Some of the most rapidly expanding Third World churches have, in fact, been movements that broke away from churches dominated by missionaries (that is true, for example, of the Pentecostal Church of Chile, which found the Methodist Church too tightly restricted by Methodist missionaries). Some Third World churches have sprung up seemingly in isolation from any existing church structures, based upon the preaching and charismatic leadership of particularly strong local leaders. That pattern has produced phenomenal recent growth among the independent churches of Nigeria, to take one example. So the question whether Christians should actively seek conversions in predominantly non-Christian countries is not exactly a question to be decided in New York or London.

Still, the attitude of all Christians everywhere toward that question will affect church strategy. Western Christians may not be in a position to be effective evangelists (in the narrow sense) themselves, but their attitude toward proselytizing as a goal is bound to influence church strategy. It will often affect priorities for resource allocation, even when Western churches are careful to avoid dominating the financial decisions of Third World churches. Apart from the attitudes of Western Christians, this is an issue that Third World Christians themselves cannot avoid.

Surely the goal of the Christian Church cannot simply be to expand its own numbers. The larger the church is, the greater its institutional power is likely to be. But the church does not exist for the sake of institutional power. It exists to be an anticipation in its own life of the meaning of God's purposes for the whole human family and to be an instrument for those purposes beyond itself. Its exists to expand the reality of loving trust in this world, to bring people to a fuller awareness of their ability to trust in and respond to God's unbounded love, and to fashion human institutions and practices that are responsive to that reality. Where the church keeps its focus clear on this objective, it can be somewhat more relaxed about issues related to its own institutional power. (Indeed, it had better!) A church that is preoccupied with enlarging its own numbers and increasing its own political power and economic strength cannot speak clearly to the really central questions plaguing humanity in this or any other time. These have to do with the meaning of life, not with who will be winners and who will be losers in the warfare among religions. Most people can sense it readily enough when their conversion is being sought for instrumental reasons, and not as an expression of real caring. Other religions may be expected to be defensive to the extent they are exposed to frontal attack by aggressive Christianity.

It is interesting that the resurgence of some Third World religions coincided with the rise of new nationalism in the 1950s and 1960s. Indigenous religion—like indigenous language and other cultural symbols—became identified with the human dignity and self-determination of a number of societies. Christian mission, identified with proselytizing efforts, had the appearance of being the religious cloak of Western imperialism. Where proselytizing is the main goal, that identification is strengthened and it becomes more difficult to speak of the real objectives of Christian faith.

Some have concluded from such observations that the church should be concerned only with good works, such as the building of hospitals and schools and in other ways seeking to improve the life of people. Such activities are indeed important for the sake of well-being of people. But active witness to the Christian understanding of reality is also important, notwithstanding Mahatma Gandhi's commentary on this problem. In a discussion of Western missions in India (and anticipating the coming independence of that country), Gandhi wrote that

> current missionary activities are of three kinds, good works, education and religious propaganda. In the India of tomorrow the first two will be allowed to go on without hindrance and will even be welcome but, if the missionaries continue to bend their efforts towards religious proselytizing through medical and educational work and so on, I shall certainly insist that they leave free India. The religions of India are right for her people: we have no need of spiritual conversion.[16]

Such a statement is doubtless a legitimate reaction against manipulative efforts by many missionaries. But the implied rejection of all efforts to influence the religious thinking of India's people is a surprisingly illiberal viewpoint, coming from Gandhi (particularly in view of the great influence the New Testament had over his own life). The church, if it cares about the central problem facing all humanity, namely, how to understand and relate to ultimate reality, cannot be limited to a ministry of good works alone.

The essential question may not have changed very much from the first years of Christianity until now: Should Christianity attempt to spread the influence of the gospel? Should it make converts? Should it enlarge the church? Implicit in the observation that the question has not changed very much is the point that if it has been desirable for Christianity to spread in the past, it may be desirable for it to spread further in the future! For the Christian perspective to be effective in the lives of individuals and in the construction of society it has had to have institutional embodiment in the church. Even though the church, as we have seen, is also prone to sinfulness along with all other institutions, it has still been the social incarnation of the meaning of Christ.

But the form of church life has varied immensely through the centuries of the Christian era. It is worth mentioning that the great movements of Christian expansion have often begun within an institutional framework which then became outgrown. That was, in fact, the original situation. The Christian movement began as a deep stirring within the community of Israel; it could almost be described in its origins as a kind of Jewish sect. The proclamation of the Christian message was not, at least originally, an effort to get Jews to abandon their Jewish identity. Rather it was to suggest that the true meaning of that identity was to be found in Jesus Christ. It turned out that the Jewish cultural and institutional framework could not contain the explosive power of this new movement; but that is not because Christians set out in the beginning to change their institutional affiliation. Somewhat analogously, the Wesleyan revival in eighteenth-century England did not intend the creation of a new church, any more than the Lutheran reform of the sixteenth century had. But in both cases, the new reality could not finally be contained within the old structures. Neither Luther nor Wesley originally intended to establish a new "church"; rather, they sought to call the existing church back to a more authentic faithfulness to Christ.

The point of this may be that if Christians focus primarily upon the proclamation of the faith itself and the demonstration of its relevance to the life experience and problems of all people in the present age, the response to that may not be entirely predictable. True, people who accept Christian faith as organizing basis for their lives and their world vision will always need some kind of social support, some group or communal life together with others who share that vision. But that does not have to take the form of any presently existing church as long as it is an expression of the Christian faith.

The insistence upon particular forms of church life seems more relevant to a view of "salvation" that is far removed from the Christian cup as we have discussed it in these pages. It seems more relevant to a conception of Christianity as an individualistic saving of one's soul in the afterlife, with particular forms and sacraments considered necessary to that end. But if one understands the faith as the proclamation of God's absolutely dependable love, then one is relieved of having to earn that love through correct institutional observances. Then it is a matter of how one can structure one's life so as to be able to live out the implications of grateful response.

In light of that, I am not sure I would spend the energy of the church in the largely ineffectual attempt to gain converts from, say, Islam. It might be more important to explore with Moslems how Christian faith brings life into focus and to work toward the reinterpretation and restructuring of Islam itself. Insofar as Christian faith proved to have creative spiritual power in that environment one could either expect success or the emergence of movements and groups of those Moslems who, in the final analysis, found themselves captivated by a new way of looking at things. Under such circumstances, even baptism might prove to be a secondary question. The baptism of heart and mind is more important than the symbolic baptism with water. What really *matters* is whether people come to trust the loving God and to reconstruct their lives and their world in light of the reality of God.

## CONCLUSION

In some respects, this chapter must conclude with ambiguity befitting the complexity of the present religious pluralism. I wish only to make the summary point that the case for the Christian cup does not depend in any way upon everybody being conducted into a great, united world church. Christian faith, while continuing to trust the reality of God's loving covenant with humanity as revealed in Christ, is in principle open to rich variety in human experience. It helps bring into focus the truth about human love and human responsibility in all situations and insofar as that truth is to be encountered in other religions. The viability of the Christian cup does not even depend upon its being recognized or accepted by all people. It does depend upon its being capable of bringing life fully into integrated wholeness for those who are open to it.

# 11

## TREASURE IN EARTHEN VESSELS

Each day the first day; each day a life. Each morning we must hold out the chalice of our being to receive, to carry, and give back. It must be held out empty—for the past must only be reflected in its polish, its shape, its capacity.
—Dag Hammarskjold, *Markings*

We conclude, as we began, with the figure of the cup, and we repeat the question: Is the Christian cup, like that of which the old California Indian chief spoke, broken and doomed to pass away? In the twilight of the second millennium of the Christian era, is Christian faith also in twilight? Is this faith perspective able to bear the weight of profound human experience in this most challenging, most troublesome epoch of history?

### THE INTEGRITY OF CHRISTIAN FAITH

We have tried to be honest throughout this book with those who no longer consider Christianity supportive of truth and goodness as it is now given us to see. Their questions probe deeply, whether into the human self, the social problem, the scientific frontiers, or the persistence of evil. In response to critical questions it is clear that not every belief entertained by Christians can honestly be held and not every interpretation of Christian faith can serve to respond fairly to the most searching problems. Christians must be lovingly ruthless in discarding elements of tradition that stand in the way of the essential points of faith and in refusing to offer humanity stones when it hungers for bread. Christians must not convey falsehood in order to cheer up a bewildered age or to serve the church's own institutional interests; Christians should not suppose they can tell lies to the greater glory of God. We have noted the fragmentary character of much Christian life, not out of lack of compassion for those who are compensating for loss of wholeness but for the sake of wholeness itself.

Having said such things, is it really true that the Christian cup is broken? The integrity, the wholeness of Christian faith rests finally upon foundations that cannot be demonstrated beyond dispute; but so does every other perspective on ultimate reality. Christians do not have a monopoly on human finitude. Everybody is limited in mind and experience in face of the vast expanses of the universe and the incredible complexity underlying even commonplace occurrences. Everybody is also prone to enough egoism to distort the vision. All of us alike must finally find our refuge in our confidence that certain aspects of our experience point dependably to the character of the depth and wholeness of reality. Those experiences touch us with the force of revelation. They bring other things into focus and, if the revelation be sufficiently profound, they make it possible for us to find wholeness in every aspect of life.

The Christian revelation is centered in the overwhelming reality of God: God the creator and sustainer of all that exists; God the personal Being who calls us into covenant; God whose gracious love is revealed in Jesus Christ. Christians thus find personhood and relationship to be the decisive points of revelation. Reality, when it is deeply understood, is understood to be like *that*. We are not misled about the character of reality when we take our own personhood and the best aspects of our relationships as the best clues. More specifically, the experience of Jesus Christ is the truly decisive clue, the best revelation of what personhood and relationship mean. God is revealed in Christ.

This Christian basis of understanding reality is deeply attuned to the rational assumptions of science and to the realities of our own selfhood. It brings perspective on the mystery of how natural process and personhood can coexist in the same universe so that our selfhood does not need to be seen as a simple function of material causes. Its fundamentally optimistic theme is relevant to the facts of personal and social experience. Its account of sin and evil, the tragic side of human experience, is not superficial. It does not require surrender to tragedy or complacency about evil.

Christian faith does not "explain" everything. But it provides a frame of reference within which explanation can be sought and within which it will mean something when it is found. Christian faith does not issue precise marching orders, but it locates the fundamental life purpose for each of us. It does not provide exact criticism of competing philosophies and religions, but it poses the questions we need to ask about them. And meanwhile it provides a sure foundation for positive pluralism and for interreligious dialogue.

In short, Christian faith does exactly what a "cup" is supposed to do. It *contains* the ongoing stream of our experience. It is a cup of life. Those who live in this faith need not exist in fragments. They need not operate on the basis of contradictory values and perceptions of reality which ultimately tear life apart or force it into malaise among those who have not discovered a basis of wholeness.

## LIFE IS MORE THAN THE CUP

Dag Hammarskjold's words are a good reminder that life itself is more than even the most integrated perspective on life. Christian revelation and tradition form the cup, but they do not fill it. One of the frustrations every theologian faces in writing about issues of faith and life is the recognition that the subject matter is always more than the words can possibly convey. Paul Tillich pointed to this one day following a lecture when a student asked him about the prayer life of the theologian. "The theologian," he responded, "must pray twice as much as anybody else." His point was that those who objectify the subject matter of religious faith are most in danger of alienating themselves from the reality itself. They are in greatest need of returning to the living reality. If one does not think and write about the fragmentation of faith and the sources of its wholeness and renewal, life can persist in its distortion. But God is more than our little cups, no matter how well we polish them. As Tennyson put it,

> Our little systems have their day
> They have their day and cease to be;
> They are but broken lights of thee,
> And Thou O Lord, are more than they.

Those could be hard words if we did not have confidence that the God who is more than "our little systems" is the one, finally, who gives the life and love that constitute our being. It is this God who makes it possible for us to affirm, in the language of the Twenty-third Psalm, that "my cup overflows" and "surely goodness and mercy shall follow me all the days of my life"—even though much of that life must also exist in "the valley of the shadow of death" and in the presence of seemingly intractable evil.

## THE RENEWAL OF FAITH

Clearly Christianity, while not broken by the tides of history, is in need of renewal if it is to serve as ground of hope and purpose for the world beyond this century. In spite of the enormous problems of the present time, one can detect signs of renewal in many quarters. Some of it is in the liturgical movement sweeping Catholic and Protestant churches. At its best, this movement seeks to bring the language of worship to an expression of faith and love in twentieth-century terms while maintaining continuity with the great traditions of Christianity. Renewed liturgy encourages us to bring our whole selves to the point of worship, thus to integrate every aspect of our being around the center of our faith. Some signs of renewal can also be found in the ecumenical revolution (that is not too strong a term) of the twentieth century. After many generations of bitter confrontations, Catholics, Protestants, and Orthodox Christians have discovered one another as fellow Christians. In the unity of faith, in overcoming the scandal of division, there has been a return to truly fundamental points of reference on all hands. Ecumenism and renewal have gone hand in hand. This century has also witnessed an outpouring of important theological work that has made it much easier to discern the connection points between issues of faith and matters of fact. That highly sophisticated work has contributed greatly to renewal, even though great theologians often disagree about fundamentals.

There has also been renewal through the great movements for social justice that have swept through many churches. In the long run, this may be the most promising development of all. The greatest threat to the integrity of Christian faith is not, as we have seen, the scientific accomplishments of our age; it is the demonstrated powerlessness of the good in the face of massive evil. Christianity is not without answers to the problem of evil in the world, but the most convincing answer is always (to borrow from the title of a book by Carl F. H. Henry, *A Plea for Evangelical Demonstration*) Christian "demonstration." Christians do not have to win every battle against evil; but their presence or absence on the battlefield will be noted by those who struggle there for human justice. It is always difficult to live the faith in a world with much that is in profound contradiction to the faith. But that does not mean that there can be no renewal without total victory in the establishment of justice—which I fear we shall never succeed in winning. It does mean that the relativities of greater or lesser embodiments of justice weigh heavily on the scales of credibility when frail humanity assesses whether it can trust the life of love. It also means that those who give themselves wholeheartedly to the cause of human well-being, in an acting out of their response to God's love, strengthen their own faith and that of others. They engage "in work that keeps faith sweet and strong."

Christian renewal, in short, depends upon what Christians do about the great opportunities and the treasure given into their keeping. The treasure they have in earthen vessels; but if the treasure is shared, the vessels need not be broken.

# NOTES

## CHAPTER 1

1. A number of these writings have been dissected helpfully by Dewey M. Beegle, *Prophecy and Prediction* (Ann Arbor, Mich.: Pryor Pettengill, 1978).

2. Ruth Benedict, *Patterns of Culture,* Mentor Edition (New York: New American Library, 1934), 19.

3. Tom Robbins, *Another Roadside Attraction* (New York: Ballantine Books, 1971), 287.

4. Princeton Religion Research Center, *Religion in America 1982* (Princeton, N.J.: Princeton Religion Research Center, 1982).

5. "Church Global Survey Shows Startling Trends," *United Methodist Reporter* (13 July 1979): 4.

6. Ibid.

7. Gallup Opinion Index, *Religion in America 1977–1978,* 52, 58. Cited by Jeremy Rifkin, *The Emerging Order* (New York: G. P. Putnam's Sons, 1979), 99.

8. Ibid. On the basis of similar objective data five years later, Gallup remarked that "only about one person in four says religion is the *most important* influence in his or her life." *Religion in America 1982,* 3. This and other observations suggest that while most people affirm religious beliefs and engage in religious practices, for most it is not the integrating core of their lives.

9. Dean M. Kelley, *Why Conservative Churches Are Growing* (New York: Harper & Row, 1977).

## CHAPTER 2

1. Augustine's *City of God* was occasioned in large measure by such criticism following the sack of Rome by the barbarian Alaric in 410 A.D. Augustine argued that Rome had been corrupted fatally by self-love, a fundamentally disintegrative force.

2. Hans Küng, *On Being a Christian,* trans. Edward Quinn (New York: Doubleday & Co., 1974, 1976), 159.

3. T. S. Eliot, *Christianity and Culture* (New York: Harcourt Brace Jovanovich,

1949, 1960); Christopher Dawson, *The Historical Reality of Christian Culture* (New York: Harper & Brothers, 1960).

4. Küng, *On Being a Christian,* 145.

5. The fact that this church, along with many others, is now open to persons of all races may be less attributable to the "happy Sunday nights" than to deeper theological and social currents and to the courage of those who risked much in order to challenge racial segregation.

6. See Gordon W. Allport, *The Nature of Prejudice* (Cambridge, Mass.: Addison-Wesley, 1954), 449–53. Allport also found, however, that profound religious commitment can correlate with tolerance.

7. The New Testament, as such, did not take canonical form until late in the fourth century A.D., and even as late as the sixteenth century Luther could challenge the inclusion of one book (James) in the authoritative New Testament canon. The actual development of the New Testament canon was largely occasioned by doctrinal struggles within early Christianity and the felt need (on both sides of doctrinal battle lines) to designate the writings that could be approved for use in worship.

8. "The Virgin Birth Is Vital," *Good News: A Forum for Scriptural Christianity within the United Methodist Church* 2 (Nov.–Dec. 1977): 32.

9. Quoted by William E. Phipps, "Darwin, The Scientific Creationist," *Christian Century* (14–21 Sept. 1983): 809.

10. Form letter dated 17 June 1982 from Jerry Falwell, The Moral Majority. See also Falwell, *Listen America* (New York: Doubleday & Co., 1980).

11. Robert Bellah, "Civil Religion in America," *Daedalus* 96 (1967): 1–21. See also Elwyn A. Smith, ed., *The Religion of the Republic* (Philadelphia: Fortress Press, 1971) for other essays in the American civil religion.

12. John H. Dietrich, "Who Are These Agnostic Humanists," *Humanist World Digest* 26 (1954): 7.

13. Liberation theology is sometimes accused of this kind of truncated approach to ultimate questions. In the case of major figures such as Gutierrez, Segundo, and Bonino, the charge is difficult to sustain. Some of their rhetorical flourishes may convey an impression of fragmentation along these lines, and it is arguable that their work as a whole may not supply us with a broad and deep enough perspective. But it is also clear that such figures are wrestling with ultimate issues of faith and not exclusively with questions of social location and social action. Indeed, they would argue that it is their concern with the latter that makes it possible to deal with the former without ideological distortion. Of course, not all that goes by the name of liberation theology shares a concern with ultimate issues of faith. In an important document issued in 1984, the Vatican criticized some versions of liberation theology for being insufficiently concerned about the primary need for all humanity to be liberated from personal sin. Of course that is exactly the point at which much Marxist writing can be challenged by Christians: The failure to recognize that sin has roots that go deeper than any forms of institutionalized oppression—indeed, that the latter is caused by the former as much if not more than the former by the latter. The Vatican statement was widely (and perhaps correctly) interpreted as a reprimand of the liberation theologians and, if so, it certainly overshot the mark.

See Sacred Congregation for the Doctrine of the Faith, *Instruction on Certain Aspects of the "Theology of Liberation"* (Vatican City, 1984).

14. William Hamilton's book *The New Essence of Christianity* (New York: Association Press, 1961) shares this dependence upon Feuerbach, although not unambiguously. Hamilton continued to search for ways to express the transcendence of the human essence beyond the purely historical plane. He acknowledged quite explicitly, however, the fragmentary character of the resulting theological perspective: "I suspect that we have come to a time when theology should try to give up its structural pretensions and be content with not much more than a collection of fragments or images, not too precisely related to each other, indirectly rather than directly put forth. . . . The form and structure of a new essence of Christianity will be fragmentary." Pp. 13–14. Feuerbach had declared that "the personality of God is nothing else than the projected personality of man." Ludwig Feuerbach, *The Essence of Christianity* (New York: Harper & Brothers, 1957, 1841), 226.

15. Thomas J. J. Altizer, *The Gospel of Christian Atheism* (Philadelphia: Westminster Press, 1966): "God's death has actualized in our history a new and liberated humanity." P. 111.

16. See especially Jean-Paul Sartre, *Existentialism,* trans. Bernard Frechtman (New York: Philosophical Library, 1947) and *Being and Nothingness,* trans. Hazel Barnes (New York: Philosophical Library, 1956).

17. See, e.g., William K. Frankena, *Ethics* (Englewood Cliffs, N.J.: Prentice-Hall, 1963) and John Rawls, *A Theory of Justice* (Cambridge, Mass.: Harvard Univ. Press, 1971).

## CHAPTER 3

1. " . . . all the choir of heaven and furniture of the earth, in a word all those bodies which compose the mighty frame of the world, have not any subsistence without a mind . . . their *being* is *to be perceived or known.*" George Berkeley, *A Treatise on the Principles of Human Knowledge* (London, 1710).

2. David Hume, *Treatise of Human Nature* (1739), Bk. I, Pt. I.

3. See especially Friedrich Engels, *Anti-Duhring* (1880).

4. Albert Einstein, et al., *Living Philosophies* (New York: Simon & Schuster, 1931), 6–7.

5. John Rawls, *Theory of Justice.*

6. *Smithsonian* magazine has, however, supplied us with the name of one Corsebus who seems to have won the very first Olympic race in 776 B.C. See Lionel Casson, "The First Olympics: Competing for the Greater Glory of Zeus," in *Smithsonian* 15 (June 1984): 65.

7. The nineteenth-century philosopher Arthur Schopenhauer, who held a consistently pessimistic view of human meaning, reduced life to the simple will to live. Beyond that blind will and its attendant needs there is no real meaning. Life, therefore, is finally ennui. Schopenhauer found evidence for this unhappy portrayal of life in the fact that people can find some meaning in the intrinsically meaningless activity of playing card games.

8. "We can now see why it is impossible to find a criterion for determining the

validity of ethical judgments. It is not because they have an 'absolute' validity which is mysteriously independent of ordinary sense-experience, but because they have no objective validity whatsoever. If a sentence makes no statement at all, there is obviously no sense in asking whether what it says is true or false. And we have seen that sentences which simply express moral judgments do not say anything. They are pure expressions of feeling and as such do not come under the category of truth and falsehood. They are unverifiable for the same reason as a cry of pain or a word of command is unverifiable—because they do not express genuine propositions." Alfred J. Ayer, *Language, Truth, and Logic* (New York: Dover Publications, 1952), 108–9.

9. See J. Philip Wogaman, "The Integrity of Christian Ethics," in American Society of Christian Ethics, *Selected Papers, 1977* (Waterloo, Ontario: Council on the Study of Religion, 1977) for more extended discussion of the ontological basis of the good.

10. I have used the word metaphor rather than the word symbol because the latter can suggest (despite Tillich's distinction between "sign" and "symbol") an arbitrary relationship between the reality and that which conveys its meaning to us. Those who are accustomed to purely literary uses of the word metaphor will recognize that I am employing the term broadly.

11. Quoted by Mark Sherwin, *The Extremists* (New York: St. Martin's Press, 1963), 110.

12. See James Luther Adams, *On Being Human Religiously* (Boston: Beacon Press, 1976), 131–32. Adams here cites Whitehead's classroom lectures at Harvard University. See also Alfred North Whitehead, *Process and Reality: An Essay in Cosmology* (New York: Macmillan Co., 1941, 1929), 7.

13. Whitehead, *Process and Reality,* 7.

14. Ibid., 8.

15. Edward O. Wilson, *Sociobiology: The New Synthesis* (Cambridge, Mass.: Harvard Univ. Press, 1975); B. F. Skinner, *Beyond Freedom and Dignity* (New York: Alfred A. Knopf, 1971). See also Arthur L. Caplan, ed., *The Sociobiology Debate* (New York: Harper & Row, 1978).

16. Albert Einstein, *Out of My Later Years* (New York: Philosophical Library, 1950), 22–23.

17. Sallie McFague, *Metaphorical Theology: Models of God in Religious Language* (Philadelphia: Fortress Press, 1982), 15. McFague suggests a number of refinements in the use of metaphor, including a distinction between metaphor and symbol.

18. Ibid., 18.

19. H. Richard Niebuhr, *The Meaning of Revelation* (New York: Macmillan Co., 1941), 109.

20. Karl Barth, *Church Dogmatics,* I/1 (Edinburgh: T. & T. Clark, 1956), 350.

21. Heb. 11:1, 3.

22. 1 Cor. 13:12.

23. Aurelius Augustinus, *The Confessions of St. Augustine,* trans. Edward B. Pusey, Harvard Classics (New York: P. F. Collier, 1909, 1937), see esp. the Seventh Book.

24. Richard Grossman, ed., *The God That Failed* (New York: Harper &

Brothers, 1950) includes autobiographical essays by six such writers: Arthur Koestler, Ignazio Silone, Richard Wright, Andre Gide, Louis Fischer, and Stephen Spender. These essays are particularly compelling in revealing the painfulness of the authors' disillusionment and their refusal to substitute a facile anticommunism for the rejected Marxism.

25. An illustrative passage from Nietzsche: "[The church] has at all times laid the stress of discipline on extirpation (of sensuality, of pride, of the lust to rule, of avarice, of vengefulness). But an attack on the roots of passion means an attack on the roots of life: the practice of the church is hostile to life." Friedrich Nietzsche, *Twilight of the Idols* (1888).

26. See esp. Edgar Sheffield Brightman, *An Introduction to Philosophy*, rev. ed. (New York: Henry Holt & Co., 1951), 68–73.

27. Whitehead, *Process and Reality*, 12.

28. Ibid., 9.

29. I have discussed this dual, individual/social understanding of human nature more fully in *A Christian Method of Moral Judgment* (Philadelphia: Westminster Press, 1977), 136–39.

## CHAPTER 4

1. Einstein, et al., *Living Philosophies*, 6. In another writing, Einstein speaks positively of a form of religious feeling "which knows no dogma and no God conceived in man's image." Albert Einstein, *Ideas and Opinions* (New York: Dell Pub. Co., 1954, 1930), 48.

2. Carl Sagan, *Dragons of Eden: Speculations on the Evolution of Human Intelligence* (New York: Random House, 1977), 221.

3. Gibson Winter, *Elements for a Social Ethic: Scientific and Ethical Perspectives on Social Process* (New York: Macmillan Co., 1966), 23–29.

4. F. H. Bradley, *Ethical Studies* (Oxford: At the Clarendon Press, 1927).

5. The point was made with particular vigor by the Boston personalists Borden Parker Bowne, Edgar S. Brightman, and Peter A. Bertocci.

6. See Skinner, *Beyond Freedom and Dignity*.

7. Bertrand Russell, *Why I Am Not a Christian, and Other Essays* (New York: Simon & Schuster, 1957), originally published in the 1903 essay, "A Free Man's Worship."

8. Werner Jaeger, *Paideia: The Ideals of Greek Culture*, trans. from the 2d German ed. by Gilbert Highet (New York: Oxford Univ. Press, 1939, 1945), 1:153.

9. McFague, *Metaphorical Theology*, 20.

10. One of the curious ironies about some forms of twentieth-century personalism is that actual personhood appeared to be subordinated to concepts about personhood. Consequently, such personalism was not able to accommodate forms of existentialism and dialectical theology that were not inherently inconsistent with it.

11. H. Richard Niebuhr, *Meaning of Revelation*, 151–53.

12. Karl Barth, *Church Dogmatics* I/1, 350.

13. T. F. Torrance, *Space, Time and Incarnation* (New York and London: Oxford Univ. Press, 1969), 75.

14. Ibid., 76.

15. Ibid., 90.

16. John Hick, ed., *The Myth of God Incarnate* (London: SCM Press, 1977).

17. Maurice Wiles, "Christianity without Incarnation?" in Hick, ed., *Myth of God Incarnate*, 9.

18. Torrance, *Space, Time and Incarnation*, 76.

19. Bernard Lonergan, *Method in Theology*, 2d ed. (New York: Herder & Herder, 1973), 123.

## CHAPTER 5

1. Carl Sagan, *Cosmos* (New York: Random House, 1980), 196.

2. Ibid., 265.

3. Russell Stannard, *Science and the Renewal of Belief* (London: SCM Press, 1982), 137.

4. Sagan, *Cosmos*, 257.

5. See esp. Paul Tillich, *Systematic Theology*, vol. 1 (Chicago: Univ. of Chicago Press, 1951).

6. While not questioning the rationality of the universe as such, the Nobel Prize–winning biochemist Jacques Monod has raised serious questions about whether any of the actual contents of the universe reflect overall design or purpose. See esp. Monod, *Chance and Necessity: An Essay on the Natural Philosophy of Modern Biology*, tr. Austryn Wainhouse (New York: Vintage Books, 1972 [1970]). As I understand Monod's point, it is that every specific mutation, from the most elemental to the most complex, in the sequences of biological evolution, is a result of pure chance: "Pure chance, absolutely free but blind, at the very root of the stupendous edifice of evolution: this central concept of modern biology is no longer one among other possible or even conceivable hypotheses. It is today the *sole* conceivable hypothesis, the only one that squares with observed and tested fact" (pp. 112–13). He concludes from this that "the ancient covenant is in pieces; man knows at last that he is alone in the universe's unfeeling immensity, out of which he emerged only by chance" (p. 180). Monod's work is a good reminder that we be cautious in attributing specific intention to any of the particular forms taken by the evolution of life. Still, the potentialities for all of the existing forms (and an infinite number of other forms which never came into existence because circumstances were not right) were present from the very beginning—and that is my own central point.

7. "One can be grateful," Gustafson writes, "for the divine governance, for all it sustains and makes possible, without conceptually personalizing the Governor. . . . I agree with Tillich that we can be personally related to the divine governance without conceiving of God as a person." James M. Gustafson, *Ethics from a Theocentric Perspective* (Chicago: Univ. of Chicago Press, 1981), 271.

8. In this respect, it is interesting to compare the individualistic cultural portrayals of Jesus in Charles Sheldon's *In His Steps* and Bruce Barton's *The Man Nobody Knows: A Discovery of Jesus* of an earlier North American generation with the picture emerging from the Nicaraguan campesinos in Ernesto Cardenal's *El Evangelio en Solentiname*. The former could almost be characterized as bourgeois idealizations, the latter as perfectly suited for a socialist vision of humanity.

9. H. Richard Niebuhr, *Radical Monotheism and Western Culture* (New York: Harper & Brothers, 1960).

## CHAPTER 6

1. Nietzsche, *Twilight of the Idols.*

2. Karl Marx, *Toward the Critique of Hegel's Philosophy of Right.* Edition cited is Lewis S. Feuer, ed., *Marx and Engel's Basic Writings on Politics and Philosophy* (Garden City, N.Y.: Doubleday Anchor Books, 1959), 263.

3. Ludwig Feuerbach, *The Essence of Christianity* (1841).

4. Sigmund Freud, *The Future of an Illusion,* trans. W. D. Robson-Scott (New York: Liveright Pub. Corp., 1928, 1949), 58. Freud compares religion to childhood neurosis and expresses the hope that "mankind will overcome this neurotic phase, just as so many children grow out of their similar neuroses." Ibid., 92.

5. Peter L. Berger, *A Rumor of Angels: Modern Society and the Rediscovery of the Supernatural* (Garden City, N.Y.: Doubleday & Co., 1969), 71.

6. Ibid., 65–66.

7. Nineteenth-century German bourgeois/Christian culture was not noted for its libertarian tendencies, and with an upbringing in a Lutheran parsonage Nietzsche may have experienced the more restrictive aspects of that culture. His recurrent emotional problems suggest that Nietzsche never finally came to terms with the conflicts engendered by a too-restrictive childhood.

8. T. S. Eliot, "Murder in the Cathedral," in T. S. Eliot, *The Complete Poems and Plays* (New York: Harcourt Brace Jovanovich, 1952), 196.

9. Dietrich Bonhoeffer, *The Cost of Discipleship,* trans. R. H. Fuller (New York: Macmillan Co., 1963, 1937), 45, 54. See also John D. Godsey, *The Theology of Dietrich Bonhoeffer* (Philadelphia: Westminster Press, 1960).

10. Thomas A. Harris, *I'm OK, You're OK: A Practical Guide to Transactional Analysis* (New York: Harper & Row, 1969).

11. This is not to say, of course, that there is no place for what I have called secular psychology. Wise pastors and priests know that some psychological disorders require referral to highly trained therapists.

12. Peter A. Bertocci, *Religion as Creative Insecurity* (New York: Association Press, 1958).

13. The secular theology movement was based primarily on the writings of Friedrich Gogarten and Dietrich Bonhoeffer, largely as popularized by Harvey Cox, *The Secular City* (New York: Macmillan Co., 1965).

14. From Luther's *Open Letter to the German Nobility* (1520).

15. Wogaman, *A Christian Method of Moral Judgment,* 1–5.

16. The work of James M. Gustafson and Stanley Hauerwas illustrates both the grounding of ethics in personal virtue and (in my judgment) the relative neglect of social ethics. Hauerwas's *A Community of Character: Toward a Constructive Christian Social Ethic* (Notre Dame, Ind.: Univ. of Notre Dame Press, 1981) attempts to ground a social ethic in Christian character and the Christian "story," but it seems limited both in the scope of issues considered and in its (to me) ambiguous portrayal of the relationship between the church and social power. Nevertheless, such Christian ethicists are right in emphasizing the fundamental significance of the moral self.

17. Victor Hugo, *Les Miserables,* tr. Charles E. Wilbur (New York: Modern Library, 1931 [1862]), 90.

## CHAPTER 7

1. See especially Robert K. Merton, *Social Theory and Social Structure* (Glencoe, Ill.: Free Press, 1957), 225–286.

2. See Ayn Rand, *The Virtue of Selfishness: A New Concept of Egoism* (New York: New American Library, 1964).

3. L. Harold DeWolf, *Responsible Freedom: Guidelines to Christian Action* (New York: Harper & Row, 1971), esp. 107–9.

4. Paul Lehmann, *Ethics in a Christian Context* (New York: Harper & Row, 1963).

5. Joseph Haroutunian, *God with Us: A Theology of Transpersonal Life* (Philadelphia: Westminster Press, 1956), 17.

6. See, e.g., Martin Luther King, Jr., *Strength to Love* (Philadelphia: Fortress Press, 1981) and *Where Do We Go from Here: Chaos or Community* (New York: Harper & Row, 1967).

7. The nineteenth-century philosopher Hegel made essentially this point in a perceptive criticism of slavery, noting that the institution depersonalizes the master quite as much (if not more) than the slave. See Georg W. F. Hegel, *The Phenomenology of Mind,* 2d rev. ed., trans. J. S. Baillie (London: G. Allen and Unwin, 1949), 229–40.

8. King, *Where Do We Go from Here,* 101.

9. St. Augustine, who certainly believed in the transmission of original sin through the birth of successive generations, also disavowed the idea that our physical nature, per se, is evil. See *The City of God,* Books XIII and XIV.

10. Reinhold Niebuhr, *The Nature and Destiny of Man,* vol. 1 (New York: Charles Scribner's Sons, 1943). See also a somewhat similar analysis in Ernest Becker, *Escape from Evil* (New York: Free Press, 1975).

11. Niebuhr, *Nature and Destiny of Man,* 178–79. In criticism of Niebuhr's view of sin, it has sometimes been argued that its presentation is too bounded by the cultural proclivities of white male theologians—a point which may have some truth to it. Still, it seems to me that his insight reaches beyond the particularities of that cultural limitation to the more generic or universal plight of human anxiety and inability to trust God as the source of "sin." Possibly original sin expresses itself in more forms than Niebuhr or Becker imagined, but I think they were not far off the mark in exploring its roots.

12. Both Gutierrez and Bonino are particularly influenced by the Leninist doctrine of imperialism, utilizing it substantially in their analysis of the causes of poverty and oppression in Latin America. Both are sympathetic to the call for revolution. However, neither accepts Marxist metaphysical conceptions. In his recent writing, Bonino gives more emphasis to the Christian doctrine of sin, to the moral importance of avoiding violence except when justified by extreme situations, and to the prima facie claims of political democracy. See Gustavo Gutierrez, *A Theology of Liberation* (Maryknoll, N.Y.: Orbis Books, 1973), Jose Miguez Bonino,

*Christians and Marxists: The Mutual Challenge to Revolution* (Grand Rapids: Wm. B. Eerdmans, 1976), and Bonino's more recent book *Toward a Christian Political Ethics* (Philadelphia: Fortress Press, 1983).

13. David M. Paton, ed., *Church and Race in South Africa* (London: SCM Press, 1958), 100–101.

14. I have been struck by how astutely Reinhold Niebuhr anticipated the success of this movement of the 1960s by his comment in *Moral Man and Immoral Society* (New York: Charles Scribner's Sons, 1932), published thirty years earlier: "The technique of non-violence . . . will, if persisted in with the same patience and discipline attained by Mr. Gandhi and his followers, achieve a degree of justice which neither pure moral suasion nor violence could gain. . . . One waits for such a campaign with all the more reason and hope because the peculiar spiritual gifts of the Negro endow him with the capacity to conduct it successfully. He would need only to fuse the aggressiveness of the new and young Negro with the patience and forbearance of the old Negro, to rob the former of its vindictiveness and the latter of its lethargy." P. 254.

15. In *Where Do We Go From Here,* King had to conduct a rear-guard struggle against the seemingly more militant proponents of "black power" who had become very impatient with the apparently weaker strategies of nonviolence and racial inclusiveness. But King perceived two realities better than they: First, that real power required coalition building in an overwhelmingly white society and second, that by asserting moral and tactical leadership in the emerging black/white "coalition of conscience" the black was asserting his or her dignity and personhood far more powerfully than a separatist or purely adversarial program could possibly hope to do.

16. See, e.g., Elizabeth Möltmann-Wendel, *Liberty, Equality, Sisterhood: On the Emancipation of Women in Church and Society,* trans. Ruth Gritsch (Philadelphia: Fortress Press, 1978) and Naomi R. Goldenberg, *Changing of the Gods: Feminism and the End of Traditional Religions* (Boston: Beacon Press, 1979). Publication of the National Council of Churches' *An Inclusive Language Lectionary* in 1983 dramatized the struggle over sexist language by offering alternative phrasings for familiar scriptural texts.

17. Feminist theologians, such as Mary Daly, who feel that patriarchal conceptions are essential (and not tangential) aspects of Christian tradition can cite an abundance of references from all periods of Christian history in support of their position. Some, including Daly, appear to have abandoned Christian faith altogether for that reason. They may feel that the power of the masculine identification of God is just too great to be overcome in Christian symbolism. But if Christian faith is to be abandoned on such grounds, one is left with the question what one is to substitute for it. If one retains faith in a personal God and the overall vision of reality discussed in this book, then the question may only be semantic and strategic. If one abandons that more basic faith too, however, then something more than feminism must explain it. For the faith in a personal God and the confidence in the ultimate goodness of reality which (I believe) is at the heart of Christian faith is beyond gender.

18. Robert M. MacIver, *The Web of Government* (New York: Macmillan Co., 1947), 94. The sociologist Talcott Parsons remarks similarly that political power "is

capacity to control the relational system as a system." *The Social System* (Glencoe, Ill.: Free Press, 1951), 126.

19. Franz Neumann, *The Democratic and Authoritarian State* (New York: Free Press, 1957).

20. Leo Tolstoy, *My Religion* (New York: Crowell and Co., 1885).

21. Jacques Ellul, *Violence: Reflections from a Christian Perspective* (New York: Seabury Press, 1969) and John Howard Yoder, *The Politics of Jesus* (Grand Rapids: Wm. B. Eerdmans, 1972).

22. Reinhold Niebuhr, *The Children of Light and the Children of Darkness* (New York: Charles Scribner's Sons, 1944), xiii.

23. Wogaman, *Christian Method of Moral Judgment,* chap. 4.

24. The growing ecumenical tradition has already made substantial contributions to political thought. In particular, the discussion of the "Responsible Society" at the 1948 and 1954 assemblies of the World Council of Churches and the formulation of the "just, participatory, and sustainable society" at the assemblies of 1975 and 1983 can be cited. This developing tradition has emphasized the importance of the right of every person to participate in the political and economic power affecting him or her. In recent years there has been more emphasis on the rights of future generations to a legacy that has not been ruined by the selfishness and short-sightedness of the present generation.

25. Our concern, therefore, must be with *political* economy; that is, with economics as a sphere for public policy. Fundamental economic decisions must be subject to the collective will of the whole community.

26. Robert Benne, *The Ethic Of Democratic Capitalism: A Moral Reassessment* (Philadelphia: Fortress Press, 1981) and Michael Novak, *The Spirit of Democratic Capitalism* (New York: Simon & Schuster, 1982).

27. This point is made strikingly by the British economist John Hicks in his essay, *The Crisis in Keynesian Economics* (Oxford: Basil Blackwell & Mott, 1974). Hicks observes the tendency of lower-paid groups of workers (or managers or investors) to strive for greater equality. But the more "catching up" occurs the more those who are being caught up with feel that they are proportionately losing ground. Equality is the goal of the former, maintaining existing relationships that of the latter. Besides providing a very helpful biblical analysis, Bruce C. Birch and Larry L. Rasmussen's *The Predicament of the Prosperous* (Philadelphia: Westminster Press, 1978) suggests in world terms how disproportionate wealth and power have distorted economic relationships of all kinds.

28. Robert L. Heilbroner, *An Inquiry into the Human Prospect* (New York: W. W. Norton, 1975), 169ff.

29. J. Philip Wogaman, *The Great Economic Debate: An Ethical Analysis* (Philadelphia: Westminster Press, 1977), chap. 2.

30. Heilbroner, *Inquiry into the Human Prospect,* p. 175.

31. The subtitle of Hardin's essay, "Lifeboat Ethics: The Case against Helping the Poor" (in *Psychology Today* [September 1974]: 38–43, 124–26) may make the point. Hardin argues that it is a mistake for affluent countries to help poor countries unless they can be sure that the population growth rates of the latter will not simply expand and absorb the additional food that is given to them without improving the overall quality of life. He pictures the affluent countries as occupying "lifeboats" in

a turbulent sea. The poor countries are floundering in the water nearby. If those in the lifeboats (the prosperous) yield to compassionate but misguided feelings by bringing the swimmers (the poor) on board they will only sink the boats and all will be lost. For contrasting perspectives on the applicability of the lifeboat metaphor to the relationship of rich and poor nations, see George R. Lucas, Jr. and Thomas W. Ogletree, eds., *Lifeboat Ethics: The Moral Dilemmas of World Hunger* (New York: Harper & Row, 1976).

Rawls's theory of justice is not, on the face of it, as self- or group-interested as the "lifeboat ethics," since what is sought in his work is an overall conception of justice to serve as a norm for all of society. Nevertheless, Rawls's celebrated conceptual device of the "original position" appears to presuppose pure self-interest. Rawls suggests that the clearest, most defensible conception of justice would emerge if all people were to adopt the social arrangements they would consider to be in their best interest without knowing, in advance, what their own personal situation would turn out to be. Rawls concludes that the rational person would opt for a society in which equality would be the norm except for those inequalities found to serve the interests of the least well-off members of the community. See John Rawls, *A Theory of Justice* (Cambridge, Mass.: Harvard Univ. Press, 1972).

## CHAPTER 8

1. S. Paul Schilling, *God in an Age of Atheism* (Nashville: Abingdon Press, 1969), 122. See also his *God and Human Anguish* (Nashville: Abingdon Press, 1977) for a penetrating discussion of the theological problems posed by human suffering.

2. "A Time to Remember the Holocaust," *Washington Post* (17 April 1978): B3.

3. Richard Rubenstein, *After Auschwitz* (Indianapolis: Bobbs-Merrill, 1966).

4. William R. Jones, *Is God a White Racist?* (Garden City, N. Y.: Doubleday & Co., 1973).

5. Becker did, however, believe in God. In a fascinating interview shortly before his death, he indicated that it was the wonder of the birth of his first child that, for him, pointed to the reality of God. See "The Heroics of Everyday Life: A Theorist of Death Confronts His Own End," *Psychology Today* (April 1974): 71ff.

6. Ernest Becker, *Escape from Evil* (New York: Free Press, 1975), 136.

7. Ibid., 1.

8. Alfred Lord Tennyson, "In Memoriam," *The Poetic and Dramatic Works of Alfred Lord Tennyson* (Cambridge, Mass.: Houghton, Mifflin, The Riverside Press, 1898), 176.

9. Epicurus, "Letter to Menoeceus," in W. T. Jones, et al., eds., *Approaches to Ethics*, 3d ed. (New York: McGraw-Hill, 1977), 78.

10. From Dylan Thomas, *The Collected Poems of Dylan Thomas* (New York: New Directions, 1957), 128.

11. Raymond A. Moody, *Life After Life* (New York: Bantam Books, 1975, 1976) and *Reflections on Life After Life* (New York: Bantam Books, 1977). The tremendous public fascination with this theme is illustrated by the fact that the first of these books sold more than two million copies in its first three years. See also L.

Harold DeWolf, *Eternal Life: Why We Believe* (Philadelphia: Westminster Press, 1980).

## CHAPTER 9

1. The expression was a kind of working slogan of the 1937 Oxford Conference. See Ruth Rouse and Stephen Charles Neill, eds., *A History of the Ecumenical Movement 1517–1948* (London: SPCK, 1967), 591.

2. See Robert Merton, *Social Theory and Social Structure,* rev. ed. (Glencoe, Ill.: Free Press, 1957) for an excellent analysis of reference group behavior.

3. A fascinating case study on this is provided by Thomas F. Pettigrew and Ernest Q. Campbell, *Christians in Racial Crisis: A Study of Little Rock's Ministry* (Washington, D. C.: Public Affairs Press, 1959).

4. Solomon E. Asch, "Effects of Group Pressure upon the Modification and Distortion of Judgments," in Eleanor E. Maccoby, et al., eds., *Readings in Social Psychology,* 3d ed. (New York: Henry Holt & Co., 1958).

5. The more or less conscious effort to employ social pressure to secure conformity with the group is especially noticeable among some Amish groups practicing "shunning" as an instrument of church discipline. Members of the group withhold social contact from those who have broken church discipline, and even members of the culprit's immediate family are encouraged to "shun" that person. Paul's letters to the church at Corinth show the difficulties and dilemmas involved in attempting to maintain church discipline in this way.

6. Ernst Troeltsch, *The Social Teaching of the Christian Churches,* trans. Olive Wyon (London: George Allen & Unwin, 1931, 1911). Troeltsch's typology has had to be refined to take into account the rich variety of social forms exhibited by religion. See J. Milton Yinger, *Religion, Society, and the Individual* (New York: Macmillan Co., 1957) for a more differentiated typology. H. Richard Niebuhr's *Christ and Culture* (New York: Harper & Brothers, 1951), a work in basic Christian ethics, has been influenced greatly by Troeltsch, although Niebuhr's own typology is also more carefully refined.

7. D. Elton Trueblood caught the ideal nicely in the title of his book, *The Company of the Committed* (New York: Harper & Row, 1961), even though his concept of the church is not as exclusive as that implied in Troeltsch's definition of sect.

8. *Book of Worship for United States Forces* (Washington, D. C.: Government Printing Office, 1974).

9. See, for example, Laurence H. Stookey, *Baptism, Christ's Act in the Church* (Nashville: Abingdon Press, 1982) and Geoffrey Wainwright, *Eucharist and Eschatology,* 2d ed. (London: Epworth Press, 1978).

10. Walter Rauschenbusch, *Christianizing the Social Order* (New York: Macmillan Co., 1912), 127.

11. Paul A. Carter, *The Decline and Revival of the Social Gospel: Social and Political Liberalism in American Protestant Churches, 1920–1940* (Ithaca, N. Y.: Cornell Univ. Press, 1954).

## CHAPTER 10

1. This classic statement of Victorian and post-Victorian imperialism was addressed, not to Great Britain, but to the United States. It was published in *McClure's Magazine* in 1899, shortly after the end of the Spanish-American War and was intended to speak of the duty of the United States to bring Cuba and the Philippines into protective custody.

2. Quoted by Paul A. Hopkins, *What Next in Mission?* (Philadelphia: Westminster Press, 1977), 11.

3. Emerito P. Nacpil in Anderson and Stansky, eds., *Mission Trends No. 1*, 134.

4. See especially Bonino, *Christians and Marxists*, Gustavo Gutierrez, *A Theology of Liberation* (Maryknoll, N. Y.: Orbis Books, 1973), William R. Coats, *God in Public: Political Theology Beyond Niebuhr* (Grand Rapids: Wm. B. Eerdmans, 1974).

5. See, e.g., James H. Weaver and Marguerite Berger, "The Marxist Critique of Dependency Theory: An Introduction," in Charles K. Wilber, ed., *The Political Economy of Development and Underdevelopment*, 3d ed. (New York: Random House, 1984), 45–64.

6. Regarding tensions within the African church over polygamy, see Jacob Stephens, "Church and Society: A Strategy for Ghana and A Consultation Process for the Christian Council of Ghana" (D. Min. project-thesis, Wesley Theological Seminary, 1983).

7. Francesco Ruffini, *Religious Liberty*, trans. J. Parker Heyes (New York: G. P. Putnam's Sons, 1912), 19.

8. See Paul Tillich, *The Protestant Era*, trans. James Luther Adams (Chicago: Univ. of Chicago Press, 1948).

9. William Ernest Hocking, et al., *Re-thinking Missions: A Laymen's Inquiry after One Hundred Years* (New York: Harper & Brothers, 1932), 327. The commission, made up of a distinguished group of lay leaders from several major Protestant denominations in the United States, was chaired by the eminent Harvard philosopher William Ernest Hocking. Reassessing all aspects of missionary activity, the commission undertook field studies in the Orient and was informed by expert opinion on non-Christian religions. Its conclusions show the particular influence of Hocking. A striking recent expression of the Laymen's Inquiry call for creative pluralism among the world's religions is contained in Marjorie Hewitt Suchocki's *God Christ Church: A Practical Guide to Process Theology* (New York: Crossroad, 1982), 151–60.

10. Stephen Neill, *Christian Faith and Other Faiths* (New York and London: Oxford Univ. Press, 1961), 17.

11. Hendrik Kraemer, *The Christian Message in a Non-Christian World* (London: International Missionary Council and Edinburgh House Press, 1938). See also his *Religion and the Christian Faith* (London: Lutterworth Press, 1956).

12. *The Documents of Vatican II* (New York: Guild Press, America Press, and Association Press, 1966), 662–63.

13. Arnulf Camps, *Partners in Dialogue: Christianity and Other World Religions*, trans. John Drury (Maryknoll, N. Y.: Orbis Books, 1983, 1977–78), 48.

14. Ibid.

15. I have avoided specific analysis of non-Christian religious traditions here, partly because I lack the competence to make specific comparisons in technical detail and partly because that might lead us astray from the main theme. I will record, however, that my knowledge of other world religions has not led me thus far to anything but deeper appreciation for the meaning of Jesus Christ as bearer of revelation of God. We should note, however, that Judaism presents special questions for Christians. Christian faith is in direct linear continuity with Judaism. Christians will, perhaps inevitably, interpret that heritage in light of Jesus Christ, just as they will approach an understanding of contemporary Judaism in the same light. To believe, as I do, that reality is brought into better focus when interpreted through Christ, is not to say that the covenantal tradition of Judaism is only a fragmentary faith. Some forms of Judaism may be much closer to the basic theological perspective presented in this book than some forms of Christianity.

16. Quoted in A. F. Carrillo de Albornoz, *Roman Catholicism and Religious Liberty* (Geneva: World Council of Churches, 1959), 25.

# INDEX